Violence and Democracy in India

Violence and Democracy in India

Edited by Amrita Basu and Srirupa Roy

Seagull Books
Calcutta London New York

Seagull Books
Editorial offices:
1st floor, Angel Court, 81 St Clements Street, Oxford OX4 1AW, UK
1 Washington Square Village, Apt 1U, New York, NY 10012, USA
26 Circus Avenue, Calcutta 700 017, India

ISBN 1 9054 2 231 8

British Library Cataloguing-in-Publication Data
A catalogue record for this book is available from the British Library

Typeset by Seagull Books, Calcutta, India
Printed in the United Kingdom by Biddles Ltd, King's Lynn

CONTENTS

Beyond Exceptionalism: Violence and Democracy in India

AMRITA BASU AND SRIRUPA ROY

In March 2002 the Indian state of Gujarat was the site of brutal mass violence against Muslims. As India's 'first ever televised riot'—the presence of live television cameras beaming images of death and destruction into living rooms throughout the nation was among the most distinctive features of the Gujarat violence—the details of this horrific event are all too well known. While the death toll remains a disputed figure, most reports have estimated that at least 2000 people were massacred over a relatively short time period. The initial loss of property was estimated to be in the range of three billion rupees. The figure is even higher today, as large numbers of survivors continue to be deprived of a means of livelihood and subsist under conditions of acute economic insecurity.

In at least two significant ways, the events of Gujarat stood out from the innumerable incidents of mass violence that have taken place in India over the half-century of its existence as a sovereign nation-state. First, as numerous national and international commissions of inquiry have documented, what occurred in Gujarat was not a riot that resulted from the spontaneous 'upsurge' of angry crowds. Instead, the incumbent state government led by the Hindu nationalist Bharatiya Janata Party (BJP) was directly involved in acts of commission and omission. There is overwhelming evidence that state agencies and personnel actively orchestrated and facilitated the violence, and pointedly refused to prevent its escalation. In this sense the events of Gujarat constitute an example of a pogrom or even of a genocide—theoretical and legal concepts that highlight the organized, deliberate, and institutionally sanctioned nature of the violence of March 2002.[1]

The second aspect of Gujarat's exceptionalism has to do with the specific nature of the violence. Although mass violence may be a relatively familiar occurrence in post-independence India, the scale, intensity, and brutality of the Gujarat violence was unique. The numerous incidents of sexual violence against Muslim women; the intent to inflict not just physical injury but psychic humiliation upon male and female victims; the killing of children; the dismemberment and mutilation of live bodies and corpses; and even the choice of fire as the preferred means of destruction set Gujarat apart from the earlier experience and modalities of violence in independent India.

At the time of writing—four years later—the violence of Gujarat seems exceptional in yet another way. Viewed from the perspective of the present, when the normal routines of democracy-as-usual have returned to Gujarat and to India, the events of March 2002 appear aberrant. Thus within the state itself, there have been no further incidents of large-scale violence. Although Narendra Modi still continues as the chief minister of Gujarat, his present tenure is marked by substantially different political circumstances, and his political agency is more constrained. At the national level, the Hindu nationalist-dominated coalition government was defeated in the general elections of 2004, and the new Congress coalition government has promised that events like Gujarat will never happen again. The *Sangh Parivar* or the 'joint family' of Hindu nationalist organizations is in considerable ideological and organizational disarray, and the precise coordinations and calculated long-term ideological manoeuvres that had enabled the violence of 2002 seem unlikely to be repeated in the near future. Although horrifying and unforgettable, the passage of time and the restoration of political order in India in the aftermath of March 2002 have caused the events of Gujarat to lose their unsettling immediacy. In public discourse and political consciousness, it is represented as a horrific, but increasingly distant memory: as a monstrous and relatively isolated exception that, like other incidents of extreme violence, stands outside the normal universe of democratic political practice in India.

The common scholarly understanding of the Gujarat violence as an exception or aberration for democracy is not unique to the field of Indian studies, but reflects instead a pervasive comparative-theoretical consensus in existing social science scholarship. The claim that violence is an exception for democratic politics has been advanced in a variety of different ways. The first, and most familiar variant is that of the 'Iron Law of Democracies', or 'democratic peace': this applies the argument—in the field of international relations—that democracies do not fight each other to the arena of domestic politics.[2] For instance, several scholars have argued on the basis of comparative studies of cross-national variations in violence, that democracies are less violence-prone than non-democracies.[3] The contemporary foreign policy of the United States also reflects this perspective. Both in official rhetoric and in the supportive media discourses of neo-conservative commentators, the goal of 'regime change' in Afghanistan and Iraq is justified in terms of the pacifying effects of 'bringing democracy' to these otherwise violent and 'unstable' countries.

While such theories of democratic peace are statements of observable tendencies rather than explanations, other variants of the argument that violence is exceptional in democracies do in fact offer a causal explanation for why this may be the case. Thus, a second variation of this thesis specifies a particular subset of democracies within which this holds true. The classical statements of modernization theory from scholars such as Samuel Huntington, and more recently, the work of theorists of post-socialist transitions to democracy have identified how political violence erupts in collapsing, unstable, emerging, or weakly institutionalized and de-institutionalized democracies.[4]

A third and related strand of scholarship specifies a more fine-grained set of institutional and political-economic variables that determine the occurrence of violence within a democratic political system. A range of different factors are seen to be causally influential, such as the type of electoral system and the nature of political incentives that it creates; the size of population; the distribution of social-economic cleavages; and the institutional density of civil society and inter-ethnic associations. The vast majority of comparative political science scholarship may be classified within this category, and recent scholarship has included, among others, the influential writings of David Laitin and James Fearon, Stathis Kalyvas, Donald Horowitz, Paul Brass, Ashutosh Varshney, Steven Wilkinson, and other theorists of ethnic violence in India and elsewhere.[5]

Clearly there are substantial theoretical and methodological differences between these approaches. At the same time, they all reflect the common belief that democratic norms preclude violence. Thus, when violence occurs in a democratic polity, it is an anomaly: what needs to be explained is how and why this deviation from democratic norms has occurred.[6]

It is this understanding of violence as an exception or aberration that this book seeks to interrogate. As we argue below, much is lost, both theoretically and politically, if we exceptionalize violence; that is, treat each manifestation of violence as a discrete and unique event that is insulated from, and intrinsically opposed to, the norms and practices of modernity and democracy. In what follows, we explore instead what we want to claim is the constitutive relationship between the 'normal' and the 'exceptional' practices and processes of political life, and locate our inquiry into the causes and consequences of extreme, visible violence within the everyday, banal, often invisible configurations of politics and power in contemporary India.

Each chapter in this volume accordingly offers a commentary on the violence of Gujarat by going beyond the specific time-space of its occurrence. Taken together, they advance the argument that the enabling mechanisms for the Gujarat violence are located in long-term processes unfolding in a variety of arenas that took place well before March 2002, and are continuing to take place well after the return of apparent normalcy to the Indian political arena. In sum, this book is a consideration of how the roots of exceptional violence can lie in politics-as-usual. It seeks not so much to make events in Gujarat appear 'normal' as to inquire into the conditions under which normal politics becomes exceptional politics; into why and how democratic polities can countenance, and even facilitate, acts of extreme violence.

The remainder of this introduction expands on these propositions. Through a discussion of the specific case that prompted this volume, namely the violence of Gujarat in March 2002, Section I establishes what it means to locate violence 'beyond exceptionalism' and to reconceptualize the relationship between violence and democracy as enabling rather than inherently oppositional. Section II maps the common themes that weave through the individual chapters of this volume, and considers their broader theoretical implications both for scholars of India and for those interested in the relationship between democracy and violence in a comparative and global context.

SECTION I: RECONSIDERING GUJARAT

In October 2001, Narendra Modi, the newly appointed chief minister of the Indian state of Gujarat, declared at his inaugural press conference: 'I have come here to play a one-day [cricket] match. I need fast and performing batsmen to help me score runs in the limited-over game.[7] Four months later, in March 2002, Modi's state was the site of what many observers[8] have referred to as post-colonial India's first organized pogrom or even genocide, conforming as it did to the United Nations' definition of such an act: 'the intent to destroy, in whole or in part, a national, ethnical, racial or religious group.'[9] Following news reports about how a group of 'Muslim miscreants'[10] had set fire to a train compartment that was carrying *kar sevaks* or temple volunteers who were returning to their homes in Gujarat after participating in a campaign to build a Hindu temple at the site of the demolished Babri mosque in the north Indian town of Ayodhya, a wave of 'revenge killings' against Muslims engulfed the state.

Unremarkable at the time, Modi's call for 'fast and performing batsmen' to 'score runs' has chilling connotations as we reflect on it today, in the shadow of the events that took place a mere four months after his press conference. However the real significance of Modi's statement is not to be found in his exhortation to perform in a particular way. It lies instead in the larger metaphoric logic that he deploys: *the one-day match is to the game of cricket as Modi's stewardship of Gujarat is to constitutional democracy in India.*

The relatively recent, made-for-television innovation of the one-day, limited-over cricket match has its own rules and strategies for winning that are in many ways very different from the classic five-day test match.[11] However, it is still recognized as cricket. Accordingly, with the metaphor of politics as cricket, Modi positions his governance of Gujarat within the larger rule-bound universe of democratic politics-as-usual in India. He establishes a connection, however mediated or tenuous, between what has gone before and what is; between the existing rules of the game, and apparent departures from them.

This book takes Modi's cricket metaphor seriously, suggesting that its logic—how the Hindu nationalist movement in India is playing a familiar yet different game—echoes Antonio Gramsci's argument about the dynamics of political, social, and ideological continuity and change that were set in motion by the rise of Italian fascism in early 20th-century Europe, and by earlier 19th-century liberal-constitutional movements as well. According to Gramscian theory, Hindu nationalism's ascendancy at the national and also at the state or local level in India does not result from a direct or frontal 'war of position' in which a new 'historical bloc' suddenly and definitively eclipses an old one. It is instead the culmination of a more gradual or incremental 'war of manoeuvre', or, to use another Gramscian turn of phrase, of the molecular transformations wrought by a 'passive revolution.'[12] Unlike the dramatically reconfigured political terrain that emerged after the 'active' revolutions of Jacobinism in France or Bolshevism in Russia, a passive revolutionary political terrain is one that is simultaneously structured by both old and new social and ideological formations; one in which upholding a distinct line of separation between secular-liberal norm and religious-illiberal aberration proves to be an increasingly difficult task.

It is precisely in such a blurred context that the violence of Gujarat has taken place, its ambiguity giving rise to a major theoretical as well as political-ethical paradox: namely, the coexistence of violence and democracy; the assertion of the freedom to live and the freedom to kill within the same polity. In an important sense, Modi is right: the events of Gujarat *have* taken place in an established constitutional democracy with a vibrant civil society. What has thus far been widely upheld as the missing factor and hence the solution to the problem of extreme violence in other contexts—democracy and its trusty metonym, civil society—can be shown to have been present at the scene of the crime in this particular instance—and to have in fact contributed to the violence.

What explains this? What do understandings of why and how extreme violence occurs within democracy tell us about the prospects for democracy after such events? These are the questions that inform this book.

A similar point about how the events of Gujarat challenge the validity of general theories about the relationship between democracy and extreme violence has been raised in a recent essay by the political and legal theorist Upendra Baxi. Expanding upon Giorgio Agamben's observation that 'every people has had its particular way of going bankrupt,'[13] Baxi calls for a critical evaluation of the mimetic terms that structure present understandings of 'holocaustian politics'[14]—the tendency to describe experiences and processes of extreme violence through implicit or explicit reference to the 'original' logics and modalities of 20th-century German fascism. This act of reading back into the German experience[15] constructs totalitarianism as the dominant 'model of bankruptcy' for extreme violence.

Such a modular narrative is not entirely devoid of nuances. For instance, it takes into account the substantial differences between the organized efficiency of the Third Reich's bureaucratic-industrial death factories and the weakness and incoherence of state power in polities such as Rwanda, Cambodia, post-communist Yugoslavia, and the Ottoman Empire during its terminal days. Nevertheless, such acknowledgements of institutional divergence and significant variations in state capacity continue to be accompanied by assertions of commonality at a higher-order level of regime-type—i.e. the fact that these are all non-democracies of a certain kind.

It is precisely this democratic ellipsis that serves as the point of departure for theorists such as Agamben and Baxi. Their call to recognize that there are many different ways of going bankrupt calls into question the prevailing conceptualization of mass violence as a scripted politics of exception that occurs only in recognizably deviant places where democracy is absent. Instead of partaking in mutually exclusive universes, the aberration of holocaustian politics and the norm of democratic politics may well have significant points of convergence. Simply put, there are democratic ways of going bankrupt as well.

The most obvious confirmation of the thesis of democratic bankruptcy comes from the bare facts of the case itself. As we have already noted, the violence of March 2002 and the aftershocks thereafter took place within a stable constitutional democracy that guarantees its citizens an impressive array of rights and protections, and in the context of a vibrant and flourishing civil society. More significantly, however, and here is where Modi's cricket metaphor comes into play, the historical emergence and consolidation of Hindu nationalism has occurred in and through the workings of electoral democracy, through its ability to establish a diversified presence within civil society, and through the appropriation of many of the existing cherished and authorized discourses of civic nationhood and popular sovereignty. In other words, the solution of democracy and civil society can be shown in many ways to be intimately associated with the emergence of the problem. Let us now elaborate on this claim in further detail by discussing some of the specific aspects of Hindutva's war of position or the ways in which it has transformed from within, gradually, the existing rules of a familiar and normative game.

The electoral route: First, and at a very basic level, the trajectory of Hindutva's ascendancy can be plotted along a paradigmatically democratic axis whose intervals are parliamentary and assembly election results.[16] If the political wing of the Hindu nationalist family of organizations was in power at the time of the Gujarat violence as the leading member of a coalitional government, it was because electoral campaigns had been fought and won across the nation. More specifically, it was because the peculiar structural mechanisms and aggregational logics of a first-past-the-post electoral system and a highly fragmented party system enable political parties to come to power at the national level without necessarily having secured a majority of the votes polled, and to gain a share of legislative seats that are disproportionate to the actual percentage of the vote received. Moreover, as scholarship on the electoral strategies of the BJP has noted, the votes garnered by the party in state assembly elections and national parliamentary elections often derive from systemic effects such as anti-incumbency voting or the casting of a negative vote against ruling political parties rather than a positive vote for the particular ideological agenda of Hindu nationalism.[17] Indeed, the political campaigns of the BJP during the round of general elections in India in 1999 de-emphasized the Hindutva identity of the party, drawing attention instead to the 'good governance' promise of the BJP as a 'party with a difference' and to the ways in which it would invigorate the existing political system by attending to secular concerns about corruption, the economy, and law and order.

In sum, the structures and logics of electoral democracy can often enable rather than prevent the institutionalization of normatively reprehensible political-ideological formations. Indeed, it is a tired truism that formal democracy has no necessary relationship with substantive democracy—that guaranteeing the freedom to vote does not and cannot guarantee the desirability of the outcome. The story of how Narendra Modi became the chief minister of Gujarat as well as the sequel to the story—how and why he continues to be the honourable chief minister despite the events of 2002—is directly linked to that universal shorthand for the democratic principles of liberty and popular sovereignty: direct elections.

The incivility of civil society: Second, over the span of at least the past two decades if not longer, Hindu nationalism has been able to establish a significant presence within civil society. To state this somewhat differently, the growing strength of Hindu nationalism corresponds to the enrichment rather than the attrition of associational forms of civic life. The 'protean forms'[18] of Hindutva or the range and diversity of the organizations that are formally or informally associated with the Sangh Parivar are staggering. There are more than a hundred different kinds of organizations under the Hindutva umbrella. These range from women's organizations—the militant Durga Vahini that trains women in martial arts or the Rashtriya Sevika Samiti that encourages its members to be good Hindu mothers and wives—to organizations like the Vanvasi Kalyan Ashram that purportedly work for the welfare of tribals; from associations that only have a virtual presence, such as the Hindu Vivek Kendra which is essentially one man with an internet connection working out of a palatial apartment in Kemp's Corner, Bombay, to the raw and uninhibited muscle power and very visible street presence of the Bajrang Dal. The nodal organization of

Hindutva, the Rashtriya Swayamsevak Sangh (RSS) reflects the central importance of grassroots-level civic associational life to the movement. The internal structure of the RSS comprises of thousands of neighbourhood shakhas or branches[19] that are coordinated within an organizational framework that centres ultimate authority in the figure of the sarsanghchalak (Supreme Commander) in the national headquarters in Nagpur. At the same time, however, there is a considerable degree of manoeuvring room at the decentralized level of each individual shakha, with local swayamsevaks developing their own neighbourhood recruitment programmes and designing local variants of national campaigns that often differ significantly from one area to another.[20]

Moreover, and as scholars of Hindu nationalism have repeatedly noted, Sangh organizations do not simply have a decentralized and diffused presence in the non-state arena. In many instances, they behave like civil society actors,[21] successfully adopting and appropriating discourses and strategic practices that are usually associated with 'people-centred' oppositional social movements. There are several accounts of how Hindu nationalist organizations have effectively located themselves within the practical-cognitive universe of marginalized and alienated sections of the Indian population.[22] These studies illuminate the varied ways in which these organizations engage in a dexterous politics of needs-anticipation and needs-fulfillment, whether through addressing the material needs of schoolchildren and their families in lower-middle-class urban housing colonies,[23] or through efforts to speak to more subjective feelings of *ressentiment* (the envy and frustration that is engendered by social exclusion and blocked mobility), disorientation in the face of rapid social and economic change, and the desire for recognition on the part of the 'vernacular public' and the new middle classes of an economically liberalized India.

Such evidence of Hindutva's engagement with the minutiae of Indian lifeworlds—the ability to trade in the currency of the quotidian, the banal, and the micro-level as much as in that of the extraordinary, the spectacular, and the national—suggests that in certain contexts the proliferation of civil society associations and the increase in social movement activism can generate discourses and practices of incivility rather than civility. If the violence in Gujarat is linked to the firm entrenchment of the Hindutva world-view—the conviction that India is a Hindu nation that must be purged of its Muslims—then it is civic associational life that has made possible the digging of the ideological trenches. Many of democracy's familiar and essential components—elections, civil society networks, grassroots-level participation—seem to be implicated in the process of going bankrupt.

Discursive affinities: The third set of examples that are relevant to this discussion of how the Modi government and its allied organizations in the Sangh Parivar have been 'playing cricket'—working with existing rules and structures—relate to the uses and appropriations of normative discourses about decolonization, popular sovereignty, federalism, good governance, and the representative state: the various ideational pillars of civic nationhood and constitutional democracy in post-colonial India. In Thomas Hansen's words, 'one of the most remarkable features of . . . Hindu nationalism is the relative ease with which it has fitted into most of the authorized discourses on India and more generally on politics and culture in the postcolonial world.'[24]

Clearly, Hindu nationalism's engagement with existing social-ideological formations does not simply consist of a passive reproduction or repetition. The events of Gujarat, the nuclear testing decision of 1998, the overt agenda of 'saffronization' or the promotion of a Hindu nationalist ideology in the fields of education and culture, and the dramatically different networks of international relations (most notably the alliance between India and the United States) that have been forged in the years since the BJP came to power all point to a substantial reconfiguration of the political terrain in India.

However, such direct frontal assaults and radical changes are only part of the story of Hindu nationalism's transformative impact on the Indian polity. As Christophe Jaffrelot has documented in his study of the historical trajectory of Hindu nationalism,[25] a discussion of the overtly disjunctive, tectonic shifts associated with the direct onslaught of Hindutva—the Ayodhya campaign of the 1990s, for instance—is incomplete without a parallel consideration of Hindutva's passive revolution, or the ways in which, much like the Nehruvian state's quest for dominance in the initial post-independence period, Hindu nationalism engages in an incremental and non-spectacular 'molecular transformation' of existing social relations and ideological formations.[26] One of the distinctive features of such a molecular route to change is a dialogic engagement with rather than a direct subversion or wholesale rejection of authorized discourses. This suggests that there is some kind of continuity, an affinity even, between old and new discursive and normative formations. Differently stated, even if existing norms and agreed-upon ideals do not directly produce the Hindutva vision of India, they do not directly prevent such an envisioning either.

In this regard, as Christophe Jaffrelot and Arvind Rajagopal have pointed out, one of the significant turning points in the journey of Hindu nationalism from margins to centrestage is the alliance forged with the JP movement in the 1970s.[27] The mounting of an oppositional grassroots campaign of 'total revolution' in the name of restoring *jan shakti* or people-power, and the call to 'purify' *raj shakti* or state power of its corrupt excesses, were important instruments in the mainstreaming of Hindutva—instruments, we might add, that were in many cases not fashioned by the Sangh Parivar, but were instead part of the mobilizational arsenal of revered Gandhian socialist figures such as Vinoba Bhave and Jay Prakash Narayan. Moreover, as Richard Fox notes in his study of the synergies between Gandhian socialism and Hindu nationalism, we would be mistaken if we analysed this relationship in purely instrumentalist terms and overlooked the structural affinities between the two world-views—the ways in which the alliance was 'not so much "opportunistic" as the fruit of a real conjunction . . . in terms of certain common cultural convictions and political practice'.[28] The one-day match is a game of cricket.

There are numerous other examples of the synergy, links and common ground shared by the old and the new India. Thus, for both sets of ideological formations, the discourse of national security has come to be the dominant concern of political life, and the authorization of a strong state whose presumptions of sovereignty cannot be challenged is common to both Hindutva and secularist discourses of national identity. In this regard, there is a significant commonality or continuity between the formulation of political representation as a hierarchical relation between a transcendent, 'anti-political' state and its citizens[29] that was the hallmark of the Nehruvian national imagination, and the equivalently state-centred imagination of a Hindu *rashtra*.

Clearly, there is considerable divergence at the level of political and ethical intention and also in the kinds of policies that have been enacted after 1999, when the BJP formed the government at the national level. After all, the differential treatment of permanent minorities through protecting and preserving religious frameworks of personal law is a world apart from differential treatment as ethnic cleansing. Nevertheless, the fact that the political and cultural organizations of the Sangh Parivar have been working with familiar building-blocks—or in the terms of the structuring metaphor of this section, the fact that they are playing a recognizable game, though a much transformed version of it—still remains. This should not be glossed over, especially if the task at hand is the question of how the house of Hindutva is to be dismantled.

The problem of formulating an adequate and effective politics of opposition and transformation in the aftermath of Gujarat is rendered even more complex by Hindu nationalist appropriations of constitutional democracy. There are two main aspects to this impasse. First, the solution is a part of the problem. As the preceding discussion has endeavoured to show, democracy, civil society, and Hindu nationalism have coexisted very comfortably, working in tandem rather than in opposition. Second, and this is a stronger claim, the solution has in a certain way *enabled* the problem—i.e. the structures and discourses of constitutional democracy, civic nationalism, and civil society were used to justify, condone, and allow the violence in Gujarat to continue. For instance, in response to demands made by a wide variety of citizens' groups, media commentators, and opposition political parties for the central government to send in the Indian army to quell the violence in Gujarat, to dismiss the Modi government, and to impose a period of President's Rule on the state, the BJP responded by wielding 'the sword and shield of federalism'.[30] Citing its commitment to the principle of state's rights and democratic decentralization, the BJP argued that the proposals for top-down action violated the federalist ethos of the Indian constitution, and that intervening in the internal affairs of a popularly elected government would be a flagrant violation of existing rules and codes of fair conduct in a democracy.

Moreover, and this relates to the earlier discussion of the Sangh Parivar's concerted efforts to foster civic associational life and its adoption of 'new social movement' modes of operation, in the initial days of the violence in Gujarat, key national officials such as the prime minister and the home minister described the violence as a spontaneous 'popular upsurge' of Gujarati 'society'. In a perverse twist, the principles of democratic freedom and civil society autonomy—letting the people speak and act freely—were used to explain away the horrific violence, to justify non-intervention, and to preclude punitive bans on Sangh organizations. Arguments about democracy were also used to address the fraught issue of punishing the guilty, specifically the demand to bring Modi to justice. Here too, the BJP engaged in 'democracy-speak' by pressing for new elections almost immediately after the worst of the violence was over. In the expressed opinions of party leaders and other members of the Sangh, statutory and un-elected bodies such as the Election Commission, the Supreme Court, and the National Human Rights Commission could not adequately reflect national democratic aspirations, and any verdict they issued on matters relating to Gujarat was necessarily incomplete and flawed. The spirit of electoral democracy mandated that the people alone could decide the fate of Narendra Modi by exercising their fundamental right to vote; true justice would emerge from the ballot box alone.

Discourses of democracy and civil society do not bear exclusive responsibility for justifying the violence. Frameworks of banal and mainstream nationalism were also activated during this period, in the form of arguments about the dangers of 'Muslim terrorists and militants', and through references to the familiar spectre of the 'foreign hand'—one that, along with 'fissiparous tendencies', has haunted Indian public life long before Advani's *rath* set out on its journey. Finally, legitimization claims in the wake of Gujarat also derived sustenance from contemporary global norms and structures. India could place itself in the 'with us' camp of the post-September 11 world without directly compromising on national sovereignty, and post-colonial insecurities[31] about catching up to and being accepted by the West could be put to rest for the moment by the fact that India too had its very own Islamic terrorist demons to slay. To modify Hansen's observation: 'one of the most remarkable features of the violence in Gujarat is the relative ease with which it fits into most of the authorized discourses on politics and culture in the contemporary world.' A jarring and extreme observation, no doubt, but one that is in keeping with the dissonance of the title of this section, and by extension, the dissonance that is the reality of Gujarat: extreme violence within, and despite, democracy.

One final issue remains. If 'every people has had its own way of going bankrupt', if the violence of Gujarat demonstrates that democratic bankruptcy is a possibility as well as a reality, what does this mean for the process of becoming solvent? How does the occurrence of extreme violence within a democracy affect the prospects for democracy, peace, and justice after extreme violence?

A wide range of activities has been undertaken in the aftermath of Gujarat, reflecting the enormity and the complexity of the task of engaging with the consequences of extreme violence. Beginning in the first few days of March 2002 itself, while the violence was ongoing, several groups began to work on the most immediate and pressing task: that of providing relief and rehabilitation for victims. Although this has since become a diversified national and international campaign, with funds and other forms of assistance coming from individuals and organizations all over the world, in the initial days of terror the work of relief and rehabilitation was carried out almost exclusively by Muslim groups, who hastily pitched tents in the compounds of mosques and gathered food supplies for the thousands who had fled there seeking sanctuary.

Relief and rehabilitation efforts in those initial days focused on the provision of food, clothing, shelter, and medical care for the victims of the violence. The longer-term and ongoing effort of relief and rehabilitation includes securing employment opportunities for the thousands who lost all means of livelihood,[32] making arrangements for the present and future education of Muslim children,[33] demanding and receiving adequate compensation for the survivors, rebuilding destroyed homes and places of worship, and ensuring that essential documents such as ration cards (that serve as the only proof of residency and citizenship) are replaced.

Responses and interventions have also focused on the crucial question of securing justice. This includes assisting survivors with filing First Information Reports (FIRs) at local police stations that provide specific information on the events that had occurred—dates, names, and detailed descriptions of individual incidents of violence and crime—in order to begin procedures of criminal investigation; ensuring that these FIRs are accepted and then followed up in a timely fashion; agitating for the immediate removal of state and local officials who had been implicated in the violence; and demanding that appropriate punitive action be taken against the guilty—from local leaders of a Hindu street mob to Narendra Modi and to the national BJP leadership in Delhi (the call for the resignation of prime minister Vajpayee). These demands for justice are being pursued at multiple levels. Thus efforts are underway in local arenas such as the police station; in the national arena in the form of public interest litigation measures (PILs) filed before the Supreme Court, and finally in the international arena as well, as human rights' groups examine whether it is possible to utilize the universal jurisdiction mandate of countries such as France and Belgium and the Alien Torts Claim provision of US law in order to launch civil and criminal cases against prominent political figures such as Narendra Modi.

Finally, the question of prevention also looms large. 'Never again' in Gujarat requires grappling with the deep sense of insecurity and fear that suffuses the everyday life of Muslims in Gujarat, an insecurity that is in part mitigated through measures to ensure the dispensation of impartial and efficient law enforcement where possible—for instance, preventing Sangh organizations from continuing with their colonization of public space and their dissemination of anti-Muslim rhetoric. Other efforts at prevention have included strategic engagements within the competitive arena of electoral politics to ensure that Narendra Modi's ruling party would not be re-elected. Accordingly some groups supported the campaign of Shanker Singh Vaghela, the chief ministerial candidate of the Congress party in Gujarat when new elections were announced in late 2002. Still others have addressed the issue of social, economic, and moral-ethical collapse in Gujarat by working toward the rebuilding and re-energizing of broad-based associational and activist solidarities,[34] and the development of meaningful alternatives in education and public culture both in Gujarat and in the wider national arena that could effectively counter both the Hindutva agenda of 'saffronization' and also the increasingly hollow rhetoric of 'transcendental secularism'.[35]

Two broader trends or patterns mark this repertoire of activities, suggesting that the distinctiveness of democratic bankruptcy also occasions distinctive solutions and interventions. First, secular interventions have called into question the utility and validity of the spatialized logic of the 'state versus civil society' framework, or the assumption that state and civil society occupy different and discrete arenas. Actively engaging with state as well as non-state actors, structures, and practices, secular activists have forged strategic alliances and networks that frequently transgress the boundary between state and civil society.

For example, the adoption of the specific form of citizens' commissions to collect and convey information about what happened in Gujarat is on the one hand an example of how discourses and practices of state authority—the commission as familiar site and instrument for producing the 'myth of the [impartial] state'[36]—are used to interrogate that very authority. On the other hand, the critical or interrogatory power of citizens' commissions would be diminished if commissions were not readily recognized as weapons of the strong. In other words, the effectiveness of civil society resistance is not a product of being outside the discourses and mechanisms of the modernist state, but derives instead from intimacy, familiarity and relational engagement. It is in a similar vein that we witness, as a result of ongoing efforts to productively mine the fissures and contradictions of the state, official institutions such as the National Human Rights Commission, the Election Commission, and the Supreme Court intervening in discreet but hardly insignificant ways.

Second, groups and individuals engaged in the tasks of recovery and resistance are working with and within the existing political system. As noted earlier, they seek to mine the fissures and contradictions of the state under conditions of democratic bankruptcy, when the collapse of democratic norms and institutions is partial rather than total.

At the same time, however, they are increasingly cognizant of the limits of placing unquestioned faith in the existing 'self-correcting mechanisms' and institutions of the Indian political system. For instance, as the electoral campaign of the Congress Party in Gujarat suggests, it is not always the case that a multi-party system has a centrist or moderating influence on extreme political parties. The process of canvassing for votes can equally contribute to the formation of a new kind of 'soft Hindutva' median voter. Similarly, while the intervention of the Supreme Court over the Ayodhya dispute at the height of the Gujarat violence in 2002 lent crucial institutional support to critics of the BJP government, a year later, the activism of another layer of the judicial system—the Allahabad High Court's decision in early 2003 to call for a 'scientific archaeological investigation' of whether there was originally a temple below the Babri mosque—has very different implications.

Taken together, these unique strategies and dilemmas associated with post-violence recovery and rehabilitation suggest that familiar solutions to the problem of extreme violence cannot be transposed to situations of democratic bankruptcy without considerable revision. Thus, the examples of the interventions by the Supreme Court, the National Human Rights Commission, and the Election Commission, along with the statist form of the citizens' commissions discussed above illustrate that alternatives and interventions can indeed come from within the state.[37] This necessitates a reconsideration of predetermined understandings about how non-state arenas are necessary and sufficient spaces of hope, and how disengaging from the state and turning to decentralized, community-based initiatives of healing is the appropriate path to follow.[38]

A revision of the civil society solution to the problem of extreme violence is also in order. In recent years, scholars have argued that integrated civil societies are correlated with ethnic peace, and that ethnic violence tends to occur in non-integrated or communally insular civil societies. This argument has considerable resonance for more extreme cases of pogroms and genocide as well, with the lack of sustained social, civic, and economic interaction between ethnic groups making it easier for state institutions and political elites in such polarized societies to organize and motivate one group to commit violence against the other (or to refuse to intervene and prevent such violence). Accordingly, in post-conflict societies that have witnessed forms of mass violence ranging from riots to pogroms and even genocide, the building of an integrated civil society by fostering networks and spaces of interactions between rather than within ethnic groups (whether racially, religiously, or linguistically constituted) is an important task.[39]

However, such an emphasis on the horizontal integration of civic associations must also take into account how power is differentially distributed among civic associations. Over the past decade, Hindu nationalist associations have enjoyed state sanction, while other civic associations, particularly those formed by other religious groups, occupy a distinctly less privileged position in terms of their respective proximity to state power. In such a context, is it possible to generate and rejuvenate ties between a powerful ethnic majority and a powerless ethnic minority without addressing the imbalances of power between the two groups? What are the limitations of pursuing the horizontal integration of civil society across ethnic lines even as selective practices of 'vertical integration' into circuits of power and privilege (thus for example, the state support of Hindu nationalist organizations) proceed unchecked? And how stable is the promise of domestic ethnic peace when radical reconfigurations of global ethno-religious and racial hierarchies are underway—when the fate of the Indian Muslim is determined not only by internal political practices and ideologies but by the global construction of the threat of Islam?

To raise such questions is to unsettle the spatially demarcated and nationally bound imagination of state, democracy, and civil society that informs the model of horizontal integration—the view that a cross-ethnically integrated domestic civil society is the best guarantor of peace. As the activities undertaken in the aftermath of the Gujarat violence suggest, the process of becoming solvent after democratic bankruptcy entails instead engaging with actors and structures in state as well as non-state spaces, and forging alliances across local, national, and global scales.

Finally in terms of the post-violence situation, the partiality of the transformations wrought by Hindu nationalism's passive revolution has double-edged and contradictory implications. Constitutional frameworks of democracy, associational energies of civil society, and normative settlements about Indian nationhood in civic terms continue to structure the political terrain, and in this sense, the existing repertoire of solutions in India is considerably richer than that available in post-genocide Germany, Rwanda, or Cambodia. At the same time, the coexistence of the freedom to live and the freedom to kill means that democracy, civil society, and civic nationhood cannot be so easily separated out from the historical bloc of Hindutva and upheld as unproblematic and ready solutions to the problem of extreme violence. Simply put, there are both costs and opportunities in continuing to reproduce the rules and assumptions of the existing game, in assuming that a new team with a different winning strategy will bring about a different kind of victory.

In such a context of partial rather than total collapse or transformation, when all that is solid slowly dissolves instead of vaporizing suddenly,[40] separating solution from problem proves to be difficult. As a result, the imperative to think through the longer-term and larger-scale implications or consequences of each immediate response acquires a particular urgency. Certain questions get asked that perhaps would not be as necessary or meaningful in contexts of non-democratic bankruptcy, in which the terrain we deal with is more level or empty in comparison. For example, are there any long-term political costs in demanding a period of centrally imposed President's Rule in order to restore peace and stability in Gujarat? How might the generalized logic of such a solution impact centre-state relations in other parts of India such as Kashmir, where the continued arrogation of power to the national state at the expense of regional autonomy serves to fuel the flames of violence and disaffection? In a similar vein, what are the potential limits of continuing to deploy familiar distinctions in order to condemn the horror of Gujarat—distinctions between 'the few bad Muslims' and 'the mass of good Muslims', the 'terrorists' of Godhra versus the 'innocents' who didn't deserve to die?

By addressing such questions, not just particular outcomes of the game of democratic politics—the political party that wins, the legislative act that is implemented, the judicial decision that is handed down, the mass rally organized by a coalition of civil society groups—but the broader set of determinative rules that shapes all such outcomes becomes the subject of interrogation and evaluation. Attention is thus drawn to the costs and benefits of continuing to play a familiar game, of leaving unchallenged the normative discourses, institutions, and practices that presently structure the political field of democracy in India.

Indeed, future research on the prospects for democracy, justice, and peace in the aftermath of extreme violence would be well advised to keep in mind a version of a question posed by the Caribbean political and cultural theorist C.L.R. James, at once a fierce critic and a passionate lover of cricket: what do we gain and what do we lose when cricket is the only game we know?[41]

SECTION II: THE ESSAYS IN THIS VOLUME

Taking forward the theme of democratic bankruptcy or the fact that India's democratic polity has witnessed numerous acts of violence over the nearly sixty years of its existence as a sovereign nation-state, most of the chapters in this volume provide a different response to the question of how extreme violence can occur in India's democratic context, and how democratic institutions, ideologies and processes may actually furnish the resources for violence. Two chapters explore the relationship of modernity, democracy and violence in the broader South Asian context, with a particular focus on Bangladesh.

Not all of the chapters deal explicitly with Gujarat, but the Gujarat violence provokes all the authors to consider the relationship between democracy and violence. One calls for an approach that links local to regional and national violence, another for linking territorial and community identities, and a third for exploring how caste and gender inequality can bolster majoritarianism among subordinate groups that seek inclusion. One of the chapters relates daily violence to episodic violence, another relates pervasive human anxieties to brutal acts of sexual violence, and a third connects the state's response to violence to the likelihood that violence will recur. Taken together, they seek to move discussions of violence beyond exceptionalism through a consideration of how, when, and why normal (understood both as familiar and as valued) structures and practices of modern and democratic statecraft engender acts and experiences of violence.

Willem van Schendel's 'The Wagah Syndrome: Territorial Roots of Contemporary Violence in South Asia,' provides a powerful explanation for the unusual extent of violence in South Asia. The key, he argues, lies in the process by which four new states—Burma, India, Pakistan and Bangladesh—emerged between 1937-1971. The ambiguity that surrounded the demarcation of national borders gave rise to anxieties about territorial sovereignty to which states responded-with aggressive displays of militarism. In other words the inaccurate assumption of their complete autonomy in the face of their incomplete physical separation fanned hostilities between them. 'The Wagah Syndrome' is the only essay in this volume that examines territorially based violence rather than violence between Hindus and Muslims. However, van Schendel speculates that much violence, whatever its overt justifications, springs from the urge to territorialize religious and ethnic identities.[42] By linking violence to the expected, indeed constitutive, role of a state—namely, to secure and maintain territorial sovereignty—'the Wagah Syndrome' argues that the roots of contemporary violence lie in deeper historical processes of state-formation in post-colonial South Asia.

'The Wagah Syndrome' makes several important contributions to our understanding of violence as unexceptional. First, and echoing a theme that runs through several other chapters in the book, van Schendel dismantles the notion of a singular and discrete kind of extreme violence and engages instead the multiple forms and experiences of violence in post-colonial India. The relationships between symbolic and material violence and between everyday and episodic violence constitute important parts of van Schendel's analysis. He argues that an over-emphasis on episodic, extreme forms of violence can detract attention from violence in everyday life, and urges a focus on the quotidian rituals of violence that are connected to the actual destruction of life and goods that occurs in wars. Second, by drawing attention to the multiple and diffuse sites and agents of violence, van Schendel locates the production of violence squarely within the practices and pursuits of ordinary life and modern statecraft. Thus as he argues in the specific case of violence in the context of territorial disputes, state institutions as well as diverse sets of actors outside the state—traders, political and military entrepreneurs, cultivators, and migrant labour—enact and reproduce violence. Several other chapters in the book also take up this theme of the coproduction of violence by actors in the state as well as civil society.

Third, by locating his analysis in South Asia's borderlands, van Schendel pushes for a reconsideration of the normal spaces and sites of politics. The metaphoric significance of the borderlands as locations on the margins of time and space can potentially modify and disrupt established narratives. Ravina Aggarwal, who studies another borderland in Ladakh (chapter 5), similarly argues that the view from the border should be made more central to scholarly investigations. Ethnographies of borderlands, where latent and actual violence informs and pervades lived experience, reject the view of violence as an exceptional and aberrant phenomenon.

The lived experience of violence is the central focus of the second part of the volume. In the effort to explain the animating problem of this volume, of how, why, and with what effects, violence occurs within a democratic polity, the authors turn their analytical lens on the concept of violence itself. The next three chapters explore the meaning of violence for those who wield and experience it. While most social science scholarship has tended to discuss the context in which violence occurs rather than violence itself, these chapters identify the productive powers of violence, both materially and symbolically. Violence sharpens certain identities while dulling others, empowers some while denigrating others, provides economic rewards to some at the expense of others. Through a discussion of these varied effects and affects of violence, the three authors move beyond violence as exceptional to explore its often invisible, but enduring practices and processes. Social relations that constitute the very fabric of family and community life based on gender (as Nussbaum argues), or class and caste (as Ray and Zacharias and Devika argue), produce structures of violence within communities and in the fraught arena of Hindu-Muslim relations.

Gender figures centrally in all three essays. The very experience of humiliation is gendered female. To humiliate a man is to emasculate him. To focus on the link between humiliation and violence as Raka Ray does, helps capture the degradation to which Muslim men are subject. At the same time there is a distinctive gendered logic to sexual violence against women that stems from the notion that women belong to and exemplify community and nation. If this logic helps explain the rape of Muslim women as Martha Nussbaum argues, it also helps explain how Hindu women can build fortresses around their community identity to marginalize Muslims, as Usha Zacharias and J. Devika show.

Raka Ray's 'A Slap From the Hindu Nation', takes as its point of departure Narendra Modi's description of his electoral victory in 2002 as a 'slap in the face of pseudo-secularists'. The broader project of Hindu nationalism, she suggests, is to slap Muslims both physically and metaphorically. 'Whence does the slap derive such symbolic power that it can come to represent the relationship between Hindu and Muslim communities,' she asks. Ray argues that 'acts of violence circulate in both material and discursive realms, and thus seemingly small scale and indeed individual acts of violence may serve as powerful discursive devices through which large scale violence may be understood.' After indexing the use of the slap to describe Hindus' relationship to Muslims, she describes other contexts in which the slap denotes relations of unequal power, between parents and children, teachers and students, husbands and wives, and upper and lower castes and classes.

Ray deepens our understanding of the character of violence and its significance in daily life. Her essay underlines the extent to which Indian society is suffused by quotidian violence that we ignore when we confine our attention to episodic violence. However the violence she describes is not random but an exchange between social unequals and a method of signalling the inequality between them. The damage the slap does is more psychological than physical. The slap is meant to humiliate and put its recipient in his or her place. The person who delivers the slaps is seeking to 'set the record straight', to compensate for the sense of the being dishonoured. By identifying the psychological and symbolic dimensions of violence, Ray illuminates why people who commit brutal violence often express so little remorse or regret. Ray, like several other authors in this volume, locates the roots of exceptional, extreme moments and events of violence in the everyday practices and expressions of inequality and violence in India. She asks us to consider how the repertoires of extreme violence—killing, arson, rape—are made available, even legitimized, by the social-cultural sanction for physical violence as an instrument to assert and maintain hierarchical social relations in contemporary India.

Martha Nussbaum takes forward Ray's relational perspective on everyday and extreme violence in the specific case of Gujarat. Like Ray, she also emphasizes the social psychological underpinnings of violence; human emotions for Nussbaum are not blind surges of affect but contain deeper-rooted socially and historically constituted understandings of masculinity and femaleness. Nussbaum seeks to explain why Hindu men engaged in brutal sexual violence against Muslim women in Gujarat. Her answer focuses on the gendered dynamics of nationalism: the conflation between woman and nation and the attendant objectification of the female body by nationalist thought and practice, both secular as well as Hindu. But the analytics of female objectification do not explain the specific nature of the violence against women in Gujarat, or the question of why it took the particular gruesome form that it did. How, Nussbaum asks, can one wound, maim, and torture the body of the nation? By paying attention to the specific modalities and experiences of violence, Nussbaum expands her analysis to include a discussion of the dynamics of 'misogynistic disgust' that also played a constitutive role in the Gujarat violence.

What is notable about Nussbaum's account is her simultaneous focus on the specificity of the Gujarat violence and also on the general, enduring, long-term structures and practices of gender and communal relations. In her words, the Gujarat violence involves 'psychological dynamics that are widespread in gender relations; they took a particularly anxious and aggressive form in this concrete political context'. Instead of taking the exceptional quality of violence for granted, she inquires into the processes and mechanisms of its exceptionalization, an inquiry that relates the violence of Gujarat to the workings of non-exceptional structures and dynamics without denying its specific intensity and brutality. Nussbaum's chapter draws attention to the multiple, national as well as transnational, provenances of the violence in Gujarat. Thus, to the Indian national desire for control and ownership of the bodies of women, Nussbaum adds the element of extreme disgust towards minorities that existed in Nazi Germany. Indeed she argues that the influence of Nazism over Hindu nationalism is significant. If Hindu nationalists desire to control the bodies of Muslim women through sexual violence, transnational influences (specifically German fascism) further transform desire into violence.

The multiple arenas that constitute violence, and the reverberations of violence beyond the immediate arena of local politics, are also the focus of the next chapter, by Usha Zacharias and J. Devika. Through a collaborative historical and ethnographical investigation, they show how a local conflict in a village in coastal Kerala became a source of state level conflicts, and, as a result of subsequent global developments, became intelligible at the national level. In January 2002, five people (Hindu and Muslim) were killed in the village of Marad when a rumour spread about a boy of one community molesting a girl of another. This was followed in May 2003 by another incident in which nine men, affiliated with the RSS, were allegedly killed by the National Development Fund, a Muslim extremist organization. When the BJP demanded a national investigation of the event and the state government of Kerala refused, renewed violence broke out. Hindu families destroyed the property of Muslim families and sought to prevent those Muslims who had fled the area from returning.

The essay demonstrates the multiple logics that have led Hindu communities to support the BJP, often for reasons that are at least initially unrelated to their ideological support for Hindutva. Zacharias and Devika draw particular attention to how the dynamics of caste and gender inequality can bolster support for Hindu nationalism. The Arayas, the main protagonists in the Marad violence, are lower-caste Hindus who were seeking to improve their status and material position by aggressively asserting their community identities. Araya women played a prominent role in confronting the police and preventing resettlement of those Muslim families who had fled for fear of renewed violence. The widespread belief that the state was offering special protections to the Muslim community heightened the Arayas' long standing sense of vulnerability, stemming from their marginal location and failure to consolidate a corporate sense of community identity. Zacharias and Devika identify the modalities through which a marginal community seeks recognition by identifying itself with a national project that accords them symbolic recognition.

There are some striking connections between the violence that occurred in Marad, Kerala and just before that, in the state of Gujarat. Buoyed by its electoral victory in Gujarat, the BJP exploited local events that would enable it to expand its national reach, especially in the southern states. It also sought to capitalize on the strategy it had developed in Gujarat of drafting lower castes into its service. Thus the Marad violence provided the BJP with an opportunity to link local violence to a broader national agenda. Even if some of the conditions surrounding the Gujarat violence were exceptional, Zacharias and Devika show how it augmented the consequences of violence in diverse parts of the country.

The third part of the anthology explores what we term the 'before and after of violence'. Although much of the scholarship on riots focuses on the moment of violence, what preceded and follows the violence is often equally significant. The failure to recognize what comes before may make violence appear exceptional in places like Ladakh, which Ravina Aggarwal suggests are idealized for their tranquility. This question of representation is also an important concern for Paula Chakravartty and Srinivas Lankala who show that the media shored up menacing images of Muslim terrorists from outside India threatening the nation long after the violence in Gujarat had subsided. Zoya Hasan's chapter describes the state's failure to deliver justice and adequately compensate the victims of riots or the pogrom. All three papers in this section suggest that what makes violence unexceptional in India's democratic context can be identified by exploring prior conditions that made the violence possible and subsequent state and societal responses that permit it to continue in different forms.

In 'Once in Rangdum: Formations of Violence and Peace in Ladakh,' Ravina Aggarwal challenges narratives of exceptionalism that consider violence in Ladakh as emanating exclusively from external forces. Her point of departure is the murder of three Buddhist monks in July 2000 by unidentified assailants who were assumed to be Muslim 'enemy fundamentalists' fighting for Kashmir's independence.

The assumption that Ladakh is a naturally peaceful place and that the only violence it experiences comes from the outside is misleading in several respects, Aggarwal argues. Thanks to its location, the conflict in Kashmir has resulted in the militarization of Ladakhi society and its immersion in the conflict. Moreover the attempt by certain leaders of the Buddhist community to preserve their community and cultural heritage coincided with the RSS' growing influence in the region. These Buddhist leaders came to express increasing hostility towards the Muslim community and the state for supporting Muslims.

Aggarwal extends the analysis of violence as unexceptional in several important ways. Like van Schendel, she links community-based conflicts to territorial ones. She identifies why it is misleading to view conflicts in the border zones exclusively as cross border security threats. Attention only becomes focused on conflicts when people are killed, at which point the sudden eruption of violence seems inexplicable because it's not located in longer histories of the region. The focus on security conflicts, related in this case to Kashmir, also leaves out the position of groups who are neither Hindu nor Muslim but Buddhist. 'Once in Rangdum' also questions the assumption that conflicts between religious communities necessarily stem from religious differences. Aggarwal argues that as large landowning institutions, the monasteries' castigation of certain groups like Bakkarwals for instigating violence stemmed more from protecting their economic interests than from religious tensions. She concludes with a description of what may be a step towards a more lasting peace, namely inter-religious dialogue among groups of diverse identities.

In 'Media, Terror and Islam', Paula Chakravartty and Srinivas Lankala analyse how the Indian media sought to make sense of the events that had transpired on and around September 11 in the US through a set of 'locally resonant narratives about terror, Islam, US foreign policy and the looming military response.' Chakravartty and Lankala argue that although there was a more far-ranging debate about terror and Islam in the Indian than in the American media, the dominant trend within the Indian media was to view its own experiences through the lens of the US experiences of September 11. After an attack on the Indian parliament on 13 December by Muslim groups, the Indian media further assumed the guilt of one of the persons charged, without questioning the flimsy evidence or the violation of his constitutional rights. However by contrast, the media's role in reporting on the Gujarat violence was exemplary. They observe that the Indian media's contradictory position on these two sets of issues reflects the coexistence of two dominant ideologies that coexist uneasily, its secularism and its nationalism.

More than any of the other chapters in this volume, 'Media, Terror and Islam' suggests the importance of placing India within the global context. The BJP sought justification for anti-Muslim violence and policies by suggesting that it had long suffered from the problem that the US was now facing. Domestic problems, for which the Indian state bore major responsibility, were recast as problems caused by Islamic terrorism. What prevented the English-language press in India from engaging in a fullscale demonization of Muslims was its secularism, which included a commitment to minority rights. The normalization of violence, this chapter suggests, lies in the violence-producing potential of nationalism. The chapter also picks up on some of the themes contained in van Schendel's chapter, 'The Wagah Syndrome'. The Muslim who poses a threat, in the views of the liberal media, is not the Muslim who forms part of the nation's minorities but rather the outsider, who is identified with Pakistan and the Middle East. Anxieties around the protection of national boundaries are most apt to evoke militant responses.

In the final chapter in the section, 'Mass Violence and the Wheels of Indian (In)Justice', Zoya Hasan suggests that there is a close link between the processes responsible for extreme violence and the failure of justice in the aftermath of such violence. Drawing upon comparative material from Gujarat and Bombay, Hasan points to the systematic failure of the state to provide justice, relief and rehabilitation for the victims of extreme violence. In the case of Gujarat, the government continued to discriminate against Muslims in the aftermath of the violence. Not only has it denied them relief and rehabilitation, but it has also deprived them of citizenship rights by denying them access to municipal facilities and excluding them from electoral lists.

Hasan points to a repeated pattern of the state appointing commissions to investigate major incidents of violence and then ignoring their findings. For the findings of these commissions to be implemented would require a host of other changes, including a freeing of the judicial system from political influences, the creation of an autonomous and incorruptible police force, a check on the powers of the executive, and greater responsibility on the part of political parties. As this extensive but by no means exhaustive list suggests, the denial of justice in the aftermath of violence is symptomatic of larger flaws in the structure of democratic institutions in India. Violence cannot be rendered exceptional when it is continually reiterated through acts of omission and commission, through institutions, discourses and practices of everyday life.

The final chapter in this volume, 'Communalizing the Criminal or Criminalizing the Communal? Locating Minority Politics in Bangladesh, by Dina Siddiqi, ventures beyond India to examine anti-minority violence against Hindus during and after the 2001 parliamentary elections in Bangladesh. Contesting the view that such violence is exceptional, Siddiqi explores its multiple sites and sources. First, drawing on van Schendel's argument about the territorial uncertainty of nation-state formation in Pakistan and Bangladesh, she argues that minorities do not fit easily into the foundational narratives of the nation. Indeed, she suggests that the messiness of Partition feeds directly into the ambiguity inherent in Bangladesh's existence as an independent territorial entity. Second, she argues, a culture of violence has developed in Bangladesh, particularly around democratic elections. This, along with the state's increasing embrace of cultural majoritarianism, has fuelled anti-minority violence. Third, as the rape and abduction of Hindu women during the elections suggests, women's bodies have become prime sites for contestations over land and property. As a result, the discursive spaces available for public discussions of minority politics are extremely limited, and even those who seek to protect minority interests are ineffective in doing so.

With Siddiqi's essay we return to the central themes of this volume concerning the ways in which nationalism, electoral politics, and majoritarianism can be sources of extreme violence. That Bangladesh reproduces across the border the violence that India enacts, suggests the value of exploring comparatively the circumstances associated with extreme violence. If India has been viewed as a model of democratic stability, it might also be seen as a model of how democracy renders violence unexceptional.

Notes:

Most of the papers in this volume were presented at a workshop on 'Violence and the State in India' held at Amherst College on 30 April–1 May 2004. We are grateful to the Houston Fund at Amherst College and to the College of Social and Behavioral Sciences at the University of Massachusetts at Amherst for their financial support. The papers and discussant commentaries of David Ludden, Atul Kohli, Arjun Appadurai, Sugata Bose, Ayesha Jalal, Valentine Daniel, Uday Mehta, MSS Pandian, Kavita Khory, Atul Kohli, Sayres Rudy, Sangeeta Kamat, Nasser Hussain, Deborah Gewertz, Mary Katzenstein, and Anthony Marx have been invaluable for this volume. For their detailed comments on this introductory chapter, we thank Mark Kesselman and Tejaswini Ganti.

1 See for instance the distinctions between 'riots' and 'pogroms' developed by Paul Brass. Upendra Baxi's analysis of Gujarat goes even further, as his discussion of the 'holocaustian politics' of Gujarat classifies it as a genocide. See Upendra Baxi, 'Notes on Holocaustian Politics,' *Seminar*, May 2002, and Paul Brass, 'The Gujarat Pogrom of 2002,' available online at the website of the Social Science Research Council. http://www.conconflicts.ssrc.org/gujarat/brass.

2 The shift from externalist to internalist studies of the violence and democracy relationship has been discussed in Matthew Krain, 'Contemporary Democracies Revisited: Democracy, Political Violence, and Event Count Models,' *Comparative Political Studies,* 31:2 (1998), 139-64; especially 139-40.

3 See Krain 'Contemporary Democracies Revisited' for a review of these approaches.

4 See for instance Samuel Huntington's classic formulation in *Political Order in Changing Societies* (New Haven: Yale University Press, 1968), and Jack Snyder, *From Voting to Violence: Democratization and Nationalist Conflict* (New York: Norton Books, 2000).

5 Representative publications include James Fearon and David Laitin,

'Violence and the Social Construction of Ethnic Identity,' *International Organization* 54:4 (Fall 2000), 845-77; Stathis Kalyvas, 'The Ontology of Political Violence,' *Perspectives on Politics* 1:3 (2003), 475-94; Donald Horowitz, *The Deadly Ethnic Riot* (Berkeley: University of California Press, 2001); Paul Brass, *Riots and Pogroms* (New York: New York University Press, 1996); Ashutosh Varshney, *Ethnic Conflict and Civic Life* (New Haven: Yale University Press, 2002); Steven Wilkinson, *Votes and Violence: Electoral Competition and Ethnic Violence in India* (Cambridge and New York: Cambridge University Press, 2004).

6 In this regard, these accounts differ markedly from the historical-theoretical perspective on violence as immanent to democracy and modernity that has been advanced by political theorists and philosophers such as Hannah Arendt, Zygmunt Baumann, and in the context of India, the work of the 'critique of modernity' scholars such as Ashis Nandy. See Hannah Arendt, *The Origins of Totalitarianism* (New York: Harcourt Brace Jovanovich 1951); Zygmunt Baumann, *Modernity and the Holocaust* (Cambridge: Polity Press, 1991); Ashis Nandy, *Traditions, Tyrannies, and Utopias: Essays in the Politics of Awareness* (Delhi: Oxford University Press, 1987).

7 *Indian Express*, October 5, 2001. News reports about the conference are available at Narendra Modi's official website, http://www.narendramodi.org.

8 Such observations have been made by a wide and diverse group of organizations and individuals, including scholars, journalists, national and international civil liberties and human rights organizations and international governmental bodies such as the European Union.

9 Article II, U.N. Genocide Convention (1948).

10 *Times of India*, March 1, 2003.

11 The rules of one-day cricket were developed with the aim of maximizing the spectacle of play, and clearly favour the batting side—for example, it lays several restrictions on bowling actions that are permitted in the five-day test match. Other differences include limitations on the numbers of overs bowled (hence the 'limited over one-day match' in contrast to the five-day test match).

12 See David Forgacs (ed.), *The Antonio Gramsci Reader: Selected Writings, 1916-1935* (New York: New York University Press, 2000), 222-74 ('The Art and Science of Politics'; 'Passive Revolution, Caesarism, Fascism').

13 Cited in Upendra Baxi, 'Notes on Holocaustian Politics'.

14 Ibid.

15 As debates over the Armenian genocide of 1915 seem to suggest, that of 'reading forward' as well.

16 The political rise of the BJP resembles the trajectory of the Nazi party in Weimar Germany (the sweeping parliamentary victory of July 1932).

17 See for instance Amrita Basu's discussion of the BJP's varying electoral fortunes in different north Indian states in the early 1990s. Amrita Basu, 'Mass Movement or Elite Conspiracy? The Puzzle of Hindu Nationalism' in David Ludden (ed.), *Contesting the Nation* (Philadelphia: University of Pennsylvania, 1996).

18 We adopt this term from Biju Mathew and Vijay Prashad, 'The Protean Forms of Yankee Hindutva,' *Ethnic and Racial Studies* 23: 3 (2000), 516-534.

19 According to the RSS' own estimates there are approximately 40,000 shakhas in existence. See http://www.rss.org.

20 *The Men in the Tree* (dir. Lalit Vachani, 2002) documents some of these local variations in shakhas.

21 Sudipta Kaviraj and Sunil Khilnani provide a useful typology of different models of civil society and the kinds of activities that each model foregrounds in its definition of civic activity. See Sudipta Kaviraj and Sunil Khilnani, 'Introduction: Ideas of Civil Society,' *Civil Society: History and Possibilities* (Cambridge: Cambridge University Press, 2001), 1-8.

22 See Basu, 'Mass Movement or Elite Conspiracy?'; Des Raj Goyal, *Rashtriya Swayamsevak Sangh* (New Delhi: Radha Krishna Prakashan, 1979); Thomas Blom Hansen, *The Saffron Wave: Democracy and Hindu Nationalism in Modern India* (New Delhi: Oxford University Press, 1999); Christophe Jaffrelot, *The Hindu Nationalist Movement and Indian Politics* (New Delhi: Penguin Books, 1996) and Arvind Rajagopal, *Politics after Television: Hindu Nationalism and the Reshaping of the Public in India* (Cambridge and New York: Cambridge University Press, 2001).

23 Fulfilment in this case comes in the form of the RSS shakha and its lure of a playground—a space for daily after-school play, the offer of assistance with homework, free coaching for the Joint Entrance examinations, and free khaki shorts and white shirts for children who come from families in which buying new clothes is often an unaffordable luxury.

24 Hansen, *The Saffron Wave,* 5.

25 Jaffrelot, *The Hindu Nationalist Movement and Indian Politics*.

26 Sudipta Kaviraj and Partha Chatterjee have applied the Gramscian theory of 'passive revolution' to the anti-colonial nationalist movement and the post-colonial project of state formation and social change. See Sudipta Kaviraj, 'A Critique of the Passive Revolution in India,' in Partha Chatterjee (ed.), *The State and Politics in India* (New Delhi: Oxford University Press, 1998), 45-87; and Partha Chatterjee, *Nationalist Thought and the Colonial World* (Minneapolis: University of Minnesota Press, 1991). See also Francine Frankel, 'Avoiding Social Revolution: Caste, Class, and Peasant Mobilization in India's Nationalist Movement' (unpublished paper, 1987) for a related discussion of the strategy of 'avoiding social revolution' in India.

27 Named after its leader Jay Prakash Narayan, this was a political movement that emerged during the period of the Emergency (1975–77) in opposition to the increasingly autocratic rule of the Congress Party under Indira Gandhi. See also Jaffrelot, *The Hindu Nationalist Movement and Indian Politics* and Rajagopal, *Politics after Television.*

28 Richard Fox, 'Gandian Socialism and Hindu Nationalism: Cultural Domination in the World System,' *Journal of Commonwealth and Comparative Politics* 25:3 (November 1987), 238. Cited in Jaffrelot, *The Hindu Nationalist Movement and Indian Politics,* 263.

29 Hansen, *The Saffron Wave,* Chapter 1.

30 Upendra Baxi, 'The Second Gujarat Catastrophe', *Economic and Political Weekly*, August 24, 2002.

31 See Sankaran Krishna, *Postcolonial Insecurities: India, Sri Lanka, and the Question of Nationhood* (Minneapolis: University of Minnesota Press, 1999) for an extended discussion of the discourses and practices of 'postcolonial insecurity'.

32 This task was made particularly difficult by the fact that in the aftermath of the violence several local Sangh organizations organized a 'social and economic boycott' of Muslims that was upheld in numerous villages, making it impossible for returning residents to find any opportunities to make a daily living.

33 The immediate task at hand was to demand a postponement of the secondary school examination that was scheduled to take place in April that year, so that the thousands of Muslim school children living through the terror would have the opportunity to take the examination and receive their school-leaving diploma. The state education ministry could not be persuaded.

34 For example, the membership recruitment campaigns that were run by the largest national women's organization, All India Democratic Women's Association (AIDWA), in rural Gujarat after March 2002. See Kalindi Deshpande, 'AIDWA Makes Efforts to Rebuild Confidence. Available online at: http://pd.cpim.org/2002/dec15/12152002_gujarat_aidwa.htm

35 We borrow this phrase from Akeel Bilgrami. See his 'Secularism, Nationalism, and Modernity' in Rajeev Bhargava (ed.), *Secularism and Its Critics* (New Delhi: Oxford University Press, 1998), 380-417.

36 Thomas Hansen, 'Governance and Myths of State in Mumbai' in C. J. Fuller and Veronique Benei (eds.), *The Everyday State and Society in Modern India* (Delhi: Social Science Press, 2000), 31-67.

37 This possibility of turning to the state in the aftermath of extreme violence calls for a transformed understanding of the state itself, from a monolithic and spatially discrete entity that is separate from society to a multi-layered institutionalized ensemble of contradictory social relations.

38 Such arguments are presented by the 'critique of modernity' school discussed earlier.

39 Varshney's recent book makes such a case.

40 Marx's famous description of modernity, as an era in which 'all that is solid melts into air': *Communist Manifesto* (1848), 51-2.

41 C. L. R. James, *Beyond a Boundary* (Durham: Duke University Press, 1993), Preface. The original question: 'what do we know of cricket if we only cricket know?'

42 Indeed, questions of territoriality are just under the surface of Hindutva speeches that claim that Muslims' primary allegiances are to Pakistan or that even if not all terrorists are Muslim, all Muslims are terrorists.

The Wagah Syndrome: Territorial Roots of Contemporary Violence in South Asia

WILLEM VAN SCHENDEL

Is there a special relationship between violence and the state in South Asia? Many social theorists have posited that a monopoly of the major means of violence is a defining characteristic of states. Some have also described the modern state as a form of 'violence directed towards a space.'[1] With respect to these two general aspects of state violence—military as well as territorial—the states of South Asia are comparable to all modern states. But it is not this general relationship that we will be concerned with here. I will argue that there is, in addition, a specifically South Asian connection between states and violence—the outcome of a regional process of state formation that has few if any parallels in the world.

The process in question is the disintegration of the colonial state of British India and the eventual creation, out of its ashes, of no less than four major new states, a unique occurrence in the history of 20th-century decolonization. This process of end-of-empire state formation spanned the period between 1937 and 1971. It created the states of Burma (Myanmar), Pakistan, India and Bangladesh. Historians have usually disassembled this period by constructing three distinct and seemingly unrelated 'events': a) the 'breakaway' of British Burma (1937), b) the 'Partition' of the remaining rump of British India (1947), and c) the 'Liberation War' of Bangladesh (1971). It may be more helpful to look at these moments of rupture as connected to each other in a process of decolonization in which formal state control was handed over to four new state elites.

In this paper I am especially concerned with some spatial effects of this process and the implications for the ways in which these states relate to violence. The disintegration of British India has often been described in terms of necessary violence, as a form of surgery. This is a misleading analogy because of its connotations with precision, professionalism and healing.[2] Decolonization in South Asia was not a series of clinical operations producing four well-defined national bodies. On the contrary, the four post-colonial states found that their physical separation was incomplete and that they had inherited ill-defined nations and frayed territories.[3]

FRAYED TERRITORIES AND CONUNDRUMS OF SOVEREIGNTY

Like other modern states, the post-Partition states of South Asia are founded on the notion of territorial power: each state strives to exercise exclusive sovereignty over a delineated, self-enclosed geographical space.[4] Like other modern states, South Asian states employ strategies of *territoriality*, spatial strategies to 'affect, influence, or control resources and people, by controlling area.' Territoriality is a form of enforcement that involves the active use of geographic space to classify social phenomena.[5]

What makes the post-Partition states in South Asia unusual, however, is that they have to pursue this strategy with their hands tied behind their backs. The geographical spaces over which they preside are anything but clearly delineated, self-enclosed, or undisputed. On the contrary, they are stuck with territories that have very rough edges indeed. For this reason, sovereignty, territoriality and violence all take on specific forms in this region. It is important to develop tools to analyse these regional specificities. Let us begin by distinguishing three types of territorial ambiguity in post-Partition South Asia.

Mcmahonian issues: These are a group of territorial disputes arising from failed border-making exercises in the colonial period. In 1914 the expanding British-Indian state tried to create an enclosed geographical space for itself by settling the location of its northern Himalayan borders with China and Tibet. After tripartite deliberations, a preliminary agreement was reached over the location of these borders (known as the McMahon Line, after the chief British negotiator[6]) and maps were drawn up showing these.

The British colonial state was keen to set these decisions in stone but China was not; it soon repudiated the agreement.[7] As a result, the Himalayan borders remained undefined up to and beyond the time of Partition, when the area fell to India and Pakistan. Despite high hopes that the issue could be resolved by the new states, this turned out to be too optimistic an assessment—all McMahonian issues remain unresolved today.

In terms of the geographical space contested, these issues are truly enormous. China and India (and possibly Pakistan[8]) dispute each other over areas covering approximately 120,000 sq. km, roughly the size of the combined territories of Switzerland, the Netherlands and Denmark. Some of these areas are currently occupied by India, others by China (Plate 1).[9] In terms of sovereignty, McMahonian issues have poisoned relations between these two countries, especially after 1962 when they led to the India-China War.[10] There have been many false starts in resolving this geographical quarrel and it continues unabated today.

McMahonian issues are the oldest type of territorial ambiguity in contemporary South Asia and they involve the largest territorial claims and counterclaims. Predating Partition, they form a colonial legacy that post-colonial states have been unable to shake off. These issues continue to be extremely relevant in inter-state relations in Asia because they involve three very large states, India, China, Pakistan. In addition another state, Nepal, and a former state, Sikkim, have also become ensnared in the McMahonian problematic.[11]

Radcliffian issues: I propose this term to refer to a group of territorial disputes that emerged from the crudeness of the Partition of 1947. In June 1947, two boundary commissions were formed to determine where the borders between India and East and West Pakistan were to be drawn. Cyril Radcliffe headed both commissions who submitted their decisions by mid-August 1947, and hence it is fitting to name the resulting territorial ambiguities after him.

The commissions did not base their decisions (or 'awards') on detailed personal knowledge of the territories to be divided. The members of the commissions were all jurists who lacked specialist knowledge of geography, cartography or boundary making. No surveys

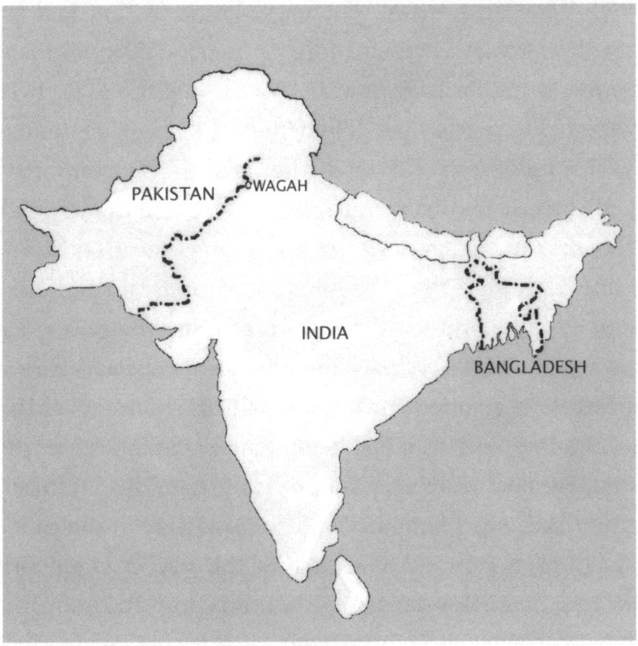

Plate 1 (Top): McMahonian Issues.
Plate 2 (Bottom): Radcliffian Issues

or field visits informed their deliberations, which were based largely on maps that were often out of date. Not surprisingly, their decisions bore more resemblance to a mad butcher's chopping than to incisions made by a surgeon's scalpel.[12] The Radcliffe awards created jagged edges to Pakistan and India: their new borders were riddled with geographical uncertainties and areas of disputed sovereignty. Despite attempts by the new states to sort these out (e.g. the Bagge Tribunal in the 1950s), and some successes, many territorial anomalies persist and these continue to act as 'flash points' of violent confrontations.

Radcliffian issues have resulted from hasty bureaucratic boundary making in 1947. They involve much smaller territories than McMahonian ones but there are many more of them, and their resolution has proved to be equally intractable.

Kashmirian issues: This term refers to a third type of territorial ambiguity in post-Partition South Asia. The drawing of borders to create new state territories out of parts of the former colony in 1947 was only the first step in the construction of independent India and Pakistan. The second step was to merge areas that had been under direct colonial rule ('British India' proper) with areas that had been ruled indirectly ('Princely States'). It was only the directly ruled areas that were being partitioned. The 500-odd Princely States (covering an area of 1.5 million sq. km, or two-fifths of the subcontinent) were not touched directly by this process. They were given independence with their borders unchanged. At the same time, however, they were given only one option: to merge their territories with those of either Pakistan or India, in the process surrendering their sovereignty to the state to which they acceded. Thus the late 1940s and early 1950s saw the spectacle of hundreds of Indian princes signing over their territorial sovereignty, such as it had been, to the new state elites of India and Pakistan. In most cases this did not lead to territorial uncertainty but in some it did, most famously and destructively in the case of Jammu and Kashmir, a Princely State almost the size of Great Britain (over 220,000 sq. km), bordering both India and Pakistan. The way in which Kashmir acceded to India turned the entire area into not only a contested territory between India and Pakistan, but also a major irritant in the world state system.

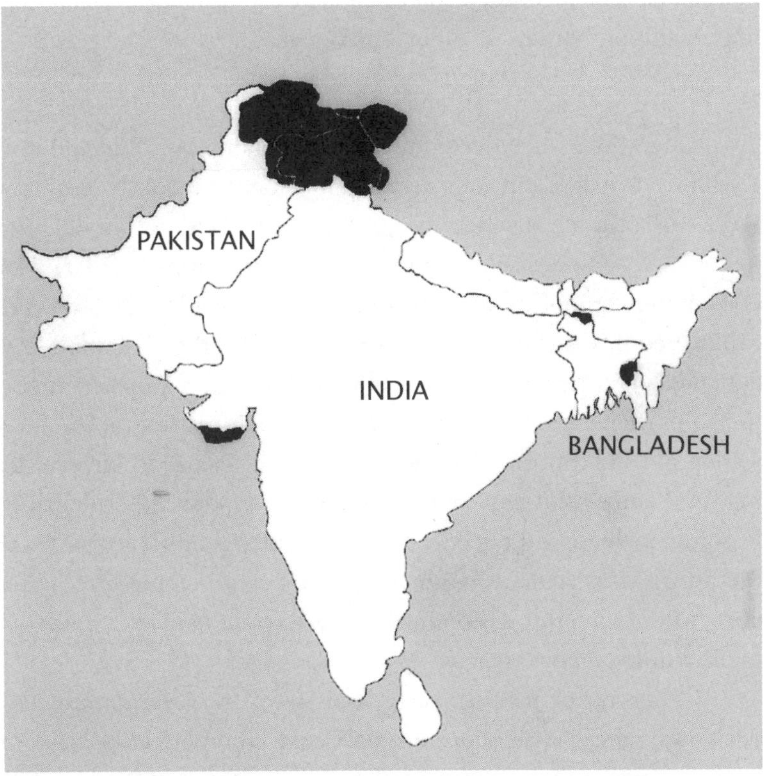

Plate 3: Kashmirian Issues

Kashmir is the best-known and largest example of territorial ambiguity resulting from the forced accession of the Princely States, and therefore it makes sense to refer to this type as Kashmirian. It is important to realize, however, that such issues occurred elsewhere as well. The accessions of other Princely States bordering both Pakistan and India (e.g. Tripura, Cooch Behar, Junagadh) threw up territorial conundrums of their own (Plate 3). In addition, the legitimacy of the merger of several other Princely States continues to be challenged (e.g. Manipur, bordering India and Burma).

THE WAGAH SYNDROME

Two generations after decolonization, McMahonian, Radcliffian and Kashmirian issues still haunt the region because South Asian states claim an exclusive sovereignty over areas that are not at all sharply-delineated, self-enclosed territories. There are simply too many loose ends. When we look at maps of contemporary South Asia, however, we cannot see this. Instead, we see a mosaic of brightly-coloured homogeneous territories, neatly joined by clean lines. Mapmakers invite us to accept their rationalization of space and their cartographic authorization of state control. Such representations are particularly misleading in South Asia, not only factually (compare the colouring of Kashmir in maps produced in India and Pakistan) but also because they suggest a 'space wherein something is accomplished, a space, even, where something is brought to perfection: namely, a unified and hence homogeneous society.'[13]

As a group of modern territorial states, however, South Asia is decidedly messy. Here states are particularly imperfect because—not having become truly undisputed sovereign territorial units— they find it very hard to employ strategies of territoriality in an effective and measured way. In a wider world of states with much more impressive territorial definition, South Asian states look weak, frayed and sovereignty-challenged. To make things worse, being neighbours they also have to face each other's territorial claims and counterclaims. Their attempts to delineate their territory and exert exclusive sovereignty over it easily lead to violent reactions from across the undefined and undemarcated border.

Plates 4 and 5: The Evening Retreat at the Wagah-Atari border. *Photographs*: *Kamal Kishore* (*Reuters*) *and K M Chaudary* (*AP*).

As a result, an inescapable geographical logic has dominated inter-state political relations in South Asia ever since Partition: state sovereignty and spatial exclusivity are anxiously flaunted in a continual regional pageantry that belies deep uncertainties.[14] I propose to call this overcompensated frailty of territorial sovereignty the 'Wagah syndrome,' after the hyperbolic choreography of male aggression daily performed at Wagah-Atari, the border-crossing between Pakistan and India near Lahore (Plates 4 and 5).

The Wagah syndrome underlies the persistently testy relations between South Asian states and permeates both inter-state and domestic politics in the region. The three types of territorial anxiety reinforce each other, and the behaviour of state elites towards their counterparts bears the mark of this triple determination.[15] Even Sri Lanka and Nepal, states without any direct connection to the Wagah syndrome, have to deal with neighbouring states that are influenced by it. The Wagah syndrome expresses itself emphatically in the form of grotesque posturing and symbolic violence at the border—epitomized by the resounding slamming of the Wagah border gates each evening, to the applause of day-trippers (Plate 6). But the Wagah syndrome is not just a choreography of symbolic violence at the border. Its anxieties express themselves in hypernationalist ideologies, state rituals, diplomatic reflexes, policies of mutual subversion and the treatment of minorities. And far from being merely the stuff of pageantry and discourse, the Wagah syndrome often results in the real destruction of life and goods.

In other words, the Wagah syndrome stands for a particular link between states and violence in South Asia. Here state sovereignty had to be built on a territorial logic that is exceptionally problematic. As a result, violent strategies of territoriality have become unusually prominent in the regional repertoire of statecraft.

RADCLIFFIAN VIOLENCE AND BORDERLANDS

Despite a burgeoning interest in both Partition and contemporary violence in South Asia, relatively little attention has so far been paid to the spatial logic determining various forms of violence today. Whatever has been written tends to concentrate on McMahonian and

Plate 6: Closing the border gate at Wagah. *Photograph: K.M. Chaudary (AP)*

Kashmirian issues, and on military violence.[16] In this essay I take a look at a region, Bengal, in which Radcliffian issues are of more direct importance than McMahonian and Kashmirian ones. McMahon's border-making did not affect this region and the merger of its two Princely states (Tripura and Cooch Behar) with independent India created only transient problems with Pakistan. But the Radcliffe awards which separated East Pakistan (now Bangladesh), India and Burma were another matter. They led to a host of persistent territorial conflicts. Although some of these have been resolved in the half century since then, many remain. These ambiguities, combined with the overcompensated sovereignty characteristic of the Wagah syndrome, have given rise to violent confrontations that we can class as Radcliffian violence.

Although Radcliffian violence originates in a process of state formation, the perpetrators of Radcliffian violence are not just states or state personnel. The relationship between states and violence in the post-colonial geography is a much more complex one. The novel geography thrown up by Partition introduced territorial uncertainties that the new state elites attempted to contain with often violent forms of territoriality. In this way, Partition introduced national social orders that were structurally violent and that will remain so as long as these ambiguities are not overcome. But these orders were not static, they have been reconfigured by over half a century of social negotiations and struggles. From the beginning, it was not only agents of the state but also traders, political and military entrepreneurs, cultivators and labour migrants who were involved in acts of violence based on the territorial ambiguities created by Radcliffe's decisions. Such acts could occur anywhere in the territory but they tended to cluster in the borderland where the national territories met and their rough edges were exposed.

Borderlands are good locations to study Radcliffian violence. Generally speaking, borderland studies can tell us much about states because borders form such an obvious link between geography and politics. It is evident that struggles in the borderlands have exerted an immense influence on the course of human events all over South Asia. And yet, the study of South Asia's borderlands lags far behind that in other parts of the world. It is not difficult to see that this academic neglect has much to do with the Wagah syndrome. The aftermath of Partition has produced intense security concerns, and these strongly influence how states and many citizens see borderlands: as the vulnerable outer rim of the national territory, which extends to the borderline, where the known world ends.[17] Writings on South Asian borderlands, such as they are, are replete with national security discourses that see border regions as landscapes of defence, as securityscapes, and as zones of subversion, interdiction and exclusion.[18] These discourses also legitimize the often horrific consequences of conflicts over spatial control.

Social scientists have left the borderlands of South Asia to military specialists and the intelligence community. As a result, these key regions for understanding contemporary conflict in South Asia have been neglected in academic research; our images of borderland society are formed by security discourses that seriously hamper our understanding of the human dynamics of borderlands. Borderland studies that are not afraid to abandon the cantonment perspective can act as a powerful corrective to the Wagah syndrome.[19]

Politically speaking, South Asian borderland studies are highly relevant in a period in which hypernationalist ('majoritarian') historical discourses are resurgent and the demonizing of Others (crossborder, as well as internal) is commonplace. Such hypernationalist histories are discursive forms of territoriality that speak to an intense fear of national disunity and fragmentation.[20] In India, Bangladesh, Pakistan and Burma alike homogenizing Grand National Narratives present the past as a triumph of Good over Evil, and the future as a Common Destiny that has little time for 'marginals' such as borderlanders.[21]

But writing histories of borderlands is not writing about margins. It is looking anew at the big stories that create fictive bonds of community by constructing a national past that is territorial, authentic, moral, unitary, linear, orderly, approved by the powers-that-be, and often self-congratulatory.[22] Borderland histories offer the possibility to modify established narratives and to escape from the 'production of ghettoised mainstream histories' because, like many other forms of alternative history, they are built around 'not foundational but recalcitrant events.'[23] The particular recalcitrance of border histories lies in their questioning of historical narratives predicated upon strategies of state territoriality. They explore how the resultant 'geographies of knowing' simultaneously create 'geographies of ignorance.'[24] For this reason alone the unfamiliar stories from borderlands are important to the practice of history-writing: they are an antidote to the partitioning of memories, the politics of forgetting, and the naturalization of exclusion that lie at the root of borderlands' political and discursive oblivion, as well as their academic invisibility.

A VIOLENT BORDERLAND

The region joining India, Bangladesh and Burma—the Bengal borderland—is a violent place but much of this violence remains unnoticed. Media attention is focused on other borders in South Asia, especially in Punjab and Kashmir, and what happens on the eastern borders appears to be of little consequence. The resulting impression of relative peacefulness is, however, seriously mistaken as a quick look at three adjoining areas along the border may illustrate.

Tripura, the Chittagong Hill Tracts and Arakan adjoin each other (Plate 7). Invaded and annexed by the British at different times during the 18th and 19th centuries, they all formed part of colonial India.[25] In the closing decades of colonial rule, they were among the more quiet corners of the colony. The aggressive cartography that accompanied the demise of British rule, however, landed Arakan in (British) Burma in 1937, the Chittagong Hill Tracts in Pakistan in 1947, and Tripura, a Princely State, in India in 1949 (Plate 8). None of these territorial allocations went unchallenged, and violence marked the moment when the new states took control.

Violence has been a very prominent feature in the subsequent history of each of these areas over the last decades: they are often referred to as 'in turmoil,' or 'out of control,' terms that indicate not only high levels of structural violence, but also serious social dislocation. Words like militarization, genocide, civil war, massacres and human rights violations are frequently used to describe conditions here. In Tripura, the Chittagong Hill Tracts and Arakan the state is deeply involved in everyday forms of violence. Various paramilitary and military forces employ counter-insurgency measures against citi-

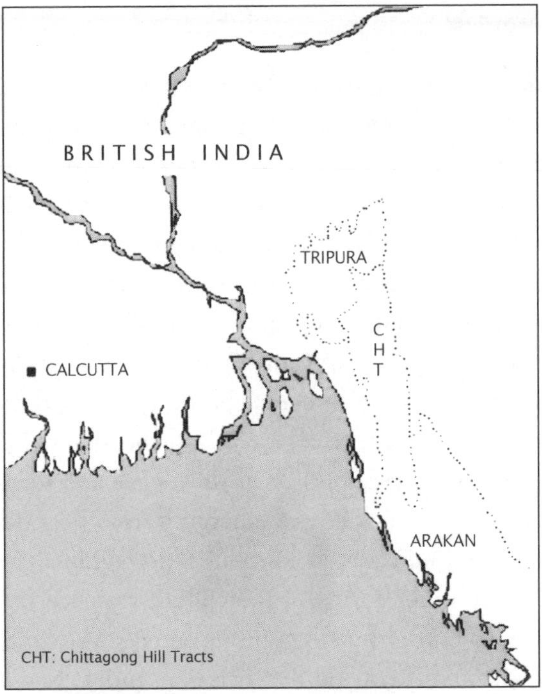

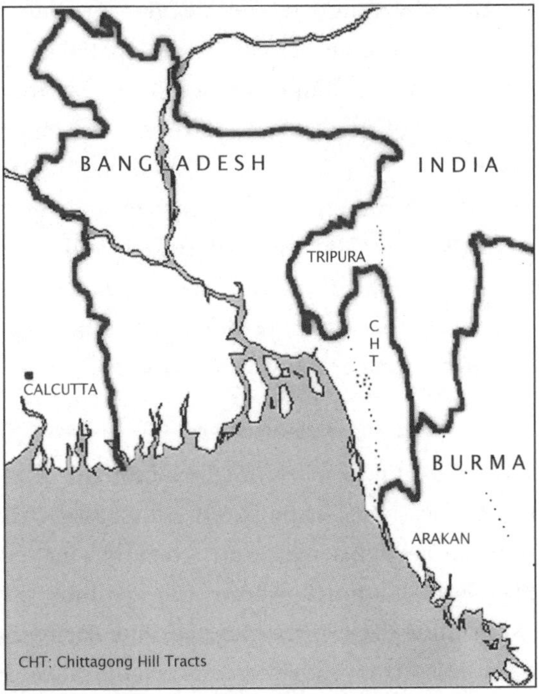

Plate 7 (Top): The Chittagong Hill Tracts and Arakan before 1937. Plate 8 (Bottom): The Chittagong Hill Tracts and Arakan today

zens, politicians set their own militias against each other, and administrators try to form vigilante groups. Ranged against them (and often against each other) are many groups of armed insurgents. In these conflicts, all of which post-date Partition, thousands of people have perished, and hundreds of thousands have sought refuge across the border.

It makes sense to describe such widespread and persistent violence as Radcliffian because it developed out of a contested and undemocratic territorial partition. Radcliffian roots of contemporary violence can also be discerned in many conflicts over citizenship, identity and resources in the entire region of Northeast India. The Indian state has interpreted these conflicts as subversive and secessionist and it has reacted with a show of force emerging from post-colonial anxiety and leading to a spiral of violence with no end in sight.

But there are other forms of Radcliffian violence that are more directly related to border making and disputed sovereignty, and these will concern us here. The border between India, Bangladesh and Burma is an unusually rough territorial edge because it is rich in spaces of disputed sovereignty. These politico-spatial anomalies result from mapping errors or unclear wording in the Boundary Commission's report of 1947. They have now become fixtures of South Asia's inter-state relations. Some have been the scene of well-publicized armed confrontations, lengthy court cases, or political negotiations. In this way Tin Bigha, Berubari, and Padua-Pyrdiwah have become widely known in South Asia. But many other disputed locations along this border are as yet little known beyond the borderland. These are not necessarily less violent places.

TERRITORIAL AMBIGUITY

Territorial ambiguity takes many forms along this 4,200 km-long border.[26] One is the *double claim*: both states assert that the area belongs to them, and violence may erupt when they insist on their sovereign rights. For example, where the Muhuri River enters Bangladesh from India the two countries dispute each other's right to a small island of little economic or strategic significance. In the 1980s and 1990s this spot has seen over 60 inconclusive gunfights between Indian and Bangladeshi border guards (see Plate 9).[27]

A second form of territorial ambiguity is the *double standoff*: Although both states formally claim the area, neither insists on taking control of it. The result is an unadministered area inhabited by people who have no idea to which state or nation they might belong.[28] For example, a group of top officials from both sides of the border visited a disputed island, Chor Ikuri, soon after Partition, and decided that it would 'be left alone to be cultivated by those who possess land on the island, the latter being free to sow, reap and carry away paddy to whichever areas or districts they belong, either Murshidabad, or Kushtia or Nadia, and police on either side would neither enter nor interfere with the life of the island.'[29] A variant of this is the *double denial*, where neither state claims an area. This appears to be the case with the border village of Chhit Bangla whose headman explained: 'We are neither Indian nor Bangladeshi nationals. We are citizens of [Chhit] Bangla.'[30]

Yet another form of territorial ambiguity is *unenforceable sovereignty*: each state has a claim on an area and this claim is recognized by the other state; yet, for reasons of logistics, sovereignty cannot be exercised. Here too the result is an unadministered area. A good example of this conundrum is the existence of almost two hundred unadministered enclaves (some belonging to India but surrounded by Bangladeshi territory, others vice versa). Although the states tried to enforce their sovereign claims to these territories in the early years after Partition, they gave up in the mid-1950s, after which the inhabitants of the enclaves effectively became both stateless and nationless.[31]

A fifth form of territorial ambiguity is known as *adverse possession*. An area is claimed by one state—a claim accepted by the other—but it is occupied by the other state. This is the case in Berubari, 'a territory about the size of an entire union' occupied by India after 1947 but claimed by Pakistan.[32] The dispute led to crossborder shootings in 1952 and it was discussed at high-level meetings till the prime ministers reached an agreement in 1958: India would give half of the area to Pakistan.[33] The agreed transfer was blocked, however, by considerable popular resistance in India against giving any territory to Pakistan, leading to a case in the Supreme Court.[34] Today, Bangladesh upholds former Pakistan's claim and India still holds half of Berubari in adverse possession.

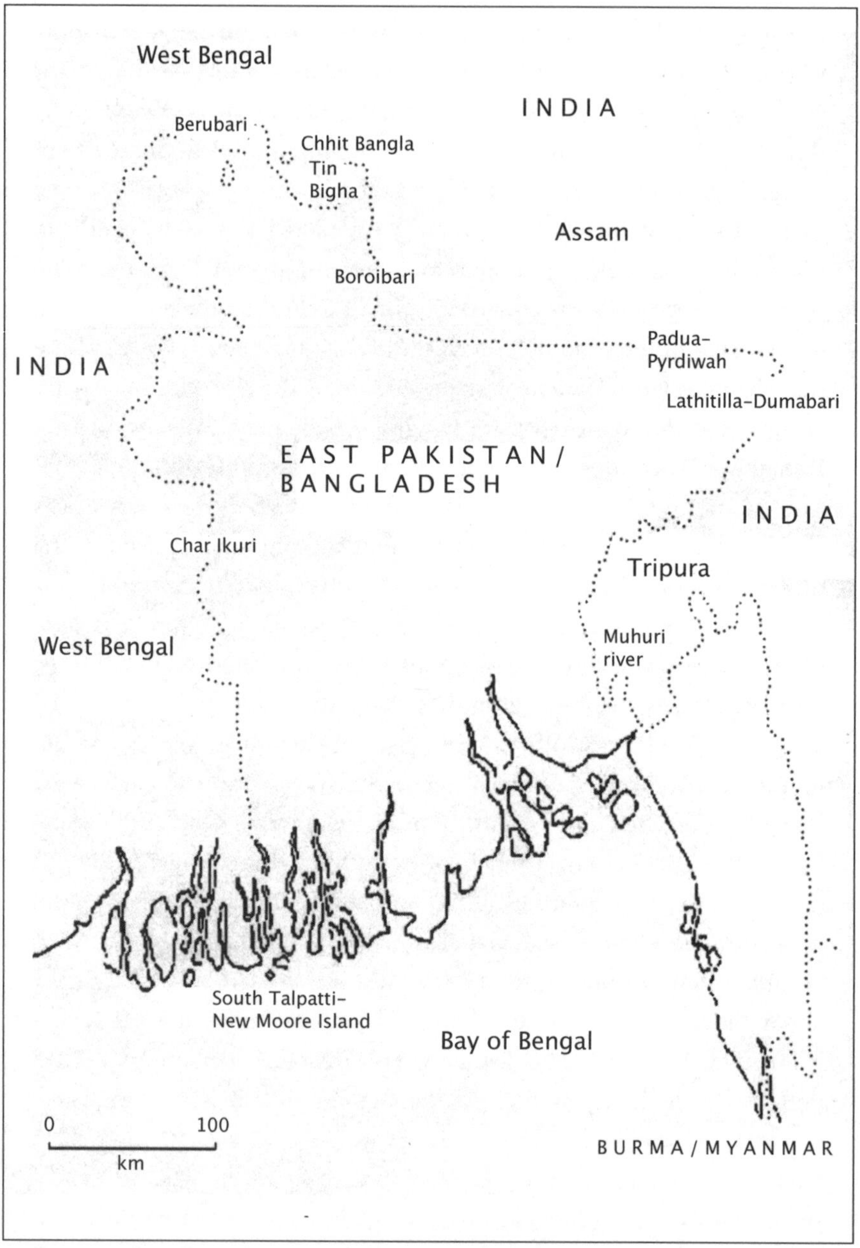

Plate 9: Locations of border violence mentioned in the text

In addition, there are several other forms of territorial ambiguity. One is disagreement about the division of the oil- and gas-rich continental shelf in the Bay of Bengal. Here the main issue is the way in which the Radcliffe line should be projected across the sea. In 1981 a dispute erupted between Bangladesh and India over the ownership of a newly emerged island. Indian authorities discovered this island—variously named (South) Talpatti/Talpatty/New Moore/Purbasha and thought to have surfaced in 1970—and claimed it in 1971. Bangladesh followed suit in 1978. In 1981, the presence of Indian surveyors on the island led to Bangladeshi gunboats entering the area. Soon the island became a focus of protest demonstrations and meetings in Bangladesh. India withdrew its presence and the two countries decided to resolve the dispute through exchange of data and, if necessary, a joint survey. No progress was made, however, and the issue continues to block any maritime boundary agreement between India and Bangladesh. A similar stalemate occurred regarding the maritime boundary between Bangladesh and Burma.

Ambiguity over territorial sovereignty can take other forms as well. My last example is an exceptional territorial invention: the part-time 'umbilical cord' linking the Bangladesh mainland with its enclave of Dohogram across a short stretch of Indian territory. India allows Bangladesh the use of a 85 metre long road, known as the Tin Bigha corridor, to access Dohogram, but only during certain hours. This arrangement does not constitute a transfer of sovereignty. The corridor remains firmly Indian. The Indian side operates the gates on its own terms, and Bangladesh government suggestions to give Bangladesh unrestricted access have been rejected.[35]

MEASURING BORDER VIOLENCE

Each of these forms of territorial ambiguity has led to violence, often repeated over many years. It is hard to capture this violence in exact figures because no records are being kept. Still, in order to get a first impression of the nature and magnitude of border violence, I have done a survey of press coverage of recent 'incidents.' The survey deals with the entire border and covers a five-year period (1998-2002) that was one of officially friendly relations. The survey shows that violence on the border was an everyday affair and that it came in small packages. Numerous incidents were reported, each typically claiming one or a few victims. The press reported 363 violent incidents in which 533 people lost their lives, 1,204 were injured and 691 were forcibly abducted.[36] Half a century after its creation, the Partition border clearly was a dangerous place.

These acts of Radcliffian violence at the border involved many different groups of people. Armed border guards played an important role, but not always in the way one would expect. A general understanding of the role of border sentinels is that they protect the territory from external threats. In the period under review, the governments of India, Bangladesh and Burma were on very friendly terms indeed and they did not pose a threat to each other's sovereignty. And yet, they shared a border that was remarkably violent. Between 1998 and 2002 border guards killed 230 civilians from the neighbouring territory and injured or abducted 636 more.[37] No less than 42 border guards were killed by their crossborder colleagues, and 32 more were injured or abducted—most of them Indians.[38]

The fact that border guards killed foreigners does not come as a surprise, although the number of victims is much higher than the image of 'friendly neighbours' suggests. It is perhaps more surprising to learn that border guards killed 59 co-nationals and injured no less than 464 others,[39] or that civilians killed 46 border guards and other state employees, injuring 46 others.[40] These are forms of Radcliffian violence that are rarely highlighted.

An even more complicated picture of Radcliffian violence emerges when we take into account that civilians killed and wounded each other in a wide variety of altercations at the border. In the five-year period under review, 108 people died in this way and 723 others were injured or abducted.[41] Much of this violence had to do with struggles over who controlled border resources.

Counting casualties is one thing, understanding the human relations leading to them another. We need empirical research, as well as conceptual tools, to analyse the various forms that Radcliffian violence takes. In the remainder of this essay, I explore three major types of Radcliffian violence. I have selected 'flash points,' 'pushbacks,' and 'denying borderland citizenship' because these highlight different forms of state violence in contemporary South Asia.

Flash points: From the very creation of the Partition border, the term 'flash point' has been used to indicate places that were contested between the new states and where these states tried to push their own territorial self-definition at the expense of their neighbour. The usual result of this double claim was, of course, an armed clash. There are a number of locations along the border where such points have 'flashed' continually since 1947, permanently dislocating the lives of inhabitants. One such area is known as Lathitilla-Dumabari, a bone of contention that has proved resilient despite decisions of an independent tribunal and agreements between prime ministers.[42] Other flash points came up over time because of geographical change at the border. Two of these, mentioned above, were the Muhuri River conflict and the South Talpatti/New Moore Island conflict. Both developed long after Partition, when new islands formed in poorly defined border areas.[43]

The term flash point is well chosen because many places along the border are potential trouble spots. Like dormant volcanoes, they show their destructive power when least expected. A recent example is a non-descript plot of 95 hectares surrounding a sleepy hamlet known as Padua or Pyrdiwah right on the border.[44] There was a small Indian border outpost here, overlooking a quiet muddy river. In early April 2001 nothing indicated that within a week Padua would figure as an outrage on the front pages of all Indian and Bangladeshi newspapers. So how did this flash point come to be activated? And how did it then ignite another one, over a 100 km to the west?

There are, of course, two official versions of the story—one Indian and one Bangladeshi—and it is difficult to disentangle truth from rumour and propaganda. Even the name of the hamlet is in dispute: authorities in Bangladesh refer to it as Padua, Indians as Pyrdiwah. Let me give you a brief outline. The ownership of this part of the border landscape has probably been disputed from 1947. Bangladesh certainly claims that it was part of the territory of Pakistan (which Bangladesh inherited after the war of 1971). Whether India also laid claim to Padua before 1971 is not clear. The plot of this story began to thicken in 1971, when Bangladeshi guerrilla fighters operating against the Pakistan army established a training camp in Padua. These fighters left in December 1971, when the war had been won. Their camp was taken over by Indian border guards who had been supporting and training the guerrilla fighters from the beginning of the war. The Indian guards did not leave Padua but turned the now deserted camp into a regular border outpost. In this way, according to Bangladesh, 95 hectares of Bangladeshi territory came to be held in 'adverse possession' by India. This fact was virtually unknown except to locals for almost 30 years.

Things came to a head when in April 2001 a group of Bangladeshi border guards, partly in response to Indian road-building activities nearby, but apparently without the backing of their government, entered the hamlet and encircled the Indian border outpost. The action did not result in casualties but the villagers had to flee, leaving the beleaguered Indian border guards behind. The event enraged the Indian authorities and Indian media widely reported it as an 'invasion.'

A few days later, Indian border guards retaliated. As their entry point they chose Boroibari, more than 100 km to the west of Padua/Pyrdiwah.[45] Boroibari's Radcliffian history is somewhat better known. It has been disputed since 1947 and the border here remained undemarcated after joint survey parties quarrelled over its location in the early 1950s.[46] Throughout, Pakistan/Bangladesh occupied the territory, so from the Indian point of view it has been in 'adverse possession' since 1947.

The Indian border guards' plan was to occupy a Bangladeshi border outpost and to hold it, both to even the score and as a security for the return of the Padua-Pyrdiwah camp and its men. Their plan turned out to be disastrously miscalculated. In a violent confrontation, 16 Indian border guards died and 2 were injured. The attack also left three Bangladeshi border guards dead and 5 injured. About 10,000 civilians fled the area after some 24 were wounded in the shooting.

The events of April 2001 demonstrated that unresolved Radcliffian legacies could lead to wholly unanticipated outbursts of murderous violence between self-professed friendly states. The sudden flashing of Padua-Pyrdiwah and Boroibari caused enormous political and diplomatic damage.[47] Delhi and Dhaka traded bitter recriminations as well as official protests, and the news media churned out negative stereotypes about the neighbouring state and its citizens. The hypernationalist tone of these altercations provided an excellent example of what Sanjay Chaturvedi has called 'reflexive otherness.'[48]

Today the armed forces have returned to the *status quo ante* but the underlying disputes have not been resolved at all. India considers Boroibari to be in the adverse possession of Bangladesh, and Bangladesh, which retreated from Padua-Pyrdiwah after a few days, thinks that India holds that village in adverse possession. Like volcanoes, these two flash points have, for the moment, reverted to a somnolent existence. Nobody knows for how long, however, but locals insist that they can hear the rumblings announcing future clashes.

Flash points are Radcliffian jagged edges with which modern states cannot live. They are locations where armed state personnel confront each other with the intent to intimidate, kill and annex. They present us with a very distinct (para)military variant of Radcliffian violence. There are other variants, however, as the following paragraphs demonstrate.

Pushbacks, or push-ins? In the Bengal borderland, the categories of citizen and foreigner came into being at the time of Partition. International borders were a completely new phenomenon in the region, which previously had been surrounded by other areas under British colonial rule. The new border assigned a state identity to people on the basis of where they lived. Up to 1947, all borderlanders had been subjects of the British monarch but now they were recategorized as Pakistanis (later Bangladeshis), Indians and Burmese. The new states claimed authority over the movement of their citizens, both within the state territory and beyond its borders. Intense struggles ensued over that authority and over the capacity of these states to confine the lives of borderlanders spatially. The movement of people across the border became the object of continual regulation and evasion.[49] It also became a major irritant between these states and is likely to keep the relation between India and Bangladesh, in particular, volatile well into the 21st century.

The Partition border sliced through a society that had always been highly mobile. Many people continued to move back and forth across the border on a seasonal basis and some are still allowed to do so. For example, a group of Bede, a nomadic community, explained in February 2003:

> We have been travelling on well-laid out paths for generations . . . Both [Bengals] are our land, we belong to wherever we can find means to earn a living. We have seasons. Around this time, we camp in Bangladesh to collect birds and honey. A month later, when the harvest is over, we sell medicinal plants and charms to villagers. Spending much of the dry season in south-western Bangladesh, [we] return at the onset of the rainy season and . . . travel the length of Bengal, from East Midnapore [India] to North Dinajpur [Bangladesh].[50]

Such old patterns now became crossborder movements, and new ones joined them. So far, these movements have been analysed only cursorily and our understanding has been hostage to a few dramatic narratives that conceal as much as they reveal because they start from what Neil Brenner has called a territorialist epistemology: they take state territories as their preconstituted, naturalized, or unchanging scale of analysis.[51] Thus they analyse these population flows by starting from the state as a self-enclosed unit and accept the claim that it is states, and states alone, that hold the legitimate monopoly over the identity of citizens and the movement of people across international borders.[52]

The first narrative is that of *homecoming*. This is the master narrative of Partition. It epitomizes the cruelty and violence of nation building by pointing to the intense suffering of millions of uprooted people who had to cross the border in order to save their lives. In both India and Pakistan, Partition migration has been interpreted overwhelmingly within nationalist frameworks. Scholars have focused their attention on immigrants, who were seen as sons and daughters of the nation coming home, to the almost complete exclusion of emigrants, who were seen as abandoning the nation.[53] In this view, the tragedy of the immigrants was that they were members of a nation whose territory had suddenly become confined between new borders and who found themselves excluded from that territory. They were citizens by proxy and their trek across the boundary line—the spatial delimitation of the nation—was a homecoming: they joined the nation to which they belonged and in which they had full rights.[54] Their material loss, traumatic uprooting and suffering on the way were all sacrifices to the nation, and this obliged the nation to take care of them. Inevitably, the narrative of homecoming has produced two parallel, state-centred arguments that mirror each other but do not touch. The Indian variant is deeply concerned with people entering Indian territory but has nothing to say about people leaving that territory. The Pakistani/Bangladeshi variant is its exact reverse.

The second narrative is that of *infiltration.* It is equally statist in that it analyses cross-border migration only to the extent that it affects the future of the Indian state. The view that immigration was *not* a homecoming first developed in Assam and Tripura right after 1947. Here many inhabitants saw post-Partition immigrants not primarily as fellow Indians being cast out of Pakistan and in need of help but as Bengalis moving into non-Bengali areas and taking over. The language of infiltration first surfaced in official discourse in 1962 and it became widespread in Northeastern India during the Assam movement, started in 1979, which spoke to Assamese fears of 'being swamped by foreign nationals' as a result of 'misplaced notions of national commitment' and the failure of Indian laws to 'prevent infiltration from Bangladesh.'[55]

A second way in which the narrative of infiltration was elaborated was by state actors in other parts of India who, from the late 1970s, detected immigrants from Bangladesh and depicted them as lawbreakers and a threat to national security.[56] Many of these politicians and administrators were connected with the new political Hinduism (Hindutva) that held that Hindu India was under threat. They gave immigrants the appearance of destroyers of social harmony who took away jobs from Indian citizens, committed crimes, threatened the social safety net, undermined social cohesion, and subverted the Indian state.[57] Having constructed immigrants from Bangladesh as a threat to the national citizenry, they proceeded to deport them. In

1992-93, in an action code-named Operation Pushback, authorities in New Delhi and Bombay rounded up hundreds of people whom they suspected to be Bangladeshis and shipped them to the border with Bangladesh. Bangladesh refused to take them back, arguing that they were not Bangladeshi citizens, and the Indian government was forced to abandon the operation.[58] Further deportations followed in 1994, 1997, 2000 and 2003.[59] In 1998, police officers in Mumbai (Bombay) arrested 'infiltrators' and escorted them to the West Bengal-Bangladesh border to hand them over to the border guards.[60] Speaking of the deportation of 'Bangladeshi infiltrators' in the Maharashtra assembly, the Deputy Chief Minister said: 'This is a question of Indianness, nationalism and patriotism,' and he linked immigration from Bangladesh with 'a well-organised conspiracy to infiltrate ISI [Pakistani[61]] agents into the country.'[62] In 2001 the Indian Supreme Court adopted the narrative of infiltration when it declared Bangladeshi immigrants 'a threat to both the economy and the security of the country.'[63]

In short, by the 1990s the narrative of infiltration had become a core argument in national debates in India that sought to link immigration from Bangladesh with the planned subversion of India. According to this argument, the duty of any true Indian patriot was *not* to welcome immigrants as repatriates coming home, but to deport them as foreign agents out to destabilize India, Islamize parts of it, and ultimately annex these to Bangladesh. Since this narrative presents border crossing as an invasion of national space or, indeed, as a demographic attack by a neighbouring state, it is not surprising that it is confined to Indian politicians, administrators and scholars—it does not exist in Bangladesh.

By contrast, the third narrative, that of *disowning citizens*, is a purely Bangladeshi one. In East Pakistan, and later Bangladesh, successive governments developed a bizarre counter-discourse: they simply denied that *any* of their citizens migrated to India at all. In 1964, Pakistani Foreign Minister Z.A. Bhutto put it like this:

> 'It is inconceivable that . . . thousands of Muslims . . . would surrender the safety and security of their homeland in [East] Pakistan to migrate with their women and children to the

uncertainty and perils awaiting them in a hostile land beyond the border.'[64]

Thirty-four years later, echoing Bhutto's incredulity, the Prime Minister of Bangladesh stated: 'We do not accept that there is any Bangladeshi national living in India. So the question of deporting any Bangladeshi by the Indian Government does not arise.' By now this line was no longer a short-term diplomatic ploy to counter an emerging Indian discourse of infiltration. It had become a mantra of negation.[65] By the early 21st century Bangladesh officials were still in denial but some had modified their position slightly: now they claimed that there were, in their opinion, no *illegal* Bangladeshis anywhere in India.[66]

The desperate tenacity with which Bangladeshi officials clung to their discourse of denial emerged from an acute sense of vulnerability vis-a-vis their huge neighbour, India. Rooted in Partition, this feeling of being vulnerable was boosted by India's adoption of the discourse of infiltration. To the Bangladeshi state elite, acknowledging the unauthorized movement of Bangladeshi citizens across the border would reveal the inability of their state to control this movement, or, worse, suggest its complicity. In their anxiety to avoid owning up to the failure of their state's strategy of territoriality—and hence its claim to full statehood—the authorities of Bangladesh chose to disown their citizens in Indian territory. The statism of this narrative is obvious in the assumption that those who leave the state territory for India are no longer members of the Bangladeshi nation. Therefore they are of no concern to Bangladeshi politicians, nor, indeed, to scholars who treat their state's territory as the natural universe for social analysis.

This narrative of disowning citizens has had serious consequences for border crossers. Until 1982, 'while denying large-scale out-migration, Bangladesh at least took back infiltrators handed over by the Indian BSF. But after 1982, they refused pointblank.'[67] India's push-back policies could not count on any cooperation from the Bangladeshi authorities. As Indian border guards tried to push back what they termed 'Bangladeshi infiltrators,' Bangladeshi border guards tried to foil the 'push-in' of what they considered to be 'Indian citizens.' During Operation Pushback in India (which Bangladesh branded as 'Operation Push-In'[68]),

> 'The deportation process suffered a severe setback in September 1992 when 132 deportees were sent to the border. The [Border Security Force] tonsured their heads, stripped them and burnt their belongings. The event blew up into a diplomatic row when Bangladesh accused India of trying to push out West Bengal Muslims.'[69]

Clearly, both the Indian deportations and the Bangladeshi denial resulted in Radcliffian violence pitting agents of the state against individual migrants. Denied citizen's rights by either Bangladesh or India, these migrants were caught in the middle. That fate was epitomized by the experience of thousands of hapless labour migrants who, in 2003, literally found themselves marooned for weeks in the no-man's land between India and Bangladesh. Indian authorities gathered thousands of deportees at several locations along the West Bengal/Bangladesh border and for weeks they tried to drive them into Bangladesh. They did so under cover of darkness, forcing the deportees out by beating them and 'terrorising them through firing blank shots.'[70] Bangladeshi authorities refused to let them in on the ground that they were 'Bengali-speaking Indian Muslims.'[71] Bangladeshi border guards and villagers blocked the deportees' way and beat them back with sticks and gunfire. Groups of hundreds of deportees were then trapped in the no-man's land where several were injured in shootings or contracted pneumonia, and at least one old man was reported to have died of hunger and cold.

In these cases, Radcliffian violence took the form of states disowning people. Deportation and exclusion are strategies of territoriality turned against those who are unable to prove their right to be in a place over which a state claims sovereignty. South Asian states face special problems in identifying their citizens—even after half a century many of them have no state-issued proof of identity at all[72]—and conversely citizens face special problems in substantiating their rights according to state rules. The result is that authorities can decide arbitrarily to expel individuals. Such executive violence often ends in physical maltreatment. It is not surprising that this form of state violence shows its ugliest face at the Partition border.

Denying citizenship to borderlanders: States can be studied well at their borders because here they show their complexities in particular ways. The third form of Radcliffian violence that I wish to discuss has to do with the way in which state violence is turned against that state's *own* citizens who happen to live near the border. In the post-Partition borderlands, state rule is largely border guard rule, or, as borderlanders refer to it, *Rifle Raj*. It is essential to realize that border guards use violence not only against foreigners, they also turn violent against their own nationals. As one old Indian living near the border with Bangladesh expressed it: 'Our own border guards are worse than those British ever were! They push us beyond all limits of endurance . . . They should protect us, not kill us.'

We have already seen that between 1998 and 2002 border guards killed 59 co-nationals and injured no less than 464 others.[73] Quite a number of these casualties occurred in pitched battles between border guards and borderlanders. Border villages, markets and roads formed the stage. There were two main scenarios. In the first, border guards tried to apprehend smugglers whom they suspected of hiding in a border market. They would attack the market, ransack houses and indiscriminately beat up village men, women and children. Villagers would retaliate by bringing out protest processions, damaging the guards' vehicles and demanding a judicial inquiry into the atrocity.[74] If the battle took place at a border check post, local people and transport workers could barricade the border crossing in protest.[75]

The second scenario revealed an even deeper rift between the nation's sentinels and the borderlanders whom they were supposed to serve and protect. The border guards' readiness to use violence against co-nationals is demonstrated by the rapidity with which small quarrels escalate. In a Bangladeshi border town, border guard Alauddin quarrelled with a shopkeeper over the sale of a soft drink and hit him. Bystanders intervened and settled the matter. Then, however, Alauddin 'went back to his camp and returned in the area along with 25 to 30 BDR [Bangladesh Rifles] men equipped with sticks. They beat up the people standing on the road and damaged some houses, leaving 15 people injured.'[76]

In the border regions, border guards tended to rule the roost but local administrators did not always take this lying down. In 2003 tensions boiled over in West Bengal (India). Officials in Malda district accused the Border Security Force of unlawful raids on villages along the border with Bangladesh, forcing their way into houses, seizing livestock at gunpoint, gunning down villagers without any provocation, and sexually harassing local women. It was no surprise, they said, that the Indian border population regarded the Indian border guards as their enemies. The superintendent of police denounced the border guards for unleashing 'a reign of terror . . . [if they] are not taught to behave themselves, things might go out of hand any moment.' The district magistrate threatened: 'We are fed up with [the BSF] . . . If they do not stop harassing the villagers, we will lodge a complaint against the battalion with the Union Home Ministry.' In response to this campaign, Home Ministry officials intervened and the director-general of the Border Security Force announced that his men 'would attempt to arrest transborder criminals before opening fire. Even when shooting, they would target at their legs. "Shooting to kill will be the last resort," he said.'[77] Critics mocked such assurances, and a local politician scoffed:

> 'The BSF killed a middle-aged woman in cold blood a few months back when she went to give food and water to her son working in the field beyond the border fencing. Do they consider her a smuggler or an ISI operative?'[78]

What followed were border guards' attempts at winning the hearts and souls of borderlanders by means of sports tournaments and beautification campaigns.[79] Success eluded them, however. In early 2004 they detained a government minister and refused him permission to visit the border in his constituency on account of it being 'a highly sensitive area.' The minister was outraged: 'They should not have detained my car when I introduced myself as a minister . . . One can imagine the plight of ordinary people in the hands of BSF personnel if a minister had to undergo such an ordeal.'[80] Shortly afterwards, a border guard killed a woman tending her goats. This triggered a mass protest by borderlanders who demanded that the border guard be handed over to them so they could lynch him.[82]

These forms of violence at the border can be understood as instruments to classify bodies by training, clothing and arming them (e.g. border guards), by observing, categorizing, searching and approving them (authorized border crossers), or by violently opposing their movement across space (smugglers, labour migrants, or terrorists). Perpetrators of border violence can distance themselves from their victims by classifying these as bodies belonging to a particular category that the border excludes. Whether this is done in the service of the state, transnational trade, or insurrection is perhaps immaterial. A state border facilitates the dehumanizing of 'infiltrators,' 'smugglers,' 'enemy agents,' 'border guards,' etc. and provides instant ideological support for physical abuse: 'dehumanising violence perpetrated on a body is a major element of identity formation in contexts where drawing the border round the nation is in dispute.'[81]

Thus armed rebels or smugglers who set out to attack men whose bodies are clad in state uniforms have first identified these men as specimens of a category of obstructors who need to be eliminated. Similarly, Indian border guards' frequent complaint that they cannot tell Indian and Bangladeshi citizens apart translates easily into their categorizing the entire borderland population as suspect, unworthy of civil rights, and outside the nation.[83] From there it is but a small step to treating all borderlanders as subhumans and disciplining them by physical means. This allows Indian border guards to attack the bodies of *Indian* inhabitants of the borderland, by beating, shooting, raping and killing them.[84] In the process of perpetrating violence, they exclude their victims from the nation and reaffirm their own identity as definers of the nation's political borders who have a right—indeed, a duty—to destroy foreign bodies. Even though borderland politicians may object to both this arrogation of power by border sentinels and the exclusion and physical destruction of borderlanders' bodies that result from it, national politicians routinely condone it.[85]

Metropolitan disdain for borderland grievances translates into powerful protection—indeed impunity—for border guards and poses serious practical problems for borderlanders.[86] Border guards who act as 'thugs in fatigues'—who terrorize and victimize their 'own' borderlanders—appear to be above the law.[87] They enjoy the protection of their superiors and are not deemed accountable to the local civil administration, let alone to their victims' surviving relatives.[88]

The conviction that people ought to be only in a certain place, a homeland, and nowhere else—unless authorized by higher powers—leads to the violent categorization of bodies at borders.[89] Territoriality not only produces borders, by the same token it also destroys bodies. This destruction is made palatable, even laudable, by dehumanizing certain bodies as belonging to excluded and devalued categories—infiltrators, foreigners, ultras, terrorists, smugglers, anti-social elements, or, indeed, borderlanders. In this way, dead bodies at the border come to stand for a greater good: they symbolize security. Far from being an aberration, Rifle Raj exemplifies the post-Partition social order. At South Asia's borders, the violence of Partition is still happening on a daily basis.

CONCLUSION: SPATIAL DIMENSIONS TO SOUTH ASIAN VIOLENCE

It was an exercise in 'executive cartography,' or border-making-by-decree, that gave South Asia's post-colonial states their current territorial shape. As the colonial overlords handed the new state elites the reins of power, they imposed the condition that these elites would accept the spatial arrangements that came with this handover. Their acceptance in the face of the sloppiness of the arrangements allowed a distinctly South Asian connection between states and violence to emerge. For the new states, the territory came first; the consolidation of state power over it had to follow.

Those who took power applied the Westphalian model of statehood to spatial domains that were anything but Westphalian,[90] and immediately found themselves caught up in forms of violence that they could not control. The self-enclosed territorial sovereignty of a true Westphalian state—always a claim rather than a achievement in reality—is especially elusive in South Asia where half a century of post-colonial state formation faced seemingly insurmountable spatial conundrums emerging from McMahonian, Radcliffian and Kashmirian issues. Attempts to overcome territorial rough edges took various forms, many of them violent (military confrontation, subversion, deportation, exclusion[91]), others less so (negotiation, procrastination). And yet, all these failed to produce self-enclosed sovereign territories. The Wagah syndrome, a show of aggressive territoriality based on frail sovereignty, developed to compensate for this frustration. The syndrome has had a quite considerable impact on human life throughout the region. Particularly acute in Pakistan, India and Bangladesh, it turned inward as well as outward. It contributed to the authoritarian and sometimes violent behaviour of these states towards their own citizens, and it left a deep imprint on the strained relationships between these states, and also between them and other states such as China and Nepal.

In this paper I have illustrated the Wagah syndrome by exploring a number of borderland examples. These make it easy to observe the spatial underpinnings of sovereignty, citizenship and violence but such connections are in no way restricted to borderland violence. On the contrary, the Wagah syndrome underlies the particular brand of identity politics that dominates public images of violence in South Asia: 'communal violence.' Much of what is understood as communal violence today can be analysed in terms of aggressive territoriality—attempts to affect, influence, or control resources and people, by controlling area—predicated on frail sovereignty. The new territorial anxieties that were initiated during Partition, and that are still with us, created a lasting preoccupation with both physical and social borders. And this preoccupation with overcoming frayed territories is by no means restricted to states. Communal violence springs from the urge to territorialize religious and ethnic identities. Communalists who are trying to strengthen religious identities think in spatial terms. They seek purity by creating mono-religious spaces, zones, localities, or neighbourhoods. This can be done only by excluding others and by continually patrolling clear-cut social borders. Similarly, political entrepreneurs fighting for ethnic rights think in terms of exclusive and autonomous homelands, casting out those who do not fit standards of ethnic belonging based on territorial rootedness.

In South Asia the politics of belonging focus markedly on the exclusive control of space and thus reveal the territorial anxieties underlying the Wagah syndrome. The Wagah-Atari border's choreography of uncompromising aggression has become an inescapable model for numerous political actors all over the region. Their political styles, identities, strategies and institutions flow from the severe spatial insecurities permeating post-colonial societies in South Asia. The resulting enmity—whether religiously inspired rioting, border brutality, suppression of rights movements, or ethnic cleansing—points to the need to explore the spatial dimensions of everyday violence in the region.

Notes

1 Henri Lefebvre, *The Production of Space* (Oxford: Blackwell, 1991), 280.

2 In a discussion of the popularity of medical analogies in descriptions of the Partition of India and Pakistan, Chatterji calls them misleading because they present partition 1) as a necessary part of a process of healing, a surgical solution to the communal disease; 2) as something that India underwent passively without bearing responsibility for it, much as a patient undergoes the surgeon's knife; 3) as a single act, a clinically precise operation, concluded on 17 August 1947, with all loose ends tied up; and 4) as a technical affair performed by specialists armed with detailed scientific knowledge. In sum, she argues, surgical metaphors lend legitimacy and credibility to partition by containing the violence involved in it 'within an acceptable, comprehensible and even meaningful idiom.' Joya Chatterji, 'The Fashioning of a Frontier: The Radcliffe Line and Bengal's Border Landscape, 1947-52,' *Modern Asian Studies*, 33:1 (1999), 185-87, 242.

3 Cf. Timothy W. Luke and Gearóid Ó Tuathail, 'The Fraying Modern Map: Failed States and Contraband Capitalism,' *Geopolitics*, 3:3 (1998), 14-33.

4 Neil Brenner, 'Beyond State-Centrism? Space, Territoriality, and Geographical Scale in Globalization Studies,' *Theory and Society,* 28 (1999), 47.

5 James Anderson and Liam O'Dowd, 'Borders, Border Regions and Territoriality: Contradictory Meanings, Changing Significance,' in *Regional Studies*, 33:7 (1999), 598, quoting Robert David Sack, *Human Territoriality: Its Theory and History* (Cambridge: Cambridge University Press, 1986), 21-34. See also John Torpey, *The Invention of*

the Passport: Surveillance, Citizenship and the State (Cambridge: Cambridge University Press, 2000).

6 Henry McMahon, who led the British delegation at the Shimla Conference of 1913-14. The term McMahon Line is usually reserved for the eastern sector (Arunachal Pradesh/Tibet) but here I apply the adjective McMahonian to the entire India/China border. Today the McMahon Line is often referred to as the 'Line of Actual Control' (LAC).

7 The Survey of India did not show the McMahon Line as the official boundary till 1937.

8 The states of Pakistan and China largely seem to have ironed out their McMahonian disputes. In 1963 they signed a boundary agreement in which Pakistan ceded areas in northern Kashmir occupied by China during its war with India in 1962. In 1987 a protocol formalized the border. This is not, however, the end of the McMahonian legacy in this region. The legitimacy of the agreement and the protocol is contested by India (which claims that Pakistan illegally gave parts of Kashmir to China) as well as by groups of Kashmiri nationalists (who deny Pakistan's right to enter into agreements on behalf of Kashmir) and Tibetan nationalists (who deny China the same right on behalf of Tibet). Furthermore, it is not clear whether Pakistan actually supports the Chinese claims on the region of Aksai Chin (see below).

9 The two largest disputed areas are Aksai Chin (38,000 sq.km; now under Chinese control) and (most of) Arunachal Pradesh (83,000 sq. km; now under Indian control). There are several smaller areas in dispute along the border. For details see the following maps: http://www.lib.utexas.edu/maps/middle_east_and_asia/ china_indiaw_border_88.jpg; and http://www.lib.utexas.edu/maps/middle_east_and_asia/china_indiae_ border_88.jpg

10 In October 1962 China invaded disputed territories under Indian control and easily overran the Indian armed forces. These territories were along both stretches of the India-China border, east and west of Nepal. On the western front Aksai Chin and part of Pangong (according to India: Ladakh, Kashmir), as well as the Bara Hoti Pass (according to India: Uttar Pradesh), afterwards remained in Chinese hands, but other disputed areas in Kashmir, Himachal Pradesh and Uttar Pradesh (Demchok, Kauirik, Nelang, Topidunga) are currently under Indian control. On the eastern front, Chinese troops entered deep into the North-East Frontier Agency (NEFA, now

Arunachal Pradesh). After a month and about 500 killed on either side, the Chinese declared a unilateral cease-fire and retreated without relinquishing their claims on Arunachal Pradesh. Rumours of Chinese invasion crop up occasionally. For a recent panic, see e.g. 'Open Sino-Indian border worries Arunachal CM,' *The Sentinel* (11 October 2002); 'India's equivocal policy towards China,' *Daily Mail* (Islamabad) (22 June 2003); 'Govt aware of LAC violations by Chinese army,' *The Assam Tribune* (25 July 2003); Manoj Joshi, 'Map interpretation leads to confusion,' *The Times of India* (28 July 2003).

11 Nepal became involved when India, during its 'McMahonian' war with China in 1962, occupied about 75 sq. km in the area where China, Nepal and India meet (Kalapani). Nepal, referring to a border treaty of 1816, claims that three Nepali villages are now illegally occupied by India. The quarrel over the status of Sikkim is also directly linked to the conflict over the McMahon Line. India absorbed Sikkim, an independent state, in 1974 but the People's Republic of China refused to accept the legitimacy of this annexation and continued to portray Sikkim as an independent country on official maps. In 2003, during a thaw in Sino-Indian relations, China appeared to accept Sikkim's *de facto* status as a territorial part of India in exchange for India's acknowledgement that Tibet, invaded by China in 1950, was an integral part of China.

12 See Willem van Schendel, *The Bengal Borderland: Beyond State and Nation in South Asia* (London: Anthem Books, 2005).

13 Lefebvre, *Production of Space*, 281.

14 Krishna captures this in his notions of 'postcolonial insecurities' and 'cartographic anxiety.' Sankaran Krishna, *Postcolonial Insecurities: India, Sri Lanka and the Question of Nationhood* (Minneapolis: University of Minnesota Press, 1999); Sankaran Krishna, 'Cartographic Anxiety: Mapping the Body Politic in India,' in Michael J. Shapiro and Hayward R. Alker (eds.), *Challenging Boundaries: Global Flows, Territorial Identities* (Minneapolis: University of Minnesota Press, 1996), 193-214.

15 For example, McMahonian and Kashmirian conflicts interact in the three-cornered dispute between China, India and Pakistan over sovereignty of the region of Kashmir that Pakistan has ceded to China. Kashmirian and Radcliffian conflicts can be seen to interact in problems of border demarcation between the former Princely States of Tripura and Cooch Behar (now India) and Bangladesh. Cf. Willem van Schendel, 'Stateless in South Asia: The Making of the India-

Bangladesh Enclaves,' *The Journal of Asian Studies*, 61:1 (February 2002), 115-47; van Schendel, *The Bengal Borderland*.

16 For introductions to McMahonian issues, see e.g. Parshotam Mehra, *The McMahon Line and After: A Study of the Triangular Contest on India's North-Eastern Frontier Between Britain, China and Tibet, 1904-1947* (Delhi: Macmillan, 1974); Parshotam Mehra, *An 'Agreed' Frontier: Ladakh and India's Northernmost Borders 1846-1947* (Delhi: Oxford University Press, 1992); Alastair Lamb, *Asian Frontiers: Studies in a Continuing Problem* (London: Pall Mall Press, 1968); Alastair Lamb, *Tibet, China & India, 1914-1950* (Hertingfordbury: Roxford Books, 1989); and Neville Maxwell, *India's China War* (London: Jonathan Cape, 1970). For a recent overview of Kashmirian issues, see Victoria Schofield, *Kashmir in Conflict: India, Pakistan and the Unending War* (London: Tauris, 2003). Historians have written very little about Kashmirian issues in other ex-Princely States. For an example of how these issues continue to play in political debates concerning Manipur, see the Revolutionary Liberation Front of Manipur's 'Memorandum Submitted to the Secretary General United Nations . . . for De-Colonisation of Manipur from Indian Colonialism . . . and Restoration of Independence and Sovereignty of Manipur' (1999), available at http://www.geocities.com/CapitolHill/Congress/4568/memorandum/main.html.

17 Sanjib Baruah comments on 'the din of national security talk among the pan-Indian intelligentsia,' and Itty Abraham and M.S.S. Pandian similarly remark: 'What is most troubling is the all-too-easy recourse to invoking the sacred cow of national security when in trouble and the even greater ease with which so many intellectuals and commentators swallow this line.' Sanjib Baruah, *India against Itself: Assam and the Politics of Nationality* (Philadelphia: University of California Press, 1999), xv. Itty Abraham and M.S.S. Pandian, 'Autonomy of Scholarship and the State,' *The Hindu* (15 August 2001). For the image of the world ending, see Daphne Berdahl, *Where the World Ended: Re-Unification and Identity in the German Borderland* (Berkeley: University of California Press, 1999).

18 Cf. Maoz Azaryahu, 'Israeli Securityscapes,' in John R. Gold and George Revill (eds.), *Landscapes of Defence* (Harlow: Pearson Education Limited, 2000), 102-13.

19 The plea for a 'critical geopolitical perspective' with regard to South Asia's borders is most eloquently made in Sanjay Chaturvedi, 'Common Pasts and Dividing Futures: A Critical Geopolitics of Indo-

Pak Border(s),' in Paul Ganster (ed.), *Cooperation, Environment and Sustainability in Border Regions* (San Diego: San Diego State University Press/Institute for Regional Studies of the Californias, 2001), 405-22.

20 Sankaran Krishna, *Postcolonial Insecurities*, 240-41.

21 Cf. Shahid Amin, *Alternative Histories: A View from India* (Calcutta: Centre for Studies in Social Sciences/South-South Exchange Programme for Research on the History of Development (SEPHIS), 2002). Chaturvedi speaks of 'the discourse and practices of reflexive otherness.' Sanjay Chaturvedi, 'Process of Othering in the Case of India and Pakistan,' *Journal of Economic and Social Geography*, 93:2 (2002), 149-59.

22 Amin, *Alternative Histories.*

23 Ibid.

24 On 'geographies of knowing,' see Derek Gregory, *Geographical Imaginations* (Cambridge, Ma. / Oxford: Blackwell, 1994); cf. Willem van Schendel, 'Geographies of Knowing, Geographies of Ignorance: Jumping Scale in Southeast Asia,' *Environment and Planning D: Society and Space,* 20 (2002), 647-68.

25 Tripura was annexed in 1761, Arakan in 1826 and the Chittagong Hill Tracts in 1860.

26 This itself is an unresolved Radcliffian issue. No authoritative statement on the length of the border is available and various official sources quote different figures. The most detailed ones cluster around 4,200-4,300 km.

27 Including during the writing of this paper. See 'BDR Resists Construction near Border,' *The Telegraph* (19 February 2004).

28 R. Dutta Choudhury, 'Dhubri Border Farmers Live in India, Till in Bangla,' *The Assam Tribune* (17 April 2000); Faruque Ahmed, 'They are Indian but earn their livelihood in Bangladesh: With no health care centre, no post office, no grocery shop, 900 Bhogdanga villagers deprived of basic necessities,' *The Northeast Daily* (14 November 1999).

29 Home (Political) Confidential Records, B. Proceedings, 1B2-3/49 (July 1952), Government of East Bengal. These records are deposited in the Bangladesh National Archives in Dhaka. Below, I will refer to these records in this form: CR 1B2-3/49 (7-52). For similar arrangements concerning the Patharia forest, see the report of a meeting between district and forestry officials of Cachar and Sylhet in January 1949 (CR 1I-31/49 (3-49)).

30 The superintendent of police in the adjoining Indian district of

Dhubri, A.J. Baruah, added: 'Both Indian and Bangladeshi authorities do not recognize Sheet Bangla to be parts of their country. We feel sorry for the villagers.' Zarir Hussain, 'A small "country" called Sheet Bangla that India & B'desh forgot,' *The Northeast Daily* (22 May 2000); cf. R. Dutta Choudhury, 'Tale of a village trapped in no-man's land,' *The Assam Tribune* (16 April 2000). Chhit Bangla is located on the Kaljani River at the trijunction of Assam, West Bengal and Bangladesh. Despite its name (*chhit:* enclave) Chhit Bangla does not seem to be an enclave as it does not figure on the lists and maps in Brendan R. Whyte, *Waiting for the Esquimo: An Historical and Documentary Study of the Cooch Behar Enclaves of India and Bangladesh* (Melbourne: Research Paper 8, School of Anthropology, Geography and Environmental Studies, University of Melbourne, 2002).

31 At Partition 74 Pakistani and 123 Indian enclaves were created. The Pakistani (now Bangladeshi) ones are all located in Cooch Behar (India) and the Indian ones in Dinajpur and Rangpur (Bangladesh). For details, see van Schendel, 'Stateless in South Asia', 115-147; Whyte, *Waiting for the Esquimo*.

32 Pakistan's case was based on the passage in the report of the Bengal Boundary Commission that states: 'In the event of any divergence between the line as delineated on the map and as described . . . the written description is to prevail.' *Report of the Bengal Boundary Commission* (1947), 7; cf. CR 1B-39/51 (1-53).

33 The Nehru-Noon agreement of 1958, see e.g. Shreedhar and John Kaniyalil, *Indo-Pak Relations: A Documentary Study* (New Delhi: A.B.C. Publishing House, 1993), 5-7.

34 The Supreme Court dismissed the appeal to restrain the Indian government from transferring half of Berubari Union and 512 acres of nearby Chilahati village to East Pakistan. See 'Appeal dismissed in Berubari case,' *The Statesman* (August 12, 1965). In 1965 Berubari became the scene of continual crossborder firing between Pakistan and India; see e.g. '12 killed in Dahagram firing . . .,' *The Morning News* (17 March 1965); 'Fresh Pakistan firing in Berubari: West Bengal sends protest note,' *The Statesman* (3 April 1965); 'East Pakistan demands Berubari transfer,' *The Statesman* (25 April 1965). By September 1965, the West Bengal government was ready to 'undertake the Berubari demarcation on the basis of the Nehru-Noon agreement' ('Accord at eastern border talks: Demarcation to start next month,' *The Statesman*, 1 September 1965). Cf. Saroj Chakrabarty, *With Dr. B.C. Roy and Other Chief Ministers (A Record upto*

1962) (Calcutta: Benson's, 1974), 402-4, 470-73. For Indian parliamentary debates on this issue, see Avtar Singh Bhasin (ed.), *India-Bangladesh Relations: Documents – 1971-2002* (New Delhi: Geetika Publishers, 2003), vol. V, 2712-807.

35 See van Schendel, 'Stateless in South Asia.'

36 The survey was restricted to incidents that occurred *on the boundary line itself,* or very near it. It excluded the frequently reported incidence of violence away from the border, in the wider borderland, and also the many acts of border violence that did not result in the killing, maiming, or kidnapping of people. See van Schendel, *The Bengal Borderland,* chapter 11.

37 In this five-year period, Bangladesh Rifles (BDR) killed 6 Indians and injured or abducted 66 Indians; Indian Border Security Force (BSF) killed 193 Bangladeshis and injured or abducted 325 Bangladeshis; and Burmese border guards (Nasaka) killed 31 Bangladeshis and injured or abducted 244 Bangladeshis. In other words, foreign border guards killed 124 Bangladeshis, 6 Indians, and no Burmese nationals. In a few cases, the killers were other state personnel: police, forest guards, coast guards, or paramilitary personnel.

38 In this five-year period, Bangladesh Rifles (BDR) killed 33 Indian Border Security (BSF) men and injured or abducted 23 others; and BSF men killed 9 BDR men and injured or abducted 9 others. No press reports made mention of Burmese border guards (Nasaka) harming BDR or vice versa, despite frequent border shootings in this section. Shootings without casualties were excluded from the figures in the survey. See van Schendel, *The Bengal Borderland,* chapter 11.

39 In this five-year period, Bangladesh Rifles (BDR) killed 5 Bangladeshis and injured 398 other Bangladeshis at or very near the border; Indian Border Security Force (BSF) and Assam Rifles killed 48 Indians and injured 43 other Indians; and Burmese Nasaka killed 6 Burmese and injured 23 other Burmese. These figures exclude dozens of Burmese nationals being killed by anti-personnel mines laid by the Burmese army and Nasaka in the no-man's land at the Burma-Bangladesh border.

40 In 1998, there were no press reports on civilians harming state agents. According to press reports between 1999 and 2002, however, civilians killed 14 Burmese state agents, 23 Indian state agents (injuring 26 more), and 9 Bangladeshi state agents (injuring 20 more) in encounters on or very near the border line. Most of these state agents were border guards, but some were border police or customs men.

41 In this type of encounter 65 Bangladeshis were killed (and 528 others injured or abducted), 38 Indians killed (and 161 injured or abducted), and 5 Burmese killed (and 34 injured or abducted). These figures exclude one Korean national who was injured during a pirate attack on his ship.

42 On the Sylhet (Bangladesh)-Karimganj (Assam, India) border. For some in a long series of armed clashes on this disputed and undemarcated stretch of the border, see 'Indian forces withdraw from Pak territory: Heavy firing on border patrol continues,' *The Pakistan Observer* (27 March 1959); R. Dutta Choudhury, 'Fences broken, river unguarded: Indo-Bangla border still porous, aiding influx,' *The Assam Tribune* (30 November 2002); 'Bangla occupying over 750 *bighas* of Assam land,' *The Assam Tribune* (11 March 2003).

43 The island in the Muhuri River emerged around 1960 and South Talpatti/New Moore Island around 1970.

44 Padua is on the Sylhet (Bangladesh)-Khasi Hills (Meghalaya, India) border, not far from the Tamabil-Dawki border crossing. In the conflict of April 2001, the Indian authorities referred to it as Pyrdiwah. The form Padua is the more established because it is the one recorded on maps of the region.

45 Boroibari is on the border of Mankachar (Assam, India) and Roumari (Kurigram, Bangladesh).

46 CR 1B4-13/51 (9-1953).

47 All national newspapers in India and Bangladesh covered the confrontations for several weeks following 18 April 2001. The incidents were also featured widely in the international media.

48 Sanjay Chaturvedi, 'Process of Othering in the Case of India and Pakistan,' *Journal of Economic and Social Geography*, 93:2 (2002), 149-59.

49 Cf. Willem van Schendel, 'Working through Partition: Making a Living in the Bengal Borderlands,' *International Review of Social History*, 46 (2001), 393-421.

50 Alamgir Hossain, 'Nomads off beaten track,' *The Telegraph* (7 February 2003).

51 Brenner, 'Beyond State-Centrism?', 39-78.

52 They do not challenge the right of the post-1947 states to expropriate from individuals the legitimate 'means of movement' and to deprive them of the freedom to move across certain spaces without state authorization. Nor do they place this state claim in a historical context, showing how it links up with worldwide processes whereby

modern states seek to monopolize the legitimate means of movement. For an analysis of this theme for states in Europe and North America, see John Torpey, *The Invention of the Passport: Surveillance, Citizenship and the State* (Cambridge: Cambridge University Press, 2000).

53 Menon and Bhasin, *Borders and Boundaries: Women in India's Partition* (Delhi: Kali for Women, 1998) is one of the first studies to try and overcome this bias by looking at women refugees crossing the Punjab border in both directions.

54 On the concepts of citizenship and 'proxy' citizenship in India and Pakistan, see van Schendel, 'Stateless in South Asia.' On the complexities of crossborder migration and settlement in the borderland see Md. Mahbubar Rahman and Willem van Schendel, '"I Am *Not* a Refugee": Rethinking Partition Migration,' *Modern Asian Studies*, 37:3 (2003), 551-84.

55 The title of a book by the leader of this movement and later Chief Minister of Assam, Prafulla Mahanta, emphasizes the point: *The Tussle between the Citizens and Foreigners in Assam* (Delhi: Vikas, 1986) the law-abiding and Constitution-following citizens of India residing in Assam who have waged a relentless tussle against the invasion of illegal foreigners masquerading as minorities playing to the designs of the political tricksters and economic exploiters.' For a description of widespread anti-Bengali agitations in Assam in 1960-61 driving about 45,000 refugees into Jalpaiguri, Cooch Behar and Darjeeling districts, see Saroj Chakrabarty, *With Dr. B.C. Roy*, 450-60, 488-90.

56 For a slew of examples, see Ranabir Samaddar, *The Marginal Nation: Transborder Migration from Bangladesh to West Bengal* (New Delhi, etc.: Sage Publications, 1999). Cf. Avtar Singh Bhasin (ed.), *India-Bangladesh Relations: Documents – 1971-2002* (New Delhi: Geetika Publishers, 2003), vol. V, 2390-2668.

57 Cf. Sujata Ramachandran, 'Of Boundaries and Border Crossings: Undocumented Bangladeshi "Infiltrators" and the Hegemony of Hindu Nationalism in India,' *Interventions*, 1:2 (1999), 235-53. For a parallel discourse in North America, see Joseph Nevins, *Operation Gatekeeper: The Rise of the 'Illegal Alien' and the Making of the U.S.-Mexico Boundary* (New York and London: Routledge, 2002), 175.

58 Apparently, the Indian authorities had been able to 'push back' Bengali Muslims up to 1965, after which Pakistani (and later Bangladeshi) border guards started rejecting people whom the Indians sent across. Sanjoy Hazarika, *Rights of Passage:Border*

Crossings, Imagined Homelands, India's East and Bangladesh (New Delhi: Penguin Books), 60.

59 Ajoy Bose, 'Nation in migration,' *Time* (11 August 1997); Anindita Ramaswamy, 'BJP's Oust Bangladeshi drive hots up,' *Indian Express* (16 September 1998); 'Delhi police not up to "find and evict" task,' *The Times of India* (10 June 2000); Brajesh Upadhyay, 'Police find the going tough in drive against Bangladeshis,' *The Times of India* (22 June 2000). Deportations have also been reported from Uttar Pradesh: 'UP police in N Bengal to send back 225 Bangladeshis,' *The Statesman* (7 October 1999); cf. 'Haryana turns the heat on Bangladeshi migrants,' *The Statesman* (3 November 2002). For an early use of the term 'physically pushing out,' by the Indian Home Minister in 1963, see Dinesh Chandra Jha, *Indo-Pakistan Relations (1960-65)* (Patna: Bharati Bhawan, 1972), 279.

60 The government of Maharashtra claimed that it deported over 8,000 Bangladeshi 'infiltrators' between 1982 and mid-1998. In a twist to the drama, many of the deported claimed to be Muslims from West Bengal, and sympathizers tried to free them when trains reached railway stations in West Bengal, leading to exchanges of fire between Maharashtra and local policemen. The government of West Bengal also opposed the move. Rajasthan and Gujarat also deported suspected Bangladeshis. 'Joshi to deport Bangladeshis from Mumbai,' *The Daily Star* (13 October 1997); 'Bengal protests Maharashtra's action,' *The Hindu* (25 July 1998); 'Maharashtra to fight stay on deportation of "Bangladeshis,"' *Rediff on the Net* (27 July 1927); Dev Raj, 'Rights-India: Deportation of "Bangladeshis" targets Muslims,' *Inter Press Service* (3 August 1998); Udayan Namboodiri, 'Illegal Immigrants: Political Pawns,' *India Today* (10 August 1998); Kalyan Chaudhuri, 'Protest in West Bengal,' and R. Padmanabhan, 'The deportation drive,' *Frontline* (15-28 August 1998); 'India acts against alleged Bangladeshi infiltrators,' *BBC News* (4 February 1999).

61 ISI (Inter-Services Intelligence) is Pakistan's chief foreign intelligence agency. Indian politicians and journalists often suggest that Bangladesh, wittingly or unwittingly, is helping Pakistani agents to enter Indian territory. Much less frequently, Bangladeshi press reports mention activities of India's intelligence agency, the Research and Analysis Wing (RAW) in their country. See e.g. 'Report focus on ISI Dhaka hub,' *The Telegraph* (2 December 2002); 'RAW deploys hundreds of agents to watch Bangladesh defence: Monitoring Army,' *The New Nation* (1 December 2002).

62 'Deportations of illegally residing aliens will continue, says Munde,' *Times of India* (10 April 1999); 'With coal comes ISI, ultras, saboteurs too to NE,' *The Sentinel* (28 September 2001).

63 'Illegal Bangladeshis a threat to India: SC,' *The Hindustan Times* (27 February 2001). Later that year, the state of Orissa began identifying 'Bangladeshi infiltrators' with a view to driving them out of the state. '"Bangladeshis" face purge in Orissa,' *The New Nation* (6 August 2001); Imran Khan, 'Orissa to deport 4,000 Bangladeshi migrants,' *The Times of India* (26 November 2001).

64 Jha, *Indo-Pakistan Relations*, 276-277.

65 In 2000, Sheikh Hasina Wazed, then the Prime Minister of Bangladesh, was still echoing Bhutto's statement when she declared on television: 'Why should Bangladeshis go to India?' 'Hasina denies India's infiltration report,' *The Assam Tribune* (11 June 2000). See also 'No Bangladeshi immigrant in India, Hasina tells CNN,' *The Independent* (7 September 2000).

66 This is what Bangladesh Foreign Secretary Mobin Chowdhury said in 2003. 'No Bangladeshi in India illegally,' *The New Nation* (9 January 2003). However, Foreign Minister M. Morshed Khan seemed to create an opening a few months later, during a discussion at the Overseas Correspondents Association in Dhaka: 'India accused us of illegal migration. I say there is. The border is vast. But to make it an issue is ridiculous. We have found a solution to the problem—the cross-border illegal trade must be checked to control illegal migration.' 'Curbing smuggling will end illegal migration: Morshed Khan asks India, all political parties to unite to fight terrorism,' *The Daily Star* (24 April 2003).

67 Partha S. Ghosh, *Cooperation and Conflict in South Asia* (Delhi: Manohar, 1995), 84.

68 For documents on Bangladesh's official position on 'pushed-in' Bengali-speaking individuals from India, see Bhasin (ed.), *India-Bangladesh Relations*, V, 2546-548, 2565, 2569-570, 2646-658.

69 Partha Ghosh, 'Illegal immigration from Bangladesh – II,' *The Hindu* (12 August 1998). Cf. 'Presence of illegal Bangladeshis denied,' *The Hindu* (3 August 1998); 'Bangladesh terms India's claim illogical,' *The Hindu* (22 August 1998); 'Push-in bid along border in Tetulia foiled, *The Daily Star* (19 August 1998); 'Envoy summoned: Delhi urged to take steps to stop push-in attempts,' *The Daily Star* (26 August 1998); 'Dhaka not cooperating on deportation issue,' *Hindustan Times* (18 October 1998); 'BDR foils BSF's bid to push in Indian Muslims,' *The New Nation* (8 May 2002).

70 'Foreign Minister discusses push-in issue with WB CM: Unscheduled stopover in Kolkata on way back from US,' *The Independent* (1 February 2003).

71 The disagreements over the identity of deportees from India were complicated by a continual mixing of national identities (citizens of India and Bangladesh) and religious identities (Muslims and non-Muslims, particularly Hindus). Bangladesh's stand that India was pushing back Indian citizens who were Muslims, rather than Bangladeshi citizens who were Muslims, ignored the fact that India was also deporting Hindus who were thought to be Bangladeshi citizens. On the other hand, Hindu nationalist politicians in India stuck to the 'homecoming' thesis: a spokesman declared that the Vishwa Hindu Parishad (VHP) regarded 'Muslim Bangladeshis as illegal foreigners while the Hindus are refugees as they did not have any place to seek shelter except India.' See '13 Indians pushed into Meherpur,' *The New Nation* (23 May 2003); 'VHP warns against Bangla influx,' *The Assam Tribune* (26 May 2003).

72 For example, birth and death registration systems do exist in Bangladesh and eastern India but they are notoriously unreliable and bypass the vast majority of inhabitants.

73 In this five-year period, Bangladesh Rifles (BDR) killed 5 Bangladeshis and injured 398 other Bangladeshis at or very near the border; Indian Border Security Force (BSF) and Assam Rifles killed 48 Indians and injured 43 other Indians; and Burmese Nasaka killed 6 Burmese and injured 23 other Burmese. These figures exclude dozens of Burmese nationals killed by anti-personnel mines laid by the Burmese army and Nasaka in the no-man's land at the Burma-Bangladesh border.

74 After one of these attacks in a Bangladesh border market, a national daily wrote in an editorial about 'a remorseless show of strength' and 'excesses committed on innocent civilians.' It demanded that the BDR should make a formal apology to the villagers. 'We condemn the BDR action . . . People already have a somewhat negative perception of their failure to have the desired impact on smuggling, drug and arms racketeering and trafficking of women and children across the border. Such an incident of highhandedness is bound to put further dent on their credibility . . . the BDR high command should immediately initiate an investigation into the matter and take stringent disciplinary measures against the responsible jawaans [men].' 'Villagers, BDR clash in Chuadanga: 100 hurt,' *The New*

Nation (13 March 2000); 'Editorial: BDR men going haywire,' *The New Nation* (14 March 2000). For a similar case involving Indian border guards and villagers, see 'Atrocities by BSF alleged,' *The Assam Tribune* (1 May 2000). For Murshidabad, see 'Token end to border row,' *The Telegraph* (9 April 2002). Sometimes border guards clashed with people living further from the border, e.g. Indian border guards getting involved in a pitched battle with inhabitants of Gughupara, a village 5 km from the border in Murshidabad where 30 buffaloes 'were huddled together . . . for smuggling.' The guards gunned down three villagers, killing one and seriously injuring two others, and the villagers injured three guards with 'sharp weapons' and bricks. Such confrontations in the borderland, but far from the boundary line, have not been included in the figures given in this chapter. 'BSF battles rustlers,' *The Telegraph* (6 February 2002).

75 For protests at the border crossings ('land ports') of Sona Masjid, Benapol and Hili, see 'Deadlock at Sonamasjid Land Customs station continues for 10 days,' *The Independent* (16 April 2000); 'Export-import thru' Benapole suspended,' *The Daily Star* (25 November 2000); 'Trucks to Bangla held up on border,' *The Telegraph* (5 January 2001).

76 'BDR men clash with people in Joypurhat: 15 injured,' *The New Nation* (25 March 2000). For a similar case in Meghalaya (India), see 'One hurt as BSF opens fire on mob – Police to probe incident,' *The Telegraph* (6 November 2002). Cf. 'BSF jawans kill 2 near Bangladesh border,' *The Times of India* (20 January 2003).

77 'BSF steps to better relations with villagers,' *The Times of India* (15 March 2003); 'Bengali barrier in border rows,' *The Telegraph* (16 March 2003); 'BSF pledge caution on border fire,' *The Times of India* (17 March 2003); cf. Sakyasen Mitra, 'BSF plans to deploy Bangla-speaking men along border to reduce tension,' *The Daily Star* (15 June 2003).

78 Gobinda Roy, Forward Bloc MLA from North Bengal, quoted in 'BSF "firing" goes up at border area,' *The Times of India* (19 February 2003). In Cooch Behar another MLA, Nripen Roy, was equally indignant: 'The BSF reign supreme . . . we have been flooded with complaints.' Main Uddin Chisti, 'Fence bruises border villages,' *The Telegraph* (3 June 2003).

79 For BSF attempts to convince borderlanders that 'manning the international borders is not all about grim-faced jawans with fingers on the trigger, ready to shoot at the slightest provocation,' see e.g.

Bidhayak Das, 'Charity begins at the border: BSF tries to improve quality of life in interiors of Meghalaya,' *The Telegraph* (18 July 2003).

80 'BSF detains jail minister,' *The Telegraph* (8 February 2004).

81 Abhijit Chakrabarty, 'BSF guns down mother of 3,' *The Telegraph* (17 February 2004).

82 Hastings Donnan and Thomas M. Wilson, *Borders: Frontiers of Identity, Nation and State* (Oxford and New York: Berg, 1999), 141.

83 'The common man living close to the border is not treated like an Indian citizen.' Kamal Guha, the West Bengal Minister of Agriculture, quoted in 'Kamal trains guns at BSF "excesses",' *The Telegraph* (1 March 2003).

84 A similar process of dehumanizing borderlanders' bodies could be observed on the Bangladeshi side of the border. Here Bangladesh border guards (BDR) could turn violent against Bangladeshi citizens. One form of violence was rape. Zuan Rahman, a border guard of Sonatia border outpost in Panchagarh, abducted a local woman and raped her. When her co-villagers heard about this, they chased and caught him, and kept him confined in the village. Colleagues of the BDR man then rushed to the site and attacked the villagers. After wounding 5 people, including the woman who had been raped, they 'snatched the rapist from the villagers.' 'Five injured as BDR men, villagers clash,' *The Independent* (31 May 2003).

85 Cf. van Schendel, *The Bengal Borderland*, Chapter 11.

86 Bangladeshi borderlanders greeted with mixed feelings their Prime Minister's declaration that 'BDR members have been playing a commendable role in discharging their major responsibility with utmost honesty, sincerity and performance.' 'BDR members playing commendable role: Khaleda,' *The New Nation* (9 March 2002). On BDR men harassing Bangladeshi borderlanders, see Francis Rolt, *On the Brink of Bengal* (London: John Murray, 1991), 141-42.

87 The term 'thugs in fatigues' is taken from Debarati Agarwala, 'BSF jawans snare cattle booty,' *The Telegraph* (7 January 2003).

88 For some press reports, see Debarati Agarwala, 'Malda calls meet on BSF "excesses",' *The Telegraph* (14 January 2003); 'Govt draws the line for border guards,' *The Telegraph* (15 January, 2003); 'Tiller row sparks BSF fury,' *The Telegraph* (29 January 2003); '"Assault" sparks BSF boycott: Jawans beat up Congress leader, brother,' *The Telegraph* (10 February 2003); 'BSF fires on students in slap case,' *The Telegraph* (19 January 2003); 'BSF jawan shoots at student,' *The Statesman* (20 January 2003); Rousik Sen, 'BSF martial law robs villages of marital

joy,' *The Telegraph* (30 January 2003); Abhijit Chakraborty, 'Bandh to protest BSF "excesses",' *The Telegraph* (18 January 2003); Alamgir Hossain, 'Traders' ire on violent jawans,' *The Telegraph* (7 November 2002); 'Cattle battle with BSF,' *The Telegraph* (28 July 2003); Rajeev Bhattacharyya, 'Border village in dire straits,' *The Telegraph* (26 February 2003).

89 An example of territoriality at the scale of the human body. On the human body as a geographical scale, see Sally A. Marston, 'The Social Construction of Scale,' *Progress in Human Geography* 24:2 (2000), 219-42.

90 That is, the type of state that developed after the Treaty of Westphalia (1648), first in Europe and then in the rest of the world. The Treaty of Westphalia recognized 'the existence of an interstate system composed of contiguous, bounded territories ruled by sovereign states committed to the principle of noninterference in each other's internal affairs . . . This bundling of territoriality to state sovereignty is the essential characteristic of the modern interstate system.' Brenner, 'Beyond State-Centrism?' 47.

91 It was not possible to touch on technologies of violent exclusion (e.g. border fencing and anti-personnel mines) being used along South Asia's Partition borders.

A Slap from the Hindu Nation

RAKA RAY

A body is docile that may be subjected, used, transformed and improved—
Michel Foucault[1]

When Narendra Modi, the chief minister of the state of Gujarat comprehensively won the elections in December 2002, despite his involvement in orchestrating the massacre of Muslims in Gujarat earlier that year, he reportedly described his victory as 'a slap in the face for pseudo-secularists'.[2] The chat rooms of *Hindunet.org* were jammed with excited discussion about the meaning of Modi's victory. Lata Jagtiani, a regular columnist, and one of the many zealous middle-class supporters of the Sangh Parivar, celebrated the triumph of the BJP, and asked what made the 'BJP such a winner, time after time, in Gujarat?' In an article titled 'Gujarat: The Second Slap from the Nation', her answer was that there were lessons to be learnt from the events in Godhra.

> Somebody out there has been slapped twice. The first slap was the violent retaliation that spread in other parts of Gujarat. The second, more powerful slap was delivered through non-violent means: through the ballot. Both ballot and bullet have had their say. If there were any anti-national forces out there that planned to destabilize India through sudden and sporadic terrorist attacks on civilians, they must be doing a serious re-think now. The Godhra attack not only set fire to the 59 passengers, mostly women and children, it also set fire to any successful strategies of violence. Violence has been

> answered by violence and also, later, much later, by non-violence . . .
>
> It is really so simple. Violence is counter-productive and every violent act will only trigger off greater unity and cohesiveness among the threatened population. When there is a great threat there is an even greater determination to stand up to the threat.
>
> This second slap will result in an increased polarization of the Indian population everywhere. The more violent the terrorists get the greater the hardening of stands from the civilian population. A Gujarati friend aptly described this as *apni kabar khud khod rahen hain* [they are digging their own grave]. It's time for the violent ones to lay down their arms and come to the negotiating table, because that is the last way left . . . [3]

The Hindu nation's violence against Muslims—the 'someone out there'—is, Jagtiani suggests, a double lesson. The first lesson is that Hindus *will* answer violence with violence. This is the lesson of retaliation. But that is not enough. The violence, Jagtiani notes, is then followed by the non-violent embrace of the past violence through the ballot box. We may think of this as the lesson of vindication. Yet unlike the vision of democracy conjured by the ballot box, the barely hidden threat that lurks behind it is to be noted: 'the violent ones' (Muslims, again not mentioned by name because they do not need to be—they are the nation's Other) are digging their own graves (they are clearly Muslims since Hindus do not bury their dead, and the Urdu word *kabar* is explicitly used). It is Muslims who have been slapped twice. The first slap, the slap of retaliation, is physical. The second, the slap of vindication, is symbolic. In my use of the word symbolic, I do not mean to be read as saying it is 'merely' so.[4] The symbolic is rarely 'merely' so, and electoral victories have profound consequences for people's lives. I simply want to note here that the massacres and the electoral victories were both considered in the same way, even though in the second use of the word 'slap' literal physical violence was not implied. Muslims, the article suggests, must be slapped both physically/materially and metaphorically/politically. The imagery of a slap returns with astounding and chilling regularity in recent

Indian discussions of Muslims in India, and of what Muslims are doing to the national body of India. In this essay I ask why this should be. Whence does the slap derive such symbolic power that it can come to represent the relationship between the Hindu and Muslim communities?

I begin with four examples of the use of the word 'slap' to index the relationship between Hindu and Muslim communities (or India and Pakistan).[5] A weblog on *Sulekha.com* gleefully reports 'A Tight Slap to Pakistan by Bush' referring to a statement made by the US President praising Indian and other democracies in which Pakistan was not mentioned.[6] Here the writer and his over 500 respondents share in the joy that the US, Pakistan's powerful ally, has publicly shown that it does not consider Pakistan a democracy. By doing so, the US has embarrassed and humiliated Pakistan.

The word 'slap' is used to imply a weak and effeminate leadership which allows its borders to be penetrated. Thus also Vishnu Hari Dalmia of the VHP in the following quote:

> REPORTER: What do you think of the reports saying there was a Bangladesh troop build-up on the other side of the border?
> DALMIA: Of course, I am not surprised. When signals are being sent that anybody can enter India, slap its citizens in the face and spill its soldiers' blood, hostile external elements are naturally encouraged.[7]

The word 'slap' is loaded with gendered meanings of subservience, weakness, and effeminacy. The leadership of the nation is indicted for its failures of masculinity in allowing the nation under its protection to be slapped or slappeable. Indeed, as Paola Bachhetta has argued, one of the planks of the Hindu Right has been its anxiety around queerness indicated by weakness and effeminacy.[8] In the context of the hypermasculinity assigned to Muslim men, this weakness is all the more problematic. The Rashtriya Swayamsevak Sangh (RSS), the ideological 'father' of the Hindu Right, historically associated the Congress party with the sort of effeminacy that would appease Muslims and allow such a penetration to take place.[9]

Even Hindus who are sympathetic to Muslims in India have adopted the metaphor of slaps. This from a chat room discussion on

'Muslims are the problem in India':

> If u slap ur friend then the next moment u will get a slap that is the thing now happening. first we slapped them now they are slapping us. just take that slapping hand from the face to the heart. they will also give their hand to ur heart.[10]

Here however, the writer argues that it was the Hindus who first turned away from their 'friends'—the Indian Muslims. It was in retaliation for the hurt that Indian Muslims were ready to slap Hindus. It is the responsibility of Hindus to show friendship and this would be followed by a similar gesture by Muslims. Indeed, the metaphor of the slap is so powerfully resonant that the inability to slap is interpreted as a sign of inequality. Thus, Altaf Hussain Qadri writes:

> Maulana Hifzur Rahman (1901-1962), a leader of Jamiat Ulama-e-Hind, once said that he would consider India a secular country only when it became possible for a Muslim to slap a Hindu in the street without it triggering a communal riot in the city.[11]

Here Rahman refers to a personal conflict—expressed through the medium of the slap—which should remain at the level of a personal confrontation between two equal individuals and not be construed in communal terms. That a Hindu can slap a Muslim with impunity and yet a Muslim cannot do the same reveals the inequality between the two communities.

There are several questions that arise as we think through the significance of the repeated references to slaps in these discussions — questions that have both to do with its usage in quotidian Indian life as well as its rhetorical impact. In what follows, I first reflect on the symbolic significance of the slap in contemporary Indian social and political life, and second, consider slaps and other forms of routinized daily violence that form part of the everyday lived practices in India, before returning to the case of Gujarat 2002, with which this paper began. In the bulk of this brief essay, then, I move the conversation away from the large scale episodic violence which has preoccupied scholars, but yet seek to retain a connection between everyday acts of violence and violence on a larger scale on the one hand, and between physical and metaphorical violence on the other.[12] If, as Arthur Kleinman and others suggest, we must see violence as crucial to cultural processes, this applies not to just to grotesque large-scale acts of violence but to everyday acts of violence as well.[13]

There are two major ways of thinking about large scale violence, such as that which occurred in Gujarat. The first sees these episodic acts as eruptions, a breach of the normal, extraordinary in its excess.[14] Of this group, some scholars find mass violence almost untheorizable, as if there were no language with which to describe or analyse such events,[15] while others try to theorize it within the scope of categories such as collective violence or riots, or even as following the pattern of religious festivals.[16] The second sees all violence as part of the same continuum, and argues that both large- and small-scale violence may be attributed to the same underlying tensions and conflicts.[17]

It is the path between these two positions that I find most promising—one that understands routine violence as linked, but in complex ways, to non-routinized or episodic violence. With Kleinman I argue that '[v]iolence is what lends to culture its authoritativeness', and further, that the violence of everyday life must be understood 'as multiple, as normative (and normal)' (238). In this essay I attempt to understand some of the multiple meanings of a normative and routinized violence undertaken by individuals, not collectives (though the individuals who commit and those who are compelled to receive the act of violence are always seen as members and/or representatives of communities) and then to trace the discursive fields within which they may operate. I want to suggest that acts of violence circulate in both material and discursive realms, and thus seemingly small-scale and indeed individual acts of violence may serve as powerful discursive devices through which large-scale violence may be understood. Specifically I suggest that the slap, with its attendant connotations elaborated below serves as a powerful device through which the disciplining of populations can be understood.

THE SLAP

We may think of violence as a technique of governance, with a culturally specific repertoire open to extension and innovation. This technique then, must include not just its extreme forms such as mutilation and torture but its banal forms—such as a slap—as well. In the contemporary Indian context, this repertoire includes a variety of individual and collective forms such as slapping, kicking, stripping women naked, and burning. Forms of large-scale collective violence, then, may be borrowed from multiple sources, but also build from an already known and practised repertoire.[18] It is within this context that I consider the slap, a particular technique of governance whose power is disguised by its mundaneness and banality.

The slap—*thappad* (Hindi) or *chor* (Bengali)—is a ubiquitous form of daily violence used by Indian parents on children, teachers on students, policemen on perpetrators of a certain class, upper caste on dalits, and husbands on wives. The slap has two features which distinguish it from other techniques of violence.

The slap comes with it own rules about who can slap whom and when. One might say, in fact, that the slap is embedded in a political field where actors are positioned very differently vis-a-vis their ability to deliver or receive a slap. For example, the trajectory of the routine slap is down a hierarchy (teacher slaps student), while the trajectory of a non-routine slap would be in the reverse order (student slaps teacher, or Muslim slaps Hindu), which violates or subverts an accepted hierarchy. A normal slap reinforces or reasserts inequality.

The slap differs from a punch or a kick. It is aimed usually at the face, and though it may be painful, the object of the slap is not pain per se, but *humiliation*. It is this aspect of the slap which gives it its symbolic and metaphorical power. It is also this aspect that lends itself to notions of emasculation and effeminacy.[19] To allow oneself to be slapped is to be put in a vulnerable, feminine and even penetrable position. Hence when Vishnu Hari Dalmia, Pravin Togadia and Narendra Modi use the language of a slap they intend to refer to the citizens of a country, or a group being humiliated, and thus placed in a powerless and feminine position.

Given these two elements of the slap, what work can we say the slap performs? Put simply, the slap creates good subjects by marking particular subjects as bad.[20] It is an act of subject formation through discipline. The subjects being formed here are dual. In other words, by slapping someone who is not, distinctively, oneself, the deliverer of the slap creates his or her own self as different and superior to the person being slapped. The slap is thus a simultaneous recognition of inequality and the creator. It is, it may be argued, a distinctively South Asian technique of subjectification.

Through being slapped, a person or a group which has transgressed, or exceeded its bounds, is humiliated, abjected, and put back into his or her body. Such transgressions can be committed by individuals such as a particular woman, a student, a Dalit, or by an entire community. But how does it work? And whence does it derive its strength? In Althusserian terms, we could consider a slap an interpellative 'hail' not just by the state but by any authority, where we can think of a hail as a unilateral act, as Judith Butler puts it: 'as the power and force of law to compel fear at the same time that it offers recognition at an expense.'[21] While Althusser famously refers to a speech act—when a police officer calls out, 'Hey, you there!' the person being hailed is recognized as a suspect because s/he has been hailed as such by the state—the slap can just as easily fall within the realm of the interpellative hail. At the moment of being hailed, Althusser maintains, the individual recognizes his or herself and in that moment becomes a subject. While there is a temporal sequence in this example, Althusser also makes clear that 'in reality these things happen without succession . . . Individuals are always already subjects.' [22] Yet, if we are willing to put aside Althusser's 'always-already' formulation, he leads us directly to the question of the process by which subjects actually do get constituted. Thus, we can see that at the moment of a slap, the slapped one becomes a transgressor and the deliverer of the slap becomes the arbiter (the law). Indeed the slap recruits and then transforms the individual into a transgressive subject. A transgressor who has been slapped is thus reminded of his or her transgression, his or her appropriate position, and those around him are also reminded of the possible costs of transgression. The transgressor, once slapped, becomes simultaneously subjected to a higher law and a subject of it. The lesson of the slap is carried in the memory of the body.

Who gets to be the object of the slap? In other words, given that bodies exist in unequal fields of power, whose bodies are at risk of being marked by the slap? Veena Das asks, '[d]o individual members of society carry the marks of pain as the price of belonging to a society?' in the context of the industrial disaster in Bhopal in 1984. 'Pain and suffering' she continues,

> are not simply individual experiences which arise out of the contingency of life and threaten to disrupt a known world. They may also be experiences which are actively created and distributed by the social order itself. Located in individual bodies, they yet bear the stamp of the authority of society upon the docile bodies of its members.[23]

While these reflections take Das into a consideration of orientation to suffering, I proceed here by aggregating individual bodies into groups and exploring the implications of their exposure to slaps and other everyday forms of violence, and the effects of slaps in procuring docile bodies. Like a speech act or a hail, the slap confers different subject statuses to both the giver and the recipient. They serve the dual purpose of marking the social world and constituting it.

The slap does not however 'compel fear' but humiliation. In other words, it is through producing humiliation (thus it is precisely not carried out in secret but in public) that the slap achieves its goal of subjection. And it is through humiliation that the slap fulfils its disciplinary task of constituting the social order.[24] In the next section I consider four social relationships in which slaps are given, relationships which are central in many ways to the formation of Indian subjectivity and sensibility. In each case, a particular group is 'at risk' for the particular kind of social suffering that a slap imparts, while another is empowered to cause this suffering.

The inter-generational slap (parents and teachers): In the traditional relationship between student and teacher in India there is a long history of belief that students cannot or will not learn without being slapped by their teachers. Patanjali's—the 2nd century B.C. commentary on Panini's grammar—not only suggests that a student should be delivered a *chapeti* (a blow with five fingers of the hand spread out) but also that students cannot learn without the threat of a *chapeti*.[25] Since it is not the most painful punishment, the purpose of the slap here is clearly to discipline. However, as we know, school teachers routinely use slaps and other forms of punishment precisely to humiliate and discipline students (the process is actually referred to in schools as 'disciplining students').

The Calcutta *Telegraph* carried a story in 2004 about a fifteen-year old student who was punished by her teacher, who made her 'perform 150 squats [while holding her ears] in the scorching sun on Friday afternoon as punishment for talking in the class' while her classmates were asked to keep count.[26] The student finally fainted, and when the report of this reached her parents, they informed the local police which resulted in the teacher's arrest. The newspaper article uses the word 'humiliate' at least three times. No one is left in doubt about the teacher's intent. And it appears that it was precisely her refusal to act as a good subject (she was talking in class and did not show remorse when her teacher scolded her) that led him to administer the punishment. Here then, it is the humiliation rather than the pain that is intended to discipline.[27] The suffering that is to produce the docile body is not so much the painful physical exercise in the hot sun, but rather the humiliation of it.

The gendered slap: That the slap is read in profoundly gendered ways, should come as no surprise, since within the gender hierarchy, in many societies, it is the husband who is enabled to slap his wife. The literature on domestic violence reveals that there is a considerable range of grievances for which men feel entitled to slap their wives. A study on judicial attitudes to women in India found that 48% of judges agreed that it was justifiable for a man to slap his wife on certain occasions,[28] while 40% of respondents in a 2000 INCLEN study of women in four Indian states report having been slapped by their husbands.[29] Recent studies indicate that men who slap their wives are often those who are unable for one reason or another to attain in other ways a culturally sanctioned or hegemonic masculinity.[30] Indeed, Uta Klein found that in the first Gulf War in which Israeli men did not see combat, their levels of domestic violence shot up.[31] While the understanding of the authors of these studies is usually that men hit women in order to express their masculinity, I suggest that they do so in order to constitute it in a social order that seems a little shaky.

While I have been reading the literature on domestic violence in India for over two decades now, it seems to me that there is indeed a shift from beating a wife simply because one believes one has a right to do so—say because she forgets to put enough salt in the food—and beating her because that is the only way you can reassert your authority over her at a moment when she does not seem willing to accept it. In a recent study an agricultural labourer from Tamil Nadu explains:

> Because she comes to work alongside me, and comes back with me, there won't be much respect. She will not bow to my wishes. So one has to beat, to make her tow the line.[32]

In New Delhi, India, a brilliant doctor tries to commit suicide after her husband slaps her for contradicting him in front of his friends.[33]

In these cases, the slap fulfils an order creating and maintaining function. It puts the female transgressor who might have acted as if she was more than a wife or equal in some way to her husband literally back in her body. It compels humiliation and creates the 'wife' as docile subject.

But women are not slapped only by their husbands. Because women are seen to represent the honour of their communities and more specifically the honour of the men in their communities, they may be slapped as punishment for the transgression of their communities as in Gujarat, or in countless cases of upper-caste violence inflicted upon Dalit women, or indeed threatened with a slap to prevent them from speaking out in public.[34]

Yet women too slap men. What is the meaning of such a slap? It would be Pollyanna-ish of me to suggest that when a woman slaps a man, hierarchies are reversed once and for all, and new hierarchies or equalities created (though, writing her new column for the BBC, Bollywood's Preity Zinta boasts the 'one tight slap' theory of dealing with men who harass women on the street!). Depending, of course, upon the context within which the slap has been administered, a woman's slap may remind a man to perform his manly duty, or humiliate him publicly on the street by identifying him as a harasser. I can only note here that the reversed gender slap promises the possibility of change, and a brief window in the construction of an alternative gendered order, however ephemeral.

The cross class/caste slap: Two years ago, I sat in a car being driven by a 'driver' in Calcutta, as we wended our way through the city's intense stop and go traffic. After one of the stops, the driver of my car started to move before the rather new looking Ford in front if it, and thus rear-ended the car. Such accidents happen often in Calcutta, and since the speed was barely five miles an hour, I did not at that moment think it would come to anything. I was fairly sure that the little Maruti I was in would be dented, though the Ford would be unscathed. However, the Ford was brand new, perhaps an important status symbol for the young man who was driving it. He leapt out of his car and came towards us, swearing at the driver, and then reached in and slapped the driver across his face. Not to be outdone, I leaped out of the car, faced him and challenged him to slap me instead. The young man swaggered and muttered and then left. He could not slap me, of course, since I was a woman of the same class, but he had not hesitated for a second to slap the uniformed driver.

In several cases documented in the press, young Dalit men have been punished by upper caste panchayats by being slapped in public. In one particular case, two men were made to slap each other with slippers for publicizing a case of caste injustice.[35] In these cases, the slaps are administered to adult men in public, in an understood gesture of denigration and humiliation. The use of the slipper is meant to add to the insult.

In our ongoing study of servants and cultures of servitude in Calcutta, Seemin Qayum and I have found that older employers often point to how things have changed by telling us that it simply wasn't done to slap a servant any more, and yet, in the past, servants did not mind being slapped as long as it was accompanied by love. One woman told us about a song her uncle used to sing as he slapped his male servant. Another employer told us that his mother did slap servants but also looked after them when they were sick and so they loved her as they would their own mother. In this last case, the acceptability of being slapped by one's parent validates the action. And in as much as lower castes or classes are considered by upper castes and classes to be children, developmentally behind the upper castes, they are at constant risk of being slapped.[36]

One domestic worker's clear-headed words make evident that even if this is how servants once were, it is not the same any more. 'You don't stay when your husband slaps you, why should you stay when your employer slaps you? They slap you because they have more money.' While this refusal to be slapped and assertion of rights is increasingly common, we have sufficient evidence of domestic servants, especially if they are children or young women being, at least occasionally, slapped.[37]

The inter-generational slap, the gendered slap and the cross class/caste slap are delivered to different and often overlapping groups of people. These are real slaps, administered perhaps in rage, or perhaps not, in order to physically transform, control or shape the embodied subject. Precisely because they are administered down a social hierarchy, from men to women, upper caste to lower caste and from parent to child, slaps index vulnerability, femininity, and subordination—in a word, inferiority.

The nation's slap and slap as metaphor: 'Times without number we have been made to gulp down humiliation and insult at their hands' says M.S. Golwalkar.[38] Given the contexts within which the slap features as a disciplining device, we can turn now to the issue of the body of the nation. It appears that on behalf of the nation, and in order to retaliate for the past, all sorts of citizens and elected officials are willing to slap Muslims and 'pseudo-secularists'. Pradeep Dalvi, author of a play defending Nathuram Godse proclaims when told that the artist M. F. Husain had painted pictures of a naked Sita: 'Now Husain will paint pictures of Sita. You paint pictures of Fatima, then talk about freedom of expression,' he said. 'I have not yet met Husain, but the moment I will meet him, the moment I will come directly face-to-face with him, I will slap him.'[39]

If the intent of a slap is inflict humiliation and through humiliation to maintain or restore hierarchy, then the power of its use as metaphor stems from this as well. While it is not entirely uncommon to see the phrase 'a slap on the face' to describe rejection coupled with humiliation, the phrase has acquired a particularly urgent resonance in Hindutva India. If the hypermasculine Muslim has in the past been thought to have slapped, raped and penetrated the body of Hindu India, the same must now be done to him. In a historic moment when the nation is being urged to take a stand against centuries of foreign rulers (both British and Muslim), every moment of resistance or rejection is construed as a slap. Thus from the Indian Express News Service:

> Apparently buoyed by the Gujarat poll results, VHP chief Ashok Singhal today asked the Maharashtra Government to reconsider its 'dictatorial" ban on Pravin Togadia and Sadhwi Ritambara. 'Else, they will get a slap on their face (*munha ki khayenge*),' he thundered.[40]

And when in early 2005, Gujarat chief minister Narendra Modi was denied a visa to enter the US, the gesture was seen as a slap not only on the chief minister's face but on the face of every Indian.

> There is rejoicing in our secular quarters that Modi has been slapped in his face. They do not realize that a slap on Modi's face is a slap on every Indian citizen's face and some day they may know the consequences if they care. Our intellectuals are good at bowing and scraping. Their ancestors did that to the British. In turn they are doing it before the Americans.[41]

A major part of the Right wing agenda is to show Hindu India as capable of strength, resistance and retaliation against foreigners who have in the past and continue today to control and dominate India. Unlike Pakistan, 'built on the predatory desire for Hindu property and Hindu women' India was seen as, by and large, peaceful and by and large gentle and meek.[42] Within this articulation, the bowing and scraping Hindu intellectuals are not men of honour but rather, traitors. These intellectuals, along with the nation's leadership, are weak and effeminate enough to allow the nation to be invaded, penetrated and slapped. William Miller argues that to have the capacity to be or to feel humiliated there must be in place certain notions of honour and self respect.[43] It is precisely this assertion of self respect and reclaiming of honour that the Hindu Right purports to do, and which they claim the nation's secular intellectual leadership failed to do, and thus the use of the metaphor of the slap. The metaphor is at its most powerful when it refers to the Hindu nation's most significant Other, the Muslim man. The exaggerated attention paid to the slap in *public* discourse must be seen in this light. It indexes the shaking off of the tolerance and effeminacy attributed to the Hindu nation (and men), and the corresponding diminishing of the image of the hypermasculine Muslim nation (and men) by making it (and them) slappeable.[44] Thus Hindu/Indian self respect and honour can only be reclaimed at the Muslim/Pakistan's expense.

Avishai Margalit argues that a decent society is one whose members do not humiliate one another.[45] I have suggested here that humiliation is possibly a major disciplinary principle of Indian society. The slap in both its literal and discursive formulations represents humiliation and through humiliation constitutes the social world. It is intended to create not just docile bodies but docile subjects. The violence that was inflicted on Muslims in Gujarat—whether we call it a riot or a pogrom—was seen by the Sangh Parivar and its many adherents in India *not* as a series of heinous acts upon individual Muslim bodies—rather the stabbing, cutting, burning and thousands of dead and mutilated bodies were seen as a giant slap in the face of the Muslim community, which Narendra Modi, in his capacity as the guardian of the state, was entitled to deliver. All of these actions together were intended to put Muslims back into their Muslim bodies, to remind them not to be too rights-bearing and demanding, to remind them that if they had to remain in India, they must be Muslims of a certain sort. Indeed the horror of individual deaths was all but forgotten in the post election conviction that the Muslim community[46] had been chastened and enlightened.

Notes

I am grateful to Amrita Basu and Srirupa Roy for giving me this opportunity to think and write about daily violence. I'd like to thank Paola Bachhetta, Vasudha Dalmia and Gautam Bhadra for their comments on this paper as well as the participants of the seminar on Violence and the State in India held at Amherst College in 2004.

1 Michel Foucault, *Discipline and Punish: The Birth of the Prison* (New

York: Vintage, reprint edition 1995), 156

2 Narendra Modi in *India Today*, 30 December 2002

3 Lata Jagtiani, Hindunet.org, 12/15/02 08:27 AM

4 The phrase 'merely cultural' was raised by Judith Butler (1997) in the by now famous exchange between her and Nancy Fraser (1998) over the place of culture in the analysis of gender and sexuality, where Butler accused Fraser of treating sexuality as a 'merely cultural' or epiphenomenal social force. See Judith Butler, 'Merely Cultural', *Social Text* 52-53 (Fall/Winter 1997,) 265-77; and Nancy Fraser, 'Heterosexism, Misrecognition, and Capitalism: A Response to Judith Butler', *New Left Review* 228 (March/April 1998), 140-49.

5 There is a heightened tendency to equate the Muslim with Pakistan and the Hindu with India thus making Hindu/Muslim and India/Pakistan almost interchangeable.

6 Guilegusto, *Sulekha.com*, 7 November 2003.

7 *Rediff.com*, 24 April 2001

8 Paola Bacchetta, 'When the (Hindu) Nation Exiles its Queers', *Social Text* 61 (Winter 1999), 141-65.

9 This version of aggressive and masculine Hinduism can be dated to the 1920s as Sumit Sarkar, Tanika Sarkar and others have shown. Sumit Sarkar, 'Indian Nationalism and the Politics of Hindutva' in David Ludden (ed.), *Making India Hindu: Religion, Community, and the Politics of Democracy in India,* (New Delhi: Oxford University Press, 2005), 162-84.

10 http://www.reformindia.com/wwwboard/messages/1267.htm

11 http://www.geocities.com/WestHollywood/Park/6443/India/priorities.html

12 For an excellent anthology on violence, see Arthur Kleinman, Veena Das and Margaret Lock (eds.), *Social Suffering* (Berkeley, University of California Press, 1997).

13 Arthur Kleinman, 'The Violences of Everyday Life: the Multiple Forms and Dynamics of Social Violence' in Arthur Kleinman, Veena Das (eds.), *Violence and Subjectivity* (Berkeley: University of California Press, 2000), 238.

14 Upendra Baxi, The Second Gujarat Catastrophe, 27 May, 2002. http://www.sacw.net/Gujarat2002/27 May, 2002.

15 This has been particularly true around the Partition, marked as it has been by a 'zone of silence'. See Veena Das, *Critical Events: An Anthropological Perspective on Contemporary India* (Oxford: Oxford University Press, 1997), 84.

16 See, for example, the work of Stanley J. Tambiah, *Leveling Crowds: Ethnonationalist Conflicts and Collective Violence in South East Asia* (Berkeley, University of California Press, 1997).

17 Paul Brass argues that riots are themselves routinized violence, and that violence is at the heart of political practice. See Paul Brass, *The Production of Hindu-Muslim Violence in Contemporary India* (Seattle, University of Washington Press, 2003).

18 As Amrita Basu and Srirupa Roy argue in their paper 'Democracy and Genocide: A Multi-Sited and Multi-Level Aproach to Extreme Violence', 'the violence against Christians that took place in the Dangs region of the state in December 1998 established a precedent for majoritarian violence against religious minorities in Gujarat.'

19 The challenge offered by a slap on the face with a pair of gloves often ended in a duel in the many English novels of Victorian England.

20 The word slap is also used colloquially in both Bengali and Hindi in a playful manner, as in 'don't you dare do this unless you want a slap' as Gautam Bhadra reminded me, but I suggest that the playful use of the word works precisely because the serious and humiliating lurks just under the surface.

21 Judith Butler, *Bodies That Matter: On the Discursive Limits of "Sex"* (New York, Routledge, 1993), 121.

22 Louis Althusser, 'Ideology and Ideological State Apparatuses (Notes towards an Investigation)' in *Essays on Ideology* (London: Verso, 1993), 48-49.

23 Veena Das, *Critical Events,* 137-38.

24 While a slap can be used to punish or to discipline in the Foucauldian sense, I am more interested in the work performed by the disciplinary aspects of the slap.

25 I thank Pandit R. K. Shukla for locating this for me in his archives.

26 *The Telegraph,* Calcutta, 25 April 2004.

27 That this incident made the news and led to the teacher's arrest and much indignation has something to do with the form of the punishment (this 'murgi' form is perhaps seen as premodern) and the fact that it was a girl student.

28 Ammu Joseph, 'Intimate Enemy', *The Hindu*, 4 Aug 2002.

29 INCLEN, Domestic Violence in India 3: A Summary Report of Four Records Studies, 2000.

30 Henrietta Moore, 'The Problem of Explaining Violence in the Social Sciences' in Penelope Harvey and Peter Gow (eds.), *Sex and*

Violence: Issues in Representation and Experience (London: Routledge, 1994), 139-55.

31 Uta Klein, "Our Best Boys": The Gendered Nature of Civil-Military Relations in Israel", in *Men and Masculinities*, Vol. 2, No. 1, 1999, pp. 47-65.

32 T. K. Sundari Ravindran, 'Female Autonomy in Tamil Nadu: Unravelling the Complexities', *Economic and Political Weekly*,17-23/24-30 April (1999), WS34-44.

33 http://www.womensenews.org/article.cfm/dyn/aid/1591

34 T. K. Rajalakshmi, 'Caste Injustice', in *Frontline* 21: 23 (2004).

35 Ibid.

36 See Johannes Fabian, *Time and the Other: How Anthropology Makes its Object* (New York: Columbia University Press, 1983) for a brilliant typology of such classifications of Other societies by Western anthropologists.

37 I think we can extend the servant slap outward to situations in the public sphere where people who are judged to be in a more menial or subservient position also become slappable, as it were. Witness the case in 2004, when Bombay cinema's superstar, Amitabh Bachhan, was seated in the 14th row despite being an invited guest at the Zee Cinema awards. Offended, he got up to leave. In the mayhem that followed, Subhas Chandra of ZEE TV came down the aisle and slapped one of the organizers for not putting Amitabh in a VIP seat.

38 M. S. Golwalkar, *Bunch of Thoughts* (1980, 413), cited in Paola Bachhetta, 'When the (Hindu) Nation Exiles its Queers', *Social Text* 61, (Winter 1999), 152.

39 http://www.rediff.com/news/1999/oct/05us2.htm

40 *Indian Express*, 21 December 2002.

41 M. V. Kamath, *The Organiser*, 1 May 2005.

42 The *Organizer*, 1949, cited in Urvashi Butalia 'Muslims and Hindus, Men and Women: Communal Stereotypes and the Partition of India', in *Women and the Hindu Right* (Delhi: Kali for Women, 1995), 76.

43 William Miller, *Humiliation: And Other Essays on Honor, Social Discomfort, and Violence* (New York: Cornell University Press, 1995).

44 See Amrita Basu, 'Feminism Inverted: The Real Women and Gendered Imagery of Hindu Nationalism', *Bulletin of Concerned Asian Scholars* 25:4 (1993).

45 Avishai Margalit defines humiliation as any sort of behaviour or condition that constitutes a sound reason for a person to consider his or her self respect injured. By this definition, few societies are decent,

and yet I find this a curiously compelling goal—not as a claim about nations and societies as they exist, but as a reasonable goal for societies to try to achieve. Avishai Margalit, *The Decent Society* (Cambridge, MA: Harvard University Press, 1998).

46 I refer here to the re-election of Narendra Modi and the BJP in Gujarat in 2002.

Rape and Murder in Gujarat: Violence against Muslim Women in the Struggle for Hindu Supremacy

MARTHA C. NUSSBAUM

WHAT HAPPENED

One of the most horrific aspects of the Gujarat massacre was the prevalence of rape and sexual torture. The typical tactic was first to rape or gang-rape the woman, then to torture her, and then to set her on fire and kill her. Although the fact that most of the dead were incinerated makes a precise sex count of the bodies impossible, one mass grave that was discovered contained more than half female bodies. Many victims of rape and torture are also among the survivors who have testified. A close study of these terrible events reveals anxieties about masculinity, and about the body itself, that play a large role in the Hindu Right's ability to organize violence.

Sexual violence is a not uncommon part of communal violence in many areas of the world. The violence in Gujarat, however, had unusual features. Historian Tanika Sarkar, who played a leading role in investigating the events and interviewing witnesses, has argued in an important article that the evident preoccupation with destroying women's sexual organs reveals 'a dark sexual obsession about allegedly ultravirile Muslim male bodies and overfertile Muslim female ones, that inspire[s] and sustain[s] the figures of paranoia and revenge.[1] This sexual obsession is evident in the hate literature circulated during the carnage, of which the following 'poem' is a typical example:

Narendra Modi you have fucked the mother of [Muslims]

The volcano which was inactive for years has erupted
It has burnt the arse of [Muslims] and made them dance nude
We have untied the penises which were tied till now
Without castor oil in the arse we have made them cry . . .
Wake up Hindus, there are still [Muslims] alive around you
Learn from Panvad village where their mother was fucked
She was fucked standing while she kept shouting
She enjoyed the uncircumcised penis
With a Hindu government the Hindus have the power to annihilate [Muslims]
Kick them in the arse to drive them out of not only villages and cities but also the country.

[The word rendered 'Muslims'—*miyas*—is a word meaning 'mister' that is standardly used to refer to Muslims.]

As Sarkar says, the incitement to violence is suffused with anxiety about male sexuality, and the treatment of women that resulted seems to enact a fantasy of sexual sadism far darker than mere revenge. In an affidavit submitted to the Commission of Enquiry in June 2002, the leading feminist legal activist Flavia Agnes testified that although sexual crime is a common part of communal violence, the 'scale and extent of atrocities perpetrated upon innocent Muslim women during the recent violence far exceeds any reported sexual crime during any previous riots in the country in the post-independence period.'[2]

My aim in this essay is to follow Sarkar's lead, focusing on Gujarat's gruesome sexual violence and asking how it might be further illuminated with the aid of ideas drawn from feminist thought.

First, with the aid of Sarkar's important scholarship, I shall describe a history of connecting women's bodies to the idea of the Indian nation. This connection, I believe, is implicit in the events of Gujarat. But Sarkar's analysis can be taken even further if we connect her account of home as nation to the feminist analysis of objectification. Not even this analysis suffices, however, to explain the extreme gruesomeness of these sexual tortures in Gujarat. We can go further with the help of an account of misogynistic disgust that was originally sketched in Andrea Dworkin's *Intercourse*.[3] The events of Gujarat will thus be seen to involve psychological dynamics that are widespread in gender relations: they took a particularly anxious and aggressive form in this concrete political context.

WOMAN AS NATION

During the period of colonial rule the British needed to establish secure control over national political processes and criminal and commercial law. They achieved this control in part by establishing a uniform legal code for these aspects of the law. But they left family law in the hands of the different religious communities. Christians, Parsis, Hindus, and Muslims: each group had its own laws for marriage, divorce, inheritance, and succession.[4] In the case of the Hindu system, the British actively aided its codification, building a single system out of many systems of local jurisdiction. This separation of family law from other legal arenas was also the more easily accepted because it tracked a distinction between the 'public' and the 'private' realm that was traditional not only in Western political philosophy but also in Indian legal and philosophical traditions.[5]

In *Hindu Wife, Hindu Nation*, a study of the construction of gender and national identity in 19th- and early 20th-century Hindu India, Tanika Sarkar argues that this separation of domains served the purposes of empire well.[6] While establishing secure domination in the most important matters, it also quieted dissent by allowing the males of the subject population a sphere of rule: the household, where a man who had few rights in the outer world could be a king. Control over women's bodies was thus substituted for control over other aspects of daily life. And self respect that was injured in the daily encounter with the racial hierarchy of the outer world could be built up again by the experience of secure kingly rule in the sphere of the family.

As time went on, this control increasingly mimicked its source: the violence of colonial domination displaced itself onto the domination of women, which had never been all that benign, but which was permitted increasingly to express itself in violent ways. In the face of a complaint involving the rape and death of a twelve-year-old child wife, for example, British judges resisted indigenous Indian demands for the reform of laws governing marital age and consent. They argued that local traditions required deference, and the judges were not entitled to go against them.[7] Such manoeuvres had the effect of insulating domestic violence, even of this appalling and fatal sort, from criticism and change. At the same time, given that self respect and manly status were increasingly defined around the control of women's bodies, reform met with increasing internal resistance: for who would want to give up the one area of manly pride and honour? The female body simply is the nation: by controlling it, men control India, even if they don't.

This widespread image of the female body as the nation helps to explain why, during the waves of communal violence at the time of Independence, possession of women was such an important issue to the contending sides, as Muslims established Pakistan, and as Hindus and Muslims killed one another in large numbers during the mass migrations surrounding the separation of the two nations. Women were raped in huge numbers; often they were abducted as well, and forced to bear the children of the Muslim or Hindu who had abducted them.[8] The rationale of these rapes and abductions is easy to connect with the earlier history: if the female body symbolizes the nation, then, in the struggle of two emerging nations, the possession and impregnation of women is a potent weapon in consolidating power. Even when women were not abducted, but were raped and then brutally murdered, this too was an act symbolizing the power of one group to damage the domain of rule of the other group, dishonouring the group in the process.

To move from the time of Sarkar's book into the present day, the legal separation that helped to produce this situation was permitted to survive untouched in India at Independence, with the result that reform in family law is extremely slow and cumbersome. Christian women in India, for example, won the right to divorce on grounds of cruelty only in 2001. All four religious systems of personal law contain significant inequalities between the sexes; the control over women's bodies continues to be a rhetorically and politically potent issue that can block change. Each group continues to some extent to see the female body as a symbol of the nation, which its men must control in order to preserve manly honour. The struggle of the men within each group not to cede to women any sphere of rule that might weaken them in relation to the men of any other group, is a major impediment to feminist reform.[9]

This history goes some distance toward explaining the events in Gujarat, with their insistent focus on the violation of the female body. If the Muslim female body is a part of the nation that is currently dominated by one's adversary, then one must possess it to possess secure control over the nation. Murder, and hence destruction of the source of offspring, is one sure way of depriving the adversary of control over his 'kingdom'. If in the process one dishonours the adversary, all the better.

OBJECTIFICATION

The identification of the female body with the nation takes us some way into the grim darkness of Gujarat, but questions remain. If woman symbolizes nation, why are women brutally and sadistically tortured, rather than abducted and impregnated? To be sure, many people were murdered at Partition, and in the general violence many women were used simply as objects of the desire to maim and kill. On the other hand, the logic of colonial possession was also amply evident in that case, since men really did want to take these women to their country and force them to bear their children. And in large numbers, they did so. In Gujarat, we hear nothing of this sort. Women were simply tortured and killed. So we wonder how the idea of woman as symbol of nation and national rule could possibly lend itself to this particular type of violence—what can the connection possibly be between seeing a woman as a symbol of what one loves and honours, and seeing her as an object that one can break up, with indifference to her pain. Shouldn't we say that it's only to the extent that men had *lost* the connection between woman and nation that they were able to treat women in this hideous way, not even permitting the survival of the body itself, but first torturing it and then, usually, burning it to cinders?

In short, how can one maim, burn and torture the venerated body of the nation?

The feminist concept of 'objectification' provides an essential insight here.[10] Objectification is treating as a mere thing what is really not a thing. It has multiple aspects, including the denial of autonomy and subjectivity, and the ideas of ownership, of fungibility (one is just like the others), and violability (it's all right to break the thing up or abuse it). Not all forms of objectification possess all these features: for example, one may treat a fine painting as an object, thus denying it autonomy and subjectivity, without holding it to be fungible with other paintings and without holding that it is all right to break it up. In the domain of human relations, however, sinister connections begin to be woven among these different aspects. At the heart of all of them, I would argue, is the idea of *instrumentality*: a thing, unlike a person, is an instrument or means to the ends of persons; it is not an end in itself. The objectification of women is primarily a denial that women are ends in themselves. It is because one has already made that denial, at some level of one's awareness, that it becomes so easy to deny women autonomy, to deny that their subjective experience matters, and, even, to begin to ignore qualitative differences between one and another, as pornography so easily does.

What is relevant here is that the logic of instrumentality also leads powerfully in the direction of seeing women as violable. What you have already conceived of as a mere tool of your own ends, not an end in herself, can so easily be understood as something that you may beat, abuse, burn, even break up at will: it is yours to use and to abuse. Even a precious painting has legal rights against such abuses only in virtue of its connection with a human maker: the 'moral rights' of art-works under contemporary European law are not rights of the painting as such, but rights of the artist in the painting. So too, once women are understood as mere instruments of men's desires (for power, for pleasure), there would seem to be no principled limit on the ways in which one might use them. A means is a means to an end.

To bring these points back to the case of India: treating women as the nation, while apparently honorific, is already a form of objectification, and, particularly, of instrumentalization. Under colonialism, a nation is a ground on which men may gratify their desires for control and honour. By being exalted into a symbol of nationhood, a woman is at the same time reduced—from being a person who is an end, an autonomous subject, someone whose feelings count, into being a mere ground for the expression of male desire. Thus, although much of the time the male who sees a woman that way will still want her to live and eat and bear children, there is no principled barrier to his using her brutally, if that is what suits his desires. We see that connection already in the grim tales of domestic violence narrated by Sarkar.

And we see it clearly, I believe, in Gujarat. Muslim female bodies symbolize a recalcitrant part of the nation, one as yet undominated by Hindu male power. One reaction to that situation might have been to abduct the woman and to place her in one's own household. But if women are things, instruments, objects, then their bodies may also be used in gruesome ways—if *that* is what will best satisfy one's desires for power, honour, and security. Once the status of end-in-itself is denied, everything else follows on a whim.

In short, it is not simply because the logic of the domestic sphere became the logic of kingly rule, but because of the particular form this kingly rule took, involving the conception of women as means rather than ends, that nation-worship can so easily segue into woman-killing. Other forms of kingly rule—for example, most parents' relations with their very young children—do not involve instrumentalization, and do not lead to violence of the sort we see in Gujarat. But the particular way in which kingly rule over women made them into a symbol of nationhood involved instrumentalization. So the woman was reduced from a person to a mere symbol, and that symbol, however apparently honorific, was a mere tool of male ends. The road from that point to violation is short and relatively direct.

DISGUST

We have gone a little further toward understanding the logic of these tortures, but not far enough. For the logic of colonial objectification, as I have sketched it, might be satisfied—indeed seems best satisfied—with abduction, rape as impregnation, and other well-known devices through which men at war establish their domination over the subject nation. But as Sarkar says, there is something dark and unusual about the Gujarat tortures, something suggesting an obsession with the female body and especially its genital organs. Torture and abuse, particularly the insertion of large metal objects into the vagina and other forms of genital torture, play a dramatic and unusual role in these events. The feminist analysis of objectification shows why there would be no large barrier to using women's bodies in these ways. But why would men inflict such tortures? The account of objectification does not help us answer this question. This Muslim-woman hating involves something more than mere doing as one wants with an instrumental object, more even than the desire to colonize the enemy's domain and thus to inflict dishonour upon it. Although Defence Minister George Fernandes treated the rapes dismissively, as if they were nothing new, most witnesses disagreed.[11] As one commentator writes, 'The violence in Gujarat *was* different from earlier incidents of communal violence, both for the scale of the assaults and for the sheer sadism and brutality with which women and girls were victimized.'[12] This new something, I would argue, is connected to the operations of disgust, an emotion that plays a key role not only in misogyny but in many types of racial hatred.[13]

Disgust plays a powerful role in human life. Through our strong aversive reactions to substances such as feces, decaying meat, corpses, and other bodily waste, we police the boundaries of our body from contamination every day. Disgust is distinct from distaste: the very same smell arouses different disgust reactions depending on the person's conception of the object she is smelling. It is also distinct from the sense of danger, for many things are disgusting long after all danger is removed. Disgust is an emotion heavily caught up in symbolic and magical thinking. Its objects are reminders of our animality and mortality, either because they are in fact corpses or waste products or because they come through a process of association to symbolize waste, excrement, and mortality. Disgust works by shielding human beings from too much daily contact with aspects of their own humanity that are difficult to live with. Thus if we don't touch corpses or oozy decaying smelly things, we may be able to ignore our own mortality. If we neatly dispose of our bodily waste products, we more easily forget that we are made of stuffs that end up on the dungheap.

It is not enough for human beings to protect themselves from contamination by the 'primary objects' of disgust, such as feces and corpses. Humans also typically need a group of humans to bound themselves against, who come to symbolize the disgusting and who, therefore, insulate the community even further from its own animality.

Thus, every society ascribes disgust properties—bad smell, stickiness, sliminess, foulness, decay—to some group of persons, who are therefore found disgusting and shunned, and who in this way further insulate the dominant group from what they fear facing in themselves. In many European societies Jews have played that role: they were characterized as disgusting in those physical ways, and they were represented symbolically as vermin who had those same properties. In the traditional Hindu caste hierarchy, Dalits, formerly called 'untouchables', played a related role: through their contact with waste products (as people handling feces and corpses, for example) they were regarded as themselves contaminated, thus not to be touched by the pure person; their very existence in the community shielded the pure from the decay and stench involved in their own animality. (Not from danger: Gandhi points out in his autobiography that during a cholera epidemic the lower castes, who defecated in the fields far from their dwellings, were less at risk of disease than the upper castes, who used the gutters outside their windows to dispose of wastes.)

Projecting disgust onto another group subordinates the group. The group to whom disgust properties are ascribed exemplifies animality and thereby (in the eyes of the dominant group) lowness in contrast to the allegedly pure dominant ones. But because the subordination is inspired at root by anxiety and denial, it is not a peaceable subordination. Disgust-minorities are not treated like nice household pets. Instead, the rage that people feel against their own mortality and animality is often enacted toward them, whether by humiliation or, in addition, by physical violence. At its extreme point the anxiety issues in projects of ethnic cleansing: if only we could completely rid ourselves of this group, the 'thinking' goes, we would be free of our own death.

In virtually all cultures, women are among the groups to whom disgust-properties are imputed. Portrayed as hyperanimal beings, receptacles of male bodily emissions as well as the fluids associated with menstruation and birth, women are portrayed as sticky, smelly, dirty, repellent. Taboos associated with menstruation and birth are but one sign of this ubiquitous construction. But there is a subtle difference between disgust toward say, Jews, and disgust toward women: for women are, to dominant males, sexually alluring as well as disgusting, and one of the alluring things about them is the fact that they exemplify the forbidden terrain of the hyperphysical, which is the disgusting.[14] Men are revolted by the idea of their semen inside a woman's vagina, and yet they can't keep from wanting to put it there.[15]

In a brilliant analysis of Tolstoy's *The Kreutzer Sonata*,[16] Andrea Dworkin argues that this fact about disgust toward women—that men can't keep from wanting them, and then feeling sullied and disgusted by them—undergirds objectification: as Tolstoy's narrator says, he can't see his wife as a person and an end as long as he sees her as this alluring disgusting thing that he needs to use for his pleasure. But this objectification takes a particularly violent turn. For the very understanding of dominant masculinity that makes all reminders of animality disgusting is deeply threatened by sexual desire for women. The man sees, in his desire, that he is not who he pretends to be: he is an animal wanting to exercise animal functions. This deep wound to his ego can only be salved by destroying the cause of his desire. Thus Tolstoy's narrator has murdered his wife. Only after she is dead, he tells us, can he see her as a human being—because then he no longer desires her. Similarly, according to Dworkin, Tolstoy himself records in his diary violent repulsion and antagonism toward the young wife who tempts him out of his purity. Dworkin suggests that male desire is often, if not always, mingled in this way with the desire to violate and destroy.

Dworkin's analysis of disgust-misogyny would have been even stronger had she grounded it in a more general analysis of human disgust, but at any rate it is clear that she has identified a feature of misogynistic disgust that makes it (even) more violent than many other instances of disgust. My more general analysis suggests that disgust toward women of minorities already marked as animal is likely to be even more intense: thus Jewish women, in Nazi-era literature, were represented as hyperanimal and hypersexual beings, who exercised a fascinating allure but who must all the more resolutely be resisted by the pure German male, as he attempted to establish his purity and domination.

PURITY AND VIOLATION

Now we begin to be in a position to approach Gujarat again, offering a richer analysis of what we find there. All human beings experience disgust, and all use disgust to construct boundaries between themselves and their own animality. And yet some societies, and some groups within societies, learn to make disgust more central to their lives than other groups do.

For example, disgust at sexual fluids, bodily wastes, and so forth is probably more intense and more ubiquitous among males than among females; at least it does a better job of explaining the structure of sexual relations on the male than on the female side. Men, moreover, differ greatly in the degree to which their relations with women are coloured by disgust. Similarly, disgust plays a powerful role in explaining homophobic hatred and violence in the US, but we also know that many people utterly lack such motivations. Moreover, some societies strongly inhibit the projection of disgust onto vulnerable people and groups, while some actively encourage such projections.[17] Walt Whitman imagined that a democracy might exist without disgust, and therefore (he believed) without racism, misogyny, or homophobia. He movingly imagined such a society, bits and pieces of which are real. In contrast, some societies seem in general more structured around disgust and contamination than others. One might see post-World War I Germany, for example, as such a society: Klaus Theweleit's remarkable *Männerfantasien*[18] has shown the extent to which disgust at the female body is a motif underlying a great deal of the political life of that era, with its impossible fantasies of men made out of metal, uncontaminated by any fluids or blood or stickiness or stench.

In my earlier essay on Gujarat, I argued that much of the rhetoric and political culture of today's Hindu Right is appropriated from National Socialism in Germany, and plays no role in traditional Hindu understandings of identity and nationhood.[19] The founders of the Hindu right in the 1930s had studied Nazi culture closely and openly expressed their sympathy with German ideals of racial purity, and even German anti-semitism. Although admiration for Hitler went underground after World War II, textbooks written today by the Hindu Right still portray his 'achievements' in admiring terms.

Whatever the origin of such ideas, a very similar, and similarly paranoid idea of male purity has taken deep root in the culture of the Hindu Right, in a way that is unconnected to mainstream Hindu religious and cultural traditions. To be sure, there are sources in the Hindu tradition on which one could draw for the portrayal of the Hindu male as pure, lacking in lust, and uncontaminated by femaleness, and (especially in the *Laws of Manu*)[20] for the portrayal of the female as dirty and potentially contaminating. But virtually any human tradition includes such sources. And the current Hindu-Right construction of the Hindu male is terribly far removed from much that is central to the Hindu tradition historically, with its delight in sexuality, its playfulness, its sensuous enjoyment of the body. Indeed one might think of few traditions in which disgust at sexuality was as notably absent, and the body as joyously present as the tradition one of whose ancient scriptures is the *Kamasutra*. Traditionally the dominant Hindu norm of masculinity (rather like its Talmudic Jewish counterpart, as wonderfully reconstructed by Daniel Boyarin[21]) is not aggressively phallic, but, instead, sensuous, playful, artful, and even soft (by contrast to the boring and unsensuous macho stereotypes that abound elsewhere). This is one of the great attractions of that rich religious tradition.

One element of the current Hindu-Right understanding of masculinity is a sharp rhetorical opposition between the pure, chaste Hindu male, who respects women and does not have lustful desires toward them, and the lustful Muslim male, who sees women as objects for use and domination.[22] The famous television production of the *Ramayana* in 1987-88, watched by around 90% of Indian households with television sets and instrumental in constructing current Hindu-Right ideas of the tradition, shows the gods as more or less devoid of sexuality, and babies as sweet little things arriving more or less out of heaven. Even Shiva, a god profoundly connected with sexuality and the phallus, is desexualized in a most bizarre way. The narrator repeatedly insists that the Hindu tradition, unlike other religious traditions, stresses peace and purity—in combination, of course, with militant aggression against the Other, the enemy.

This same understanding of the Hindu male explains the furor, in the Hindu Right, over scholarly publications that stress aspects of sexual desire in the tradition. one terrifying example is the recent attack on Paul Courtright's scholarly book on Ganesha,[23] the god with an elephant head whose birth is closely connected to the sexual desire of the gods.[24] The attackers, mostly in online publications and public letters, show no sign of having studied the book, but focus on its Freudian reading of the relationship between Shiva and Ganesha, and Courtright's suggestion that thinking about the sexual conflicts in the human family will help us understand the Hindu gods. They particularly dislike the idea that Ganesha's sexuality is depicted (quite faithfully to the tradition) as playful and childlike, rather than as aggressive and dominating. For writing this book twenty years ago, Courtright has recently received death threats; even the public face of the opposition is extraordinarily threatening, including prominent claims in periodicals as respectable as *India Abroad* that Courtright's academic freedom should be revoked and that his university (Emory) should not allow him to teach.[25]

Similarly, when the scholar Wendy Doniger, whose work strongly influenced Courtright, recently lectured in London on sexual motifs in the stories of the gods in the classical epic Ramayana, an egg was thrown at her from the audience; and the same militant columnist in *India Abroad* attacked her right to teach the Hindu tradition.[26] More recently, the historian James Laine of Macalester College impugned the purity of a prominent woman of the past by mentioning in his biography of the 17th-century Hindu emperor Shivaji that, because Shivaji's father travelled for most of his life, there were jokes that the son was the product of an adulterous liaison of his mother's.[27] Laine did not even credit the allegation; he merely reported it. Nonetheless, the mere mention of a slur against the reputation of Shivaji's mother brought an attack on Laine's Indian collaborator, who was physically assaulted and his face painted black. Part of the institute in Pune where Laine did his research was burned; the book was banned by the state government; and its Indian edition was promptly withdrawn by a Oxford University Press. Laine has been charged with a crime against public order, and the then prime minister Vajpayee, on campaign in Maharashtra, suggested that Interpol ought to go to the US to arrest him. The death threats against Laine are obsessed with female purity; repeatedly they assert that Indian women are pure until death, whereas women in England are filthy and dirty.[28]

These examples show an obsession with treating sexuality as something Other, something foreign. Ramesh Rao, attacking Courtright, refers to the sexual aspect of Ganesha's history (an extremely important part of the traditional mythological record) as 'heathen'. One way of Othering the sexual, which Rao and Laine's attackers pursue, is to suggest that Western scholars are foisting onto Indians their own sexual obsessions. Where the scholar in question is Indian, other tactics are chosen: the distinguished historian Romila Thapar, who has insisted on presenting a balanced view of historical Hindu–Muslim relations in the medieval and early modern periods, has been attacked as a communist and an agent of Pakistan. Another revealing strategy of Othering is shown in the punishment meted out to Laine's collaborator: through blackface, he is both publicly shamed in a traditional way and turned into someone who looks Other from the dominant Hindu self-image.

We might say, then, that for whatever reason, extremists of the Hindu Right[29] currently exhibit an unusual degree of disgust-anxiety, as manifested in a fearful, even paranoid, insistence on representing the Hindu male as pure and free from lust (while being, at the same time, successfully aggressive).[30] Muslims, in contrast, are the hypersexual, the Other, the 'black'; and Muslim women, like Jewish women in the Nazi era, are doubly sexual, beings whose fertility and beauty both attracts and repels. (One repeated scare tactic of the Hindu Right is to portray Muslims as both polygamous and hyperfertile, thus as having many times more children than Hindu families, although this suggestion is not supported by demographic evidence.)

When the man who wants to be pure becomes attracted to a disgusting subordinated being, as Tolstoy and Andrea Dworkin eloquently show, the result is likely to be violent. Although Dworkin represents this violence as a cultural universal, it seems likely that it varies greatly in keeping with cultural ideologies. Sexuality and its vulnerabilities are difficult enough for any human being to deal with at any time. All cultures probably contain seeds of violence in connection with sexuality. But a person who has been taught to have a big stake in being above the sexual domain, whose political ideology insists on purity, and whose experience of cultural anxiety connects impurity with humiliation, cannot bear to be dragged into that domain. And yet, of course, the very denial and repression of the sexual create a mounting tension within. Tolstoy's diaries describe how the tension mounts inside him until he has to use his wife, and then he despises her, despises himself, and wants to use force against her to stop the cycle from continuing. The hate literature circulated in Gujarat portrays Muslim women as hypersexual, enjoying the penises of many men. That is not unusual; Muslim women have often been portrayed in this denigrating way. But it also introduces a new element: the desire that is imputed to them to be penetrated by an uncircumcised penis. Thus the Hindu male creates a pornographic fantasy with himself as its specific subject. In one way, these images show anxiety about virility, assuaging it by imagining the successful conquest of Muslim women. But of course, like Tolstoy's narrator's fantasies, these fantasies are not exclusively about intercourse. The idea of this intercourse is inseparable from ideas of mutilation and violence. Fucking a Muslim woman just means killing her. The fantasy image of the untying of the penises that were 'tied until now' is very reminiscent of the explosion of violence in Tolstoy, only the logic has been carried one small step further: instead of murder necessitated by and following sex, the murder just *is* the sex. Women are killed by having large metal objects inserted into their vaginas. In this way, the image is constructed of a sexuality that is so effective, so closely allied with the desire for domination and purity, that its penis is a pure metal weapon, not a sticky thing of flesh and blood. The Hindu male does not even need to dirty his penis with the contaminating fluids of the Muslim woman. He can fuck her with the clean non-porous metal weapon that kills her, while he himself remains pure. Sexuality itself carries out the project of annihilating the sexual. Nothing is left to inspire fear.

A useful comparison to this terrifying logic is the depiction of warlike masculinity in a 1922 novel of Ernst Jünger, *Der Kampf als inneres Erlebnis* (*Battle as Inner Experience*):

These are the figures of steel whose eagle eyes dart between

> whirling propellers to pierce the cloud; who dare the hellish crossing through fields of roaring craters, gripped in the chaos of tank engines . . . men relentlessly saturated with the spirit of battle, men whose urgent wanting discharges itself in a single concentrated and determined release of energy.
> As I watch them noiselessly slicing alleyways into barbed wire, digging steps to storm outward, synchronizing luminous watches, finding the North by the stars, the recognition flashes: this is the new man. The pioneers of storm, the elect of central Europe. A whole new race, intelligent, strong, men of will . . . supple predators straining with energy. They will be architects building on the ruined foundations of the world.[31]

In this fascinating passage, Jünger combines images of machinery with images of animal life to express the thought that the new man must be in some sense both powerful beast and god, both predatory and invulnerable. The one thing he must never be is human. His masculinity is characterized not by need and receptivity, but by a 'concentrated and determined release of energy'. He knows no fear, no sadness. Why must the new man have these properties? Because the world's foundations have been ruined. Jünger suggests that the only choices for males living amid death and destruction are either to yield to an immense and ineluctable sadness or to throw off the humanity that inconveniently inflicts pain. Disgust for both Jews and women become for such men a way of asserting their own difference from mere mortal beings.

I believe that something like this paranoia, this refusal of compromised humanity, infects the rhetoric of the Hindu Right, and, indeed, may help to explain its continuing fascination with Nazi ideas. But Jünger's novel does not connect the 'release of energy' directly to misogynistic torture and murder, although, as Theweleit shows, other documents of the period amply do so.[32] To explain that connection we need to ask what the idea of man-as-metal is an escape from, what it is denying. As in Jünger, so too in Gujarat: what seems to be denied is human vulnerability itself, the smell, the fluids, the stench of the body. The woman functions as a symbol of the site of weakness and vulnerability inside any male, who can be drawn into his own mortality through desire. The Muslim woman functions doubly as such a symbol. In this way, a fantasy is created that her annihilation will lead to safety and invulnerability (perhaps to 'India Shining', the campaign slogan that betrays a desire for a crystalline sort of domination). The paranoid anxiety that keeps telling every man that he is not safe and invulnerable feeds the desire to extinguish her.

Only this complex logic explains, I believe, why torture and mutilation are preferred as alternatives to abduction and impregnation—or even homicide. Only this logic explains why the fantasy of penetrating the sexual body with a large metal object played such a prominent role in the carnage. Only this explains, as well, the repetitious destruction of the woman's body by fire, as though the world cannot be clean until all vestiges of the female body are simply obliterated from its face.

CONCLUSION

Beginning with Sarkar's account of woman as nation, and the home as the one remaining sphere of kingly rule for the colonized male, we moved on to a more general account of the male objectification of women. I argued that we need this more general analysis to make sense of how veneration turns into brutality. But to get all the way to the grisly tortures of Gujarat, we need to think about disgust-misogyny, about the impossible project of male purity and the underside of violence that accompanies it, and about the connection between exaggerated forms of this project and cultural ideologies.

Emotions are not simply blind surges of affect. They contain images of self and Other, of masculinity and femaleness, and of what is valued most in life. Studying these images helps us go deeper in an understanding of political violence, seeing more clearly how the organizers of hate played on pervasive human anxieties, to which their specific constructs of the male and female body gave a new shape and urgency.

Why this fantasy for these people in this particular place and time? Why here a particular heightening of the need to be metallic weapons that can kill the body even while they violate it? Why this terrible and murderous vulnerability? In Germany it was easy to connect such fantasies to the devastation of World War I, the loss of a whole generation of males, and a humiliating military defeat. In the case of the Hindu Right, with Hindus in India constituting a comfortable majority of 82% percent (according to the 1991 census),[33] and Muslims around 12%, no comparable catastrophe provides an easy explanation, unless it be their perception of the long, cumulative catastrophe of being subjugated for many centuries, first by Muslims, then by the British, then by the rich developed nations of the world. But one thing seems sure enough: that such actions diminish power rather than augment it, creating not an invulnerable Hindu nation but a nation that, insofar as it allows such things to occur unpunished, is a disgrace to its own constitution and to its rich traditions of human acceptance, play, and insight.[34]

Notes

This article was originally published, in a slightly different form, in *The Boston Review* 29 (2004), 33-38. I am grateful to the editors for permission to reprint. A companion piece, discussing the legal issues in the Gujarat massacre, is 'Genocide in Gujarat: The International Community Looks Away,' *Dissent*, Summer 2003, 15-23. My forthcoming book, *Democracy in the Balance: Violence, Hope, and India's Future* (Cambridge, MA: Harvard University Press, 2007), discusses all these issues in greater detail.

1 Tanika Sarkar, 'Semiotics of Terror: Muslim Children and Women in Hindu Rashtra,' *Economic and Political Weekly*, 13 July 2002, 2872-76.

2 Flavia Agnes, 'Affidavit', in Flavia Agnes (ed.), *Of Lofty Claims and Muffled Voices* (Bombay: Majlis, 2002), 69.

3 Andrea Dworkin, *Intercourse* (New York: The Free Press, 1983).

4 This does not mean that they had separate courts: both before and after Independence, laws were separate for these communities, and religious bodies were consulted about them, but they are were adopted in the usual way: today, passed by Parliament; formerly, adopted by the Raj.

5 See my analysis in 'Is Privacy Bad for Women? What the Indian Constitutional Tradition Can Teach Us about Sex Equality,' *The Boston Review* 25 (April/May 2000), 42-47.

6. Tanika Sarkar, *Hindu Wife, Hindu Nation: Community, Religion, and Cultural Nationalism* (Delhi: Permanent Black, 2001).

7 Nehru argued that the British more generally supported the 'obscu-

rantist, reactionary' elements in Indian culture as the authentic ones, in order to prevent Indians from progressing: see Jawaharlal Nehru, *An Autobiography* (Oxford: Oxford University Press, centenary edition 1989), 449.

8 On this history, see, among other important feminist works, Kumari Jayawardena and Malathi de Alwis (ed.), *Embodied Violence: Communalising Women's Sexuality in South Asia* (London: Zed, 1993); Ritu Menon and Kamla Bhasin, *Borders and Boundaries: Women in India's Partition* (Delhi: Kali for Women, 1998); Urvashi Butalia, *The Other Side of Silence: Voices from the Partition of India* (Durham: Duke University Press, 2000); Jasodhara Bagchi and Subhoranjan Dasgupta (ed.), *The Trauma and the Triumph: Gender and Partition in Eastern India* (Kolkata: Stree, 2003).

9 See my *Women and Human Development* (Cambridge: Cambridge University Press, 2000), ch. 3.

10 See my *Sex and Social Justice* (New York: Oxford University Press, 1999). The article 'Objectification' previously appeared in *Philosophy and Public Affairs* 24 (1995), 249-91. Catharine MacKinnon and Andrea Dworkin did the fundamental work of introducing this concept and showing its importance.

11 In a speech on the floor of Parliament on 30 April 2002, he said, 'All these sob stories being told to us, as if this is the first time this country has heard such stories—where a mother is killed and the foetus taken out of her stomach, where a daughter is raped in front of her mother, of someone being burnt. Is this the first time such things have happened?'

12 Editor's Note to '"Nothing New?" Women as Victims in Gujarat,' in Siddharth Varadarajan (ed.), *Gujarat: The Making of a Tragedy* (New Delhi, London, and New York: Penguin Books, 2002), 215, rebutting Fernandes's claim. See also Flavia Agnes' Introduction, *Of Lofty Claims*, 17.

13 The discussion of disgust draws on my *Hiding From Humanity: Disgust, Shame, and the Law* (Princeton: Princeton University Press, 2004). The book draws on psychological research on the emotion of disgust by Paul Rozin and others.

14 Proto-fascist writer Otto Weininger famously argued, in his *Sex and Character* (English edition 1906) that Jews were really women: both groups share the properties of hyperphysicality and hypersexuality from which the clean German male must distance himself. His recommendation to women was to give up sex so that they might tran-

scend this destiny.

15 See also William Ian Miller, *The Anatomy of Disgust* (Cambridge, MA: Harvard University Press, 1997); although I contest most of Miller's normative conclusions, I admire much of his analysis.

16 Andrea Dworkin, 'Repulsion,' in *Intercourse* (New York: The Free Press, 1983).

17. Indeed the most serious flaw in Dworkin's analysis is her failure to consider these societal and individual variations and her consequent representation of disgust-misogyny as ubiquitous and inevitable.

18 Klaus Theweleit, *Male Fantasies*, trans. S. Conway, two volumes (Minneapolis: University of Minnesota Press, 1987 and 1989).

19 In my article 'Genocide in Gujarat'.

20. Laws of Manu, a central code of ancient Hindu law and ethics, compiled between 200 BCE and 200 CE.

21 Daniel Boyarin, *Unheroic Conduct: The Rise of Heterosexuality and the Invention of the Jewish Man* (Berkeley and Los Angeles: Unviersity of California Press, 1997).

22 For discussion and survey evidence, see Maitrayee Mukhopadhyay, in 'Between Community and State: The Question of Women's Rights and Personal Laws,' in Zoya Hasan (ed.), *Forging Identities* (Boulder: Westview, 1994), 108-29.

23 Paul Courtright, *Ganesa: Lord of Obstacles, Lord of Beginnings* (Oxford: Oxford University Press, reprint edition 1989); the new Indian edition has now been withdrawn due to pressure and intimidation.

24 One story of his birth, for example, is that Shiva and his consort Parvati saw two elephants mating. This excited them, so they turned themselves into elephants to make love in that form. Thus their child Ganesha was born with an elephant head.

25 Ramesh Rao, 'A Hindu God Must Indeed Be Heathen: What can the two million Indian-Americans do to counter the Goliath that is Western academe?' *India Abroad*, 28 November 2003, A24. See also, more recently, Rao's 'Ganesha, Shivaji and Power Play,' *India Abroad*, 16 April 2004, A22.

26 Ramesh Rao, 'A Hindu God Must Indeed Be Heathen' in the same column by Ramesh Rao, who often plays the role of spokesperson for a part of the US Hindu-Right community.

27 James Laine, *Shivaji: Hindu King in Islamic India* (Oxford: Oxford University Press, 2003).

28 Laine is a Texan, and anyone who reads the book will know it, since he repeatedly alludes to the Davey Crockett legend he absorbed in

his boyhood as a parallel to the heroic legend of Shivaji. Nonetheless, the death threats assume that he is English, effectively projecting sexual foulness onto a colonizing Other (and revealing in the process that they have not even read the chapter of the book that has occasioned controversy). It should be noted that the Laine case is rather different from the others, as it is involved with warring currents in the caste politics of Maharashtra.

29 But we should remember that this extremism derives support and comfort from the allegedly moderate politicians of the BJP: thus, as I argue in my 'Genocide in Gujarat', Vajpayee was culpably evasive about responsibility for the massacre; and although Vajpayee himself expressed some unease about the attacks on Laine and the Pune institute, he later supported the attempt to arrest Laine in very strong terms.

30 Thus Ganesha, traditionally pot-bellied and with a small child-sized penis, has been reconstructed with a 'six-pack' and a weapon-bearing arm held aggressively in the air.

31 See Theweleit, *Male Fantasies*(English edition), vol. 2, 160-62.

32 Why don't we hear more about Nazi rapes of Jewish women? As Catharine MacKinnon has demonstrated in an article in a forthcoming collection edited by Melissa Williams, contemporaneous documents give much evidence of rape, forced prostitution, and the forced exchange of sex for survival. Perhaps the Nazi bureaucrats' desire to kill like an efficient machine prevented even this much 'humanity'.

33 The religion data from the 2001 census have not yet been published.

34 Most of the information about the Gujarat riots in this article can be found in the Report of the Concerned Citizens' Tribunal, which is online at http://www.sabrang.com. See also Siddarth Varadajan (ed.), *Gujarat*, an excellent collection of documents and articles to which I am also indebted. On the funding issue, see 'The Foreign Exchange of Hate: IDRF and the American Funding of Hindutva,' also at http://www.sabrang.com. For a rejoinder by American leaders of the Hindu Right, see http://www.letindiadevelop.org/thereport. The whole issue of funding evidently deserves a thorough and impartial investigation. The volume edited by Flavia Agnes, *Of Lofty Claims*, contains a collection of testimonies from young legal activists who went to Gujarat to take down women's testimonies for future prosecutions. Another valuable report, focused on gender issues, is

Threatened Existence: A Feminist Analysis of the Genocide in Gujarat, a report by the International Initiative for Justice, available online at http://www.onlinevolunteers.org/gujarat/reports/iijg/2003/fullreport.pdf.

For conversations that have contributed to my understanding of the issues, I am grateful to Paul Courtright, Zoya Hasan, Indira Jaising, James Laine, Ramesh Rao, Tanika Sarkar, Devendra Swarup, and Romila Thapar. Some, of course, will disagree with the analysis that I have presented here.

Powers of the Weak:
Fear and Violation in the Discourse of Communalism

USHA ZACHARIAS AND J. DEVIKA

The violence of the dominated is perhaps more complex than the violence of the dominant. This paper examines how narratives and experiences of social failure, threatened symbolic boundaries, and 'weak' citizenship, form discursive spaces that can generate real acts of violence. Assumptions of what would constitute 'violence' and 'violation' are blurred in this account of how a marginal, low-caste coastal community—the Arayas of north Kerala, India—react to the Muslim/Araya killings in their area.

Although the Arayas are not *savarna* Hindus,[1] they have for long cultivated an identity that is dependent on and seeks recognition from *savarna* Hinduism, thus leading them to be included into the fold of Hindutva, or Hindu nationalist organizations and political forces. We combine historical and ethnographic work to show how the community's failure to achieve full political citizenship is complemented by a deep sense of violation and threat that is expressed through a series of imagined spatial frontiers and boundaries. The rhetorical imagination of space—or of the location of the community within symbolically shifting frontiers of danger and threat—reinforced by the killings, leads to a gray zone where distinctions of violation and violence, aggressor and victim, lose meaning. In turn, the gender politics of community works in a curious way that appears to empower Araya women, leaving them at the frontlines of the community mobilization against their Muslim opponents. The killings or the numbers of persons killed—nine, in this case—were not as significant as the quality of the political mobilization and the displacement of the Muslim community that they made possible.

Recent inter-disciplinary scholarship on violence has sought to problematize the dichotomies of wartime and peacetime violence, thus displacing traditional historiographies that assign an aberrant, disruptive quality to violence.[2] Nancy Scheper-Hughes and Philippe Bourgois describe peacetime and wartime violence as a continuum, arguing that such an approach blurs the distinctions between public/private, legitimate/illegitimate, and visible/invisible forms of violence. The approach is based on constructing gradations of violence as a meaningful social and cultural act that ranges from peacetime crimes to torture, genocide, and war. In contrast, Wenona Giles and Jennifer Hyndman favour a linking of the multiple sites of violence, that range from the home to social, political, and economic processes that are embedded in state policies, public institutions, and the global economy. In doing so, they draw on feminist arguments that deconstruct the distinction between home and nation, private and public. 'Boundaries between combatants and civilians, battlefronts and civilian spaces, cease to have much meaning in light of 9/11,' they write.[3] Although our paper does not centrally engage with the question of violence as it gets specifically rearticulated after 9/11, we think that it shifts the imaginative and rhetorical context in which Hindu/Muslim violence is interpreted in South Asia.

While both anthologies break new ground in a post 9/11 global context, they fail to attend sufficiently to scholarly work from the 'South' that has theorized both the blurring continuum of violence, and the interlinked zones of conflict since the 1990s. We refer particularly to South Asia, where the violent partition of British India was integral to nation-building processes, as were the smaller wars that involved the state, the community, and the family. South Asian feminist scholarship has pioneered the studies of these tension-ridden intersections and the gender politics that underwrite them in the historical context of the rise of imagined religious communities.[4] These anthologies theorize the intersections of state, community, and family/gender as precisely the area where multiple patriarchies gain legitimacy within the nation-state, thus complicating notions of integrated, singular, institutional identities that separate state from community and from family. These feminist anthologies have specifically foregrounded the gender politics of community construction, showing how Hindu nationalism has

(a) used particular social constructions of 'traditional femininity'
(b) deployed the violation of women as a central emotional appeal in arguing for retaliatory action; and/or
(c) succeeded in moving women to the frontlines of the conflict as active political subjects.

More recently, feminist work on displaced peoples in Sri Lanka has productively rethought the spatial imaginaries of home and belonging as well as feminist assumptions regarding peacetime gender norms.[5] Throughout our analyses here, we draw on the insights of South Asian feminist scholarly work that shows how critical gender is to the constitution of community identity; how community identity is embedded in the symbolic violence of gender domination; and how gender politics of communities are in turn only traceable through a network of power relations that criss-cross family, community, caste, and regional dynamics. In this paper, we grant a central place to both the historical constructions, and the rhetorical and discursive production of the 'spaces of violence'[6] to examine violence and its aftermath in a socially marginal community.

How does the Araya community's history of marginality and the failure to achieve full citizenship resonate with the present violence? How does the violence, occurring after 9/11, result in the rhetorical production of a landscape of fear that is constantly under siege by 'Islamic terrorism'? How does the gender politics of this fear work in a way that pits women of Araya and Muslim communities against each other? The following sections explore these questions. We begin by mapping the Marad violence at multiple sites—local, regional, national, and transnational. The next section traces the Araya community's history, reading it as a 'failed community' among socially competing communities in Kerala. The last two sections that delineate the symbolic remapping of the community in a new, rhetorically produced space of fear, and its gender politics, are based on ethnographic work in Marad.

MAPPING MARAD ON MULTIPLE SITES

Although Marad is a small coastal fishing village secluded from the city of Kozhikode in north Kerala, the violence occurring here simultaneously translated into multiple sites: local, regional, national, and global. The Marad incident occurred in a local space where *jati* institutions[7] have power and state institutions command relatively less influence in regulating civic life. Arayas, who comprise over 60% of the Marad population, are governed by the community organization known as Araya Samajam, while the Muslim self-governance begins at the local mosque. The Arayas are not part of the *savarna* Hindu community, but occupy the gray areas (as do Dalits), and qualify for special state quotas under 'Other Eligible Categories'.

The first round of violence occurred in January 2002 when five persons—three Muslims and two Araya—were killed, and fishing boats and huts were set on fire after a rumour broke about a boy of one community molesting a girl of another community during the New Year celebrations held at the local club, Sagarasarani.[8] It is not clear even now which communities the 'boy' and 'girl' belonged to, or if it was only a rumour; however, as narrated in the rumour, one was Araya, the other Muslim. This incident, in local narratives, invited the retaliatory violence of 3 May 2003, when nine men, reportedly affiliated with the Rashtriya Swayamsevak Sangh (RSS), were killed on Marad beach at sunset, allegedly by men of the Muslim extremist organization, National Development Front (NDF) and its local supporters.[9] This immediately became a source of political conflict at the regional site of the state, where Hindu nationalists, who have played relatively weak roles in both political and civil societies, have been seeking an opportunity to grow in Kerala. Electoral politics in Kerala typically swings between left and centrist coalitions, the Left Democratic Front (LDF) and the United Democratic Front (UDF) respectively. At the time of the conflict, the United Democratic Front led by the Congress was in power. The Chief Minister A. K. Anthony was clearly unwilling to risk loss of Hindu votes in an ideological atmosphere favourable to the Hindu Rightwing.

Occurring as it did in the aftermath of the Gujarat pogrom of 2002, Marad showed how a local conflict could immediately become intelligible as a national issue in the post 9/11 global context. After Gujarat 2002, and more strikingly, after the ideological victory won by Hindutva in Gujarat, Hindu nationalists had tasted political success, and were seeking opportunities to extend it further even as anti-minority discourse had reached a national crescendo. Alleging that the Muslim violence was connected to Islamic extremist groups in Pakistan/Kashmir and the Gulf region, the RSS and its electoral sibling, the Bharatiya Janata Party (BJP), demanded a Central Bureau of Intelligence inquiry that would leave the political control of the investigation in the hands of the BJP-led national coalition government.

The Kerala government's rejection of this demand, one that would hand over their regional authority to the national government, was the key turning-point in the events in Marad. Fearing police harassment and revenge killings after the violence, over 1500 Muslims fled *en masse*. Stranded Muslim women, children, and the elderly were accommodated in refugee camps within Kozhikode district set up by political parties. As these families remained displaced from their homes, the Hindutva groups proceeded to battle the government on the political front by persisting in the demand for the CBI probe, and on the local front by blocking the return of Muslim families to Marad. Araya families looted abandoned Muslim homes, carried away or destroyed consumer items such as television sets and kitchen appliances, polluted wells with garbage, literally acting as the 'physical frontiers' of the community. In a dramatic turn of events, Araya women at Marad successfully prevented the state-sponsored resettlement of Muslim families, forcing the Kerala government to abandon its rehabilitation efforts.[10] For five months, Muslim women, children, and the elderly remained uprooted in refugee camps while the men 'disappeared' under the looming threat of arrest.[11]

The Marad violence showed how acts of aggression form a powerful nexus for political and cultural mobilization due to their dynamic translatability between multiple sites, the local, regional, national, and global. The quantitative numbers of those killed, in this case, reveal little about the political forces that acts of violence can open up. In this essay, we wish to focus on the local and regional sites of the struggle, which as Zoya Hasan shows in her study of caste and community in

Uttar Pradesh,[12] is crucial to the understanding of community conflicts. What is striking about the Marad struggle is the distinctive battle fought by the Araya community, one that has always remained on the margins of Kerala society. Marad illustrated the new strategy of Hindutva that had proved to be so successful in Gujarat, that of deploying marginal castes to act as the physical frontlines of their ideological agendas.[13]

Punyani's view that the BJP offers Dalits new opportunities and greater participation is particularly relevant here.[14] In this case, we feel that a historical approach is essential to account for the community's easy submergence into Hindutva goals. Accordingly, Devika's historical research shows the Araya 'failure' in creating a community identity that was socially influential. The other important dimension of the Marad struggle is the role played by Araya women in preventing the rehabilitation of Muslim women. Usha's ethnographic work in Marad shows how Araya women perceived themselves as belonging to a threatened community, and viewed the state-sponsored rehabilitation initiatives as a sign of the power and political influence of the Muslim community.

HISTORIC FAILURE: ARAYA COMMUNITY-BUILDING

In this section we try to make sense of the pivotal role played by the marginalized Araya community in the communal mobilization of Marad, through examining the history of Araya community formation in the 20th century and taking into account the multiple contemporary contexts which shaped the antagonisms at Marad.

Both academic and non-academic accounts of Malayalee politics since the 1950s have contributed images of its exceptional character within India. They highlight the left hegemony in the political field and the presence of strongly organized communities (Nairs, Ezhavas and the Syrian Christians) as major players.[15] For many, the exceptionalism consists of political instability and communal factionalism in a 'problem state'; however, the polarization of politics between the communists and the elite-controlled community organizations is also seen to have had positive effects, especially in social development, as one highly influential account has pointed out.[16]

Many of these accounts implicitly concede that competition between communities has kept hostile religious chauvinisms in check. Thus, many authors note that in contrast to other parts of the country, Christians and Muslims are substantial, economically powerful minorities in Kerala.[17] Efforts made in 1950 to float a Hindu Maha Mandalam, supposedly to protect 'Hindu interests' against the Christian 'onslaught' were short-lived, more a product of immediate tactics than any longterm strategy. Moreover, Hindu chauvinist organizations have not been able to gain much electoral ground in the state. Thus in the 1984 elections in which the Hindu Front contested for the first time in Kerala, the BJP and the Hindu Munnani managed to garner only 1.72 and 2.17 percentage of the total votes, respectively. For all these reasons, the communal politics of Kerala has been considered to be qualitatively different from Hindu/Muslim fundamentalism, which evokes homogenous, elitist religious identities, and explicitly excludes other religious groups through hostile and often violent action.[18] In contrast, the former is shaped around community interests and aims at wresting gains from the state rather than creating and maintaining inter-community exclusions and hostilities.

While these observations are certainly valid, they overlook some crucial aspects of the historical-political scenario in Kerala. Most notably, they ignore the enactment of hostility and exclusion along intra-community (rather than inter-community) lines. For instance, Arayas continued to be excluded from the reformed Hindu community even though they embraced Hindu social norms.[19]

As *avarnas*, the Arayas were socially and economically oppressed in the traditional Malayalee caste order.[20] The strategies adopted by *avarnas* in Kerala to escape caste oppression in the 20th century, included conversion and the creation of new cults.[21] The association of 'Araya' with 'Hindu' begins quite early. Being located on the coast where substantial sections had converted to Islam and Christianity, the burden of representing the 'Hindu' often fell to the Arayas, often recognized as the leading group among the 'Hindu fishermen'.[22] Like the Ezhavas and the Nairs, Araya reformers strove hard to Hinduize marriage and family practices, eliminating, for instance, easy divorce and widow remarriage, which were the norm earlier.[23] The myth of

Araya origin from the sage Veda Vyasa was constructed, recounted in Pandit K. P. Karuppan's famous poem *Jatikkummi,* recorded by anthropologists and officials, and reiterated by contemporary Araya reformers.[24] A prominent early Araya journal was named *Vyasan* (1922); so also were several libraries, reading rooms and caste organizations.[25]

However, these efforts did not bring satisfactory gains for several reasons. First, unlike lower castes successful in community formation like the Ezhavas or the Tiyyas, the Arayas failed to decisively cut their links with traditional religious institutions and practices which were strongly mediated by *jati* hierarchies. Compared to other coastal groups, the Arayas have had stronger links with *savarna* authority structures inland. Earlier and contemporary Araya accounts of 'the glorious past' proudly recall their ritualized 'occasional inclusion' in *savarna* society, and close links with local rulers, temples and the *savarna* elite; often, these rituals have the perverse effect of reaffirming their status as subordinate helpers. Contrast this with Ezhava efforts: by distancing themselves clearly from *savarna* religious hierarchies and privileges, Ezhavas achieved both a breakdown of internal status differences and a sense of being Hindu without losing sight of the power-differentials and risks in sharing an identity claimed strongly by the *savarna*s. However, Arayas were still struggling to establish their claims within Hindu temples even in the 1960s.[26]

A related problem of Araya community identity-formation was the failure to undo internal hierarchies. Unlike the Ezhavas and the Nairs, Arayas were unable to group around a singular spiritual figure to construct a new and unified Hindu identity, although Brahmananda Sivayogi's *Anandamatam*—an anti-caste iconoclastic Hindu reformism that emphasized individual transformation through self-discipline—did attract some, educated Arayas in the early 20th century.[27] Communities like the Ezhava and Tiyya strove to establish communities of equal Ezhavas/Tiyyas, bound together within their own reformed Hinduism and distinct circuits of worship,[28] breaking down internal hierarchies within the caste group. However, Arayas were unable to achieve such a unity of the non-converted coastal groups.

Second, the Araya reform movement failed to establish an adequate and sustainable network of secular community institutions to promote education and other skills needed for modern political and economic life. The institutions were numerous but always short-lived, often for want of financial resources.[29] This seriously hampered the Araya efforts, since entering the reformed Hindu community in Kerala required not just wealth-accumulation, but also knowledge and education.[30]

Third, Araya reformers failed to wrest substantial gains from the state also because they failed to achieve numerical strength as a community. Araya reformers' failure in uniting the 'Hindu' fisher folk[31] persisted into the second half of the 20th century[32] and it is not until the late 20th century that their efforts to gain concessions from the state met with success, though such problems seem to persist even now, partially.[33] The present Araya alliance with Hindu communal forces may be read as a further move towards cultural self-assertion, having made some political gains in the late 20th century.

Fourth, the Araya community did not succeed in another significant area, the realm of gender modernization. The construct of the ideal domestic woman figured very high on all early 20th-century reform agendas in Kerala.[34] Indeed, modern gender norms are one of the standards used to assess the 'progress' achieved by each community. Women are expected to be diligent, moral domestic subjects, overseers and guardian angels of the home. Araya reformers too recognized the importance of such 'civilizing'. Araya women's associations were operating in Travancore in the thirties and the first woman graduate of the Araya community, C. Rudrani, was nominated to the Travancore's Sree Mulam Popular Assembly in 1931. While we find numerous reports of Nair and Ezhava women attaining higher degrees and employment in the newspapers of the 1930s, the same is not true of the Araya women. The major Araya success here seems to have been in dress reform. In the late 19th century, Pandit K. P. Karuppan had recommended a 'modest' style, called the 'Karuppan Kaccha'. But there are indications that this style was not always accepted, and that when women were made to conform, it was not always through persuasion, but sometimes through outright violence.[35] Araya community politics in post-independence Kerala also had little time for such issues. However, Araya reformers like Velukkutty Arayan continued to fight stereotypical representations of coastal women, which portray them as uncouth hagglers. This was one lack that the media representations of the Araya women's violence as 'sentimental' helped to cover. For when violence appears 'sentimental', it is recognized differently from, for instance, the aggressive behaviour of fish-vending women.[36] These representations justified the violence as an outpouring of grief, masking Hindu chauvinism. They also foregrounded the presence of women who seem to conform to the ideal (Hindu) womanly subjectivity in the Araya community, thus elevating it into the high-Hindu fold. Gender relations in the Araya community thus simultaneously mark the failure to modernize, and the desire for upward caste mobility.

Viewing this history alongside multiple contemporary contexts, we may identify the processes that were at work at Marad. From the mid-1980s, national conditions began to favour the rise of belligerent Hindu communalism, which had an impact in Kerala as well—evident in the emergence of the Hindu Front. As we have noted earlier, these efforts were not particularly successful in electoral terms. In this context of a weak support base within the state, the events of Marad presented Hindu nationalist organizations with a strategic opportunity to play 'champion of the oppressed'. Events at Marad were presented to the Hindu public as an illuminating case, the answer to the counterfactual question: what would happen if Muslims were more powerful in Kerala than Hindus?

These Hindu nationalist discourses on Marad played into the anxieties that dominated the regional political and cultural field at the time as a result of several conjunctural developments at the regional, and local but also the international levels. Thus in the regional political field the left cultural hegemony began to wane in the mid-80s, creating new symbolic and discursive openings for Hindutva ideology. Wary of losing Hindu votes in an atmosphere favourable to Hindu nationalist parties, the ruling Congress-led coalition was reluctant to take an overt stand against Hindutva discourses and practices of hostility and exclusion against Muslims.

In another regional-level development, the state had seen in recent years the considerable social and economic mobility of Malabar Muslims as a result of migration to and remittances from the Gulf countries. This fomented 'Hindu' fears of a future in which Muslims would equal or surpass 'Hindus' in social power.[37]

At the local level, caste structures have always regulated everyday life strongly in the state and they also provide welfare benefits to members. Historically, conversions on India's coast were not only to escape caste oppression, but also to access the (however limited) security offered by a powerful mentor, the Church or Islam.[38] For the Arayas of Marad, Hindu communal forces seemed to offer such security—indeed, researchers have noted insecurity among them over the lack of a mentor[39] in a context in which the state was increasingly unable to meet welfare commitments and political society was weakened.[40]

Developments at the national and international level were also consequential. The next section, Usha's ethnographic documentation, especially of the Arayas' evocation of a certain 'dangerous geography' establishes the impact of the post 9/11 global context and of the national ascendancy of Hindutva in shaping the violence at Marad.

SPACES OF FEAR: NARRATIVE CONSTRUCTION OF THREATENED COMMUNITY

Preliminary ethnographic work in Marad conducted by Usha in the Summer of 2005 demonstrates how the historical 'failure' of the Araya community to gain social citizenship on par with competing castes, and the subsequent Hinduization translates, in the present, to a symbolic geography where this fear and anxiety may be expressed. This symbolic geography, or spatial imagination of the community on its own 'map', is structured by the location of Marad itself on the coastline of Kozhikode district, close to the ancient port of Beypore. As Ram notes in her anthropological study of Mukkuvar women of the fishing castes, the coastal areas occupy a peculiar place in imaginative geography that is on the borderlines of mainstream society owing to both caste status and to the occupation. Ram notes that both caste segregation from *savarna* Hindus and the autonomy of fishing as an occupation allows the coastal communities to construct a distinctive identity.[41]

Always rendered peripheral to both political and economic history, the coastal communities imagine their relationship to the state, law, and processes of governance in autonomous ways that, ironically enough, in the case of Marad, allowed an increased identification with Hindutva. Conversations with older men, especially those involved with the Araya Samajam but not necessarily identified as RSS, painted a picture of Marad as a primarily Hindu coastal village under threat of siege through its vulnerable openness to the ocean and the possibility of attack from Muslim invaders. They rhetorically projected the vulnerability of the coastline as an unguarded area (by the nation-state) that was open to attack and conquest through the grand Islamic plan of capturing the entire western coastline of Kerala.

This matches the symbolic geopolitics and ideology of the RSS, which projects the threat of the Islamic takeover of the Indian coastline from, imaginably, the Middle East. In a response to the Marad violence, RSS spokesperson Ram Madhav said on 9 May 2003 that the worst fears of the RSS, that Kerala's coastline would become a 'safe haven' for 'Islamic terrorist operations . . . sponsored by the ISI' (Inter Services Intelligence, the Pakistan intelligence agency), had been confirmed. 'Kerala's coastline is open to clandestine operations from the sea. There is a systematic effort to clear the coastline of all non-Muslims. Madrasas and mosques are coming up in large numbers all along the coastline. And some of these have become hubs of anti-national activities. The very fact that the murderers at Marad beach were arrested from the local Jama Masjid and also a huge cache of deadly weapons was unearthed from the Mosque buttresses this point,' Madhav said.[42] This picture is further strengthened by rumours that many Muslim families in the area have relatives who are migrant workers in the Gulf nations, and who are collaborating with the greater Islamic project of the takeover. While this may seem an absurd notion in the era of international militarization of oceanic space, the imaginative frontier or the lack of it is a powerful symbolic grid on which the coastal community constructs its vulnerability to 'external threats'.

The whisper campaigns that gather strength among women narrators as well recount that the attackers in the violent events at Marad in May 2003 actually escaped through boats off the Marad coast, a 'fact' that the police have not attested. In fact, the entire demand for the CBI enquiry that bogged down the Marad settlement was based on the single premise that the attackers had come from 'outside'. As Uma Unni, BJP city secretary of Kozhikode, told Usha, 'We know that the Muslims in this area are not capable of waging such an assault. In fact, a single Hindu can beat up three Muslims at a time. They had outside help, and we're demanding that those forces be identified.'

Thus the symbolic figure of the post 9/11 Islamic male was cast into a possible geographical web of coast-to-coast interconnections between Kerala and the Middle East. What is particularly significant is that the nation-state or the national/international military apparatuses are seen as having little or no role in monitoring the coastal interactions. The imaginative geography moves back centuries to the time when Portuguese, Dutch, German, Christian, and Jewish traders sailed through mercantile sea routes to the treasures accessible through the coasts and harbours, without interference. Such a perception does not even have a historical precedent since Marad, at no point in its history, could have allowed boats to sail into its limited coast, which has no harbour, and which is, until today, not used even by fishing boats. The absent presence of the post 9/11 Muslim extremist and the immediately discernible violence thus translated itself into a conception of the threatened frontiers of the community, which was fighting a solitary battle against the transoceanic conspiracy, unmediated by state structures.

The essential 'powerlessness' of the Arayas then results in the necessity to build tight spaces cordoned off from the Muslims, which is incredibly difficult since they travel in the same buses, their children go to the same schools, the women participate in microcredit programmes, and since both communities share funds in longstanding local rituals such as *kurikalyanam,* a means of collective fund-raising for individual emergency needs, such as a wedding or a funeral. Usha's conversations with Araya women suggested that there were ongoing efforts to build borders, frontiers, and barriers to Muslim interactions at the local level. Neo-liberal economic programmes that foster women's cooperation for microcredit are now segregated along Hindu/Muslim lines, where Hindu women run their own cooperatives, as do Muslim women, and thus segregate different spaces for the home trades they take up. The Araya cooking hut set up with microcredit that Usha visited, where evening snacks were being prepared to be sold to the community, attested to this.

Buses and bus stops likewise provided room for hostile and separatist interactions between the communities. 'We don't sit beside them in buses,' an Araya woman told me as Usha was travelling back to Kozhikode city in a bus from Marad. Women whom Usha interviewed also said that although Muslim women seemed to want to talk to them, they would refuse to interact with them. 'We don't want any more of this treacherous friendship,' said Sreedhari, who played an active role in preventing the rehabilitation of Muslim women in their homes. Araya women also reported that children returned from school with stories of verbal threats from Muslim schoolchildren. 'We'll get back at you,' a Muslim child reportedly told an Araya child. Predictably, there was silence on the question of similar threats by Araya children.

Barriers have been erected even in connection with the *kurikalyanam*, a longstanding practice in Marad. Usually, a blackboard at the local teashop functions as an announcement space for an individual or family who needs to raise a large amount of cash for a special need. Each family in the community contributes what they can, and they list their names along with the amount donated, however small or big, on the board. Hindu and Muslim communities have traditinally ocooperated with each other in this mode of collective fundraising; however, since 2003, interviewees asserted, this is no longer the practice. Each community donates only to its own community.

HINDUTVA, GENDER, AND PRIVILEGE

The Marad events were marked not simply by the participation of the Araya community in asserting its community identity, but by the visibly aggressive role played by women as frontline protectors of the community's boundaries. The media coverage of the Marad events featured graphic scenes of Araya women actively preventing the resettlement of Muslim women who had returned to their homes under police protection. According to news reports in Malayalam papers, over 300 Muslim families fled the area soon after the killings on 9 May, while around 150 Muslim men were arrested and jailed. On 25 June, while the police, men and women, stood guard around the house of Mariayambi, who had been escorted back to Marad under police protection, hundreds of Araya women gathered at the spot with the single aim of preventing the resettlement process. News photographs show them verbally and physically confronting the police, laying waste the surrounding vegetation, and polluting the well which was the sole source of water. They also destroyed the toilet facilities that are typically located outside the home in rural areas. The Muslim family, consisting exclusively of women members, was forced to leave their home after four days, on 30 June, due to the sustained hate campaign of the Araya women.[43]

This action had the political consequence of granting power to Hindutva at the bargaining table with the United Democratic Front ministry. Thus, women of a marginal caste waged a struggle to maintain the symbolic and emotional frontiers of the community in ways that, at the level of the state, empowered the upper-caste, almost exclusively masculine, visage of Hindutva.

If one set of media images depicted aggressive Araya women in the locality, threatening the police, and successfully preventing the rehabilitation of Muslim women, another depicted the male leaders taking on the 'public voice' and visage of the community under the umbrella of the Hindu Aikyavedi (United Hindu Front). The women in the locality appeared, in the media, to be acting as empowered subjects of Hindutva, reflecting the hate ideologies against Muslims that Hindutva has popularized. The images appear to illustrate much feminist work on women in rightwing movements, specifically Hindutva, that demonstrates how Hindutva ideologies craft a new, empowered position for women in the community. In this context, we see that ethnographic work in Marad affirms the feminist position that women are empowered through their identification with Hindutva ideologies; however, it also seems that the active role taken on by women is a result of their sense of the loss of citizenship and identity as Araya, rather than as Hindu, women. That is, Araya women's aggressive postures originate from the sense of a community that has failed to construct an identity that can effectively claim social citizenship. The socially marginal caste identity of the Arayas and their dependent relationship with the *savarna* communities (described above by Devika), rhetorically play out in their present narration of the conflict as members of a threatened, vulnerable community which had no choice but to assert itself. Thus even as Muslim women were physically displaced from their homes, and left in refugee camps with no possibility of returning to their homes without inviting social conflict, Araya women saw themselves as victims of state neglect.

Araya women Usha spoke with constantly foregrounded the nature of the May 2003 violence itself as significantly different from the 'spontaneous', 'natural' violence of January 2002, when two Hindu men and three Muslim men were killed in retaliatory attacks. The January killings were described as a mutual give and take, an incident that fell into the pattern of inter-communal violence. 'When they did the job with our men, we did the job too with theirs,' said Sreedhari. The May 2003 violence, in which all nine men killed were Araya, broke this pattern as a stage-managed, planned attack that specifically targeted an unusually high number of Araya men, and was therefore a calculated strategy rather than a 'spontaneous' action. Women who had been active in countering the rehabilitation described it as a sudden, unexpected, attack that the Araya community had nothing to do with. The narrative strategy of recounting the violence as happening on the borders of the community, as 'out there' rather than as a dynamic process, fits well with Pandey's description of Partition violence, where the victims (or perpetrators, however one wishes to see them) asserted their non-involvement with this unusual turn of events.[44] And indeed, historically, such an attack is unprecedented in Marad, setting the context for a qualitatively different level of participation by the Araya women, who now positioned themselves on the frontiers of the community.

A number of women narrators who played leadership roles, and whose names are excluded at their behest, also emphasized that the decision to take on the lead role in countering the rehabilitation was not made by them, but by the larger community. The Araya Samajam, the community's own system of local governance, convened a meeting at which Araya youth had to be restrained from repaying violence in the same coin. The 'leaders' explained that this strategy would result in arrests, and more violent conflict without end. It was therefore the community that took the decision that women would lead the struggle against the resettlement of the Muslim women. In taking this decision, the Araya community seems to have gone along with the sentiments expressed by the women, that they, as mothers, would have to be at the frontline in protecting their sons. The maternal logic of seeing all men of the community as sons played a powerful role in the decision to let women take on the primary role as protectors of the community. The decision that led to the apparent, visible 'violence' by Araya women was motivated by perceptions of the 'weakness' of the community that was unable to hold its own against the sudden violence, and also against state neglect of the issue of Islamic violence.

To the Araya women, the rehabilitation of Muslim women with police protection appeared as a direct act of hostility. Komaledathi, for instance, who functioned as one of the community leaders in organizing women, said, 'We had no one. They have the police to escort them, the state to protect them; but who is there to fight for us? We had to do what we did.' The state's protective machinery, in women's narrations, appeared to be centred around the Muslims even as 'Hindus' or Arayas were coping with grief and bereavement. Given the normal class position of the Muslim families, which is one that is unable to command state protection, the government's gesture seemed extravagant and out of place. While the government could claim this as a protective measure, compared to their normal neglect of both communities of this social class, police protection in this case functioned as a signifier of privilege for Muslim women. 'There's one sub-inspector leading them into the house, another to stand guard at the door, and yet another to watch over them while they go to the bathroom,' mocked Nalini. These signifiers of 'privilege' enjoyed by the Muslim women inflamed Araya women in their forty-eight hour seige of the house of Mariyambi. It appeared to them that Muslim communities could become aggressors and then return as specially protected groups, indicating their strong influence with the state government. Ironically, then, even displaced Muslim women appeared, to the Araya women, as more privileged citizen-subjects of the state.

The visible 'privilege' enjoyed by the Muslim women in the aftermath of their community's initiation of a violent attack, provided the political, and clearly, gendered fuel of jealousy and determination that kept the Araya women, 'without food and water' as one of them said hyperbolically, awake in their struggle. The discovery of a large quantity of swords and crude bombs in the local mosque strengthened the allegation that the Muslim women, who also attend the mosque, must have been aware of the plan of attack in advance. Many Araya women described the Muslim women as neighbours and friends who had betrayed and failed them at this crucial moment. The state's involvement in the resettlement seemed to reinforce the Hindutva ideology that Hindus are a marginalized, oppressed social group, and that one of the primary oppressors is a non-Hindutva state that accords Muslims special status. In the discursive space constructed after the attacks, the Araya Hindu remained as a vulnerable community that had no state protection and no political citizenship. The women stepped into this ambiguous space, where the community appeared to lack political citizenship, in order to act as 'mothers of the community', who could assert the 'natural', maternal, protective boundaries of the community against a more privileged social group.

CONCLUSION

The historical and ethnographic work on the Araya community in the aftermath of the violence in Marad provide interesting insights into how a local conflict translates and plays out between multiple sites, real and imaginary: regional, national, and pan-national. The historical analysis of the Araya community shows its 'failure' to form a strong community as a basis to claim citizenship rewards or special status from the state. The weak social status of the Arayas—constantly dependent for caste/community status on the *savarna* Hindus—led to their alliance with Hindutva forces even as they failed to craft a strong identity 'within' Hindutva due to their permanent subordination to *jati* networks and traditional *jati* institutions. The Arayas claim to inclusion within *savarna* Hindu society was, unfortunately enough, coupled with their inability to break down internal hierarchies between coastal groups to form a political or cultural united front. Finally, the Arayas failed to develop a network of secular institutions within the community that would assure upward mobility through modernizing practices.

This is particularly evident with relation to gender norms, where the cultural battle against the stereotyping of Araya women failed to translate into any material differences in the status of women. In the context of the rise of Hindutva in Kerala from the mid-1980s, the weak social status of the Araya community allowed it all the more easily to be swept into the politics of Hindu communalism.

However, as Usha's ethnographic work shows, Hindutva's—and particularly the RSS's—presence in coastal areas was itself based on the exploitation of a felt sense of marginality of this coastal community. In the wake of 9/11, the figure of the pan-national, ocean-crossing Islamic terrorist fitted perfectly into the spatial imagination of the Arayas, who saw their community as under siege. The weak relationship of Arayas with the state, their failed claims of social citizenship, and the real absence of state institutions in administering welfare in the region, makes such an imaginary all the more real. In this context, the active role played by women in the community to 'resist' the return of Muslim women to their own homes, was, ironically enough, motivated by a perception of the 'weakness' of the community against violence—and state neglect of the issue of Islamic violence.

Feminist scholarship on women's participation in rightwing movements, specifically Hindutva, has indicated the promise of empowerment that Hindu nationalism and identity hold for women. After the demolition of the Babri Masjid, Tanika Sarkar pointed out that Hindutva was offering a powerful new subject position for women in the Ramjanmabhoomi struggle. Sita's sex, she argued, was coming to Ram's rescue, in ways that resonated with the feminist agenda of fostering women's political participation.[45] Since then, a number of feminist scholars have demonstrated the specific ways in which women gain power, identities, and subjectivities in Hindutva organizations and ideology.[46] From the Marad instance, however, we see that the caste and community affiliation of the women form a critical, if not central role, in how they constitute themselves as ambiguous, and even non-political subjects of Hindutva. Even as we examine the material and metaphoric aspects of Hindutva's gender politics[47] caste and community histories as evident in regional sites should play a critical part in the analysis of how violence is translated into the national scripts of Hindutva.

In other words, even as the women serve the larger interests of Hindutva at a site when Hindutva seeks success—such as bargaining to become a political force at the local, state, or national level—their subjective articulation of the experience is oriented primarily to regional, local, intimate affiliations of community and kin, rather than of a specific political affiliation attached to a larger political agenda. Once again, it is the Araya community's history of failure in definitively marking itself as a group positioned for social gains based on community identity, and the perception of their group as a threatened minority with vulnerable frontiers, that work toward constituting this politically ambiguous subjectivity. The history of the efforts of the Araya caste, as a failed process of community-making, may have structurally played a more critical role in etching the political agency of the activist Araya women, rather than an immediate, transversal reading of the Araya women as falling into the Hindutva agenda.

Notes

1.The *savarnas* are the uppermost sections of the varna order of Hindu society, which is recognized to be a status order (*sa-varna* literally means 'defined by a varna').

2 Nancy Scheper-Hughes and Philippe Bourgois, *Violence in War and Peace* (Oxford: Blackwell, 2004); Wenona Giles and Jennifer Hyndman (eds.), *Sites of Violence: Gender and Conflict Zones* (Berkeley: University of California, 2004).

3 Giles and Hyndman, 'Introduction: Gender and Conflict in a Global Context,' in *Sites of Violence,* 3-23.

4 Tanika Sarkar and Urvashi Butalia (eds.), *Women and the Hindu Right* (New Delhi: Kali for Women, 1995); Kumari Jayawardena and Malathi de Alwis (eds.), *Embodied Violence: Communalising Women's Sexuality in South Asia* (London: Zed Books, 1996); Neelam Hussain, Samiya Mumtaz, and Rubina Saigol, *En-gendering the Nation-State* (Lahore, Pakistan: Simorgh Women's Resource and Publication Centre, 1997); Patricia Jeffrey and Amrita Basu, *Resisting the Sacred and the Secular: Women's Activism and Politicized Religion in South Asia* (New Delhi: Kali for Women, 1999).

5 Darini Rajasingham-Senanayake, 'Between Reality and Representation: Women's Agency in War and Post-Conflict Sri Lanka', *Cultural*

Dynamics, 16:2/3 (2004), 41-168; Malathi de Alwis, 'The Purity of Displacement and the Reterritorialization of Longing: Muslim IDPs in Northwestern Sri Lanka', in Giles and Hyndman, *Sites of Violence*, 213-31.

6 Pradeep Jeganathan, 'A Space for Violence', in Partha Chatterjee and Pradeep Jegannathan (eds.), *Subaltern Studies XI: Community, Gender and Violence* (New Delhi: Permanent Black, 2000), 37-65.

7. By *jati* institutions we mean organizations focused on endogamous jati groups, the Arayas and the Mappila Muslims of Marad, respectively, like the Araya Samajam and the Mahal Committees of the Muslims. These are important as social regulatory bodies, and more often, recently, as institutions offering economic support to members in need. They must be clearly distinguished from both political parties and pan-Indian Hindu and Muslim organizations, though the boundaries may blur under specific circumstances.

8 Sanjeevan, '*Marad: Oru Kimvadanthiyil Polinjathu 14 Jeevithangal*,' (Marad: 14 Lives Lost for a Rumour), *Kerala Kaumudi*, 5 May 2003, 5.

9 *Mathrubhoomi*, 'Marad veendum akramam', 4 May 2003, 1.

10 Gita,'*Kurukkanum Kunjadum*,' (The Wolf and the Lamb), *Madhyamam*, 14 Nov 2003, 28-29.

11 For a fuller account, see Usha Zacharias, 'Intelligible Violence: Media Scripts, Hindu/Muslim Women, and the Battle for Citizenship in Kerala' in *Cultural Dynamics*, 16:2/3 (2004), 169-92.

12 Zoya Hasan, 'Community and Caste in Post-Congress Politics in Uttar Pradesh', in Amrita Basu and Atul Kohli (eds.), *Community Conflicts and the State in India* (Calcutta, Chennai, Mumbai: Oxford University Press, 1998), 94.

13 K. Balagopal, 'Reflections on "Gujarat Pradesh" of "Hindu Rashtra"', *Economic and Political Weekly* 37: 22 (2002), 2117.

14 Ram Punyani, *Communal Politics: Facts vs Myths* (New Delhi, Thousand Oaks, London: Sage, 2003), 281-82.

15 Jitendra Singh, *Communist Rule in Kerala* (New Delhi: Diwan Chand India Information Centre, 1959); D. R. Mankekar, *The Red Riddle of Kerala* (Bombay; Manaktalas, 1965); Victor M. Fic, *Kerala: Yenan of India* (Bombay: Nachiketa, 1970); P. M. Mammen, *Communalism vs. Communism: A Study of the Socio-Religious Communities and Political Parties in Kerala 1892-1970* (Calcutta: Minerva, 1981); T. Nossiter, *Communism in Kerala: A Study in Political Adaptation* (Berkeley: University of California, 1982); Robin Jeffrey, *Politics, Women and*

Well-Being: How Kerala Became a Model (New Delhi: Oxford University Press, 2003 (1992)).

16 Jeffrey, *Politics, Women and Well-Being*.

17 For instance, Nossiter, *Communism in Kerala*.

18 This is a working definition. For a fuller account of types of religiosity that may translate into rigid communal posturing, see M. Muralidharan, 'Hindu Community Formation in Kerala: Processes and Structures under Colonial Modernity', *South Indian Studies* 2 (July-December 1996), 234-59.

19 A second critical point about the existent literature is that most these accounts seem to ignore the presence (if repressed) of strident Hindu chauvinisms in Kerala, especially in Malabar after the Mappila Rebellion, which historians have pointed out: see Dilip M. Menon, *Caste, Nationalism and Communism in South India Malabar 1900-1948* (Cambridge: Cambridge University Press, 1994), 80; K. N. Panikkar, *Against Lord and State: Religion and Peasant Uprisings in Malabar 1836-1921* (New Delhi: Oxford University Press, 1989). Indeed, lower-caste Tiyya-Mappila conflicts in Malabar in the 1910s were not perceived as 'Hindu-Muslim' at that time, but by the late 1920s, communal lenses to view such happenings were in place (Menon, *Caste, Nationalism and Communism,* 80). Upper-caste community movements like the Nair Service Society (NSS) and Congress nationalists did make appeals to the 'Hindu community' posited in opposition to (and even victimized by) Christians and Muslims. The NSS tried to protect 'Hindu interests' against missionaries in the 1920s, trying to involve the 'depressed classes' in anti-caste discussions (K. M. Udayabhanu, 'The Dheevara Community and Social Change in Kerala', unpublished Ph.D. thesis submitted to the University of Kerala, Thiruvananthapuram, Kerala, 1990, 152-3). In the 1950s Hindu nationalist organizations played a role in state-sponsored Harijan uplift: *Administration Report of the Department for the Advancement of Backward Communities, 1951-52* (Ernakulum: Government Press, 1953), 16. Thus the presence of Hindu chauvinism was dormant until the mid-1980s.

20 *Avarna* means those excluded from the varna order—literally *a-varna* or 'not defined by a varna'—the so-called untouchables. A survey of the coastal village of Nayarambalam in Kochi conducted in 1935 brought this oppression out in bold relief (T. K. Sankara Menon, Report of the Economic Survey of Nayarambalam Village, Cochin: Cochin Government Press, 1935). In standard of living and

land ownership, the Arayas were just below the Ezhavas and above the Pulayas (19-20). The Nairs and Christians (many of them Syrian Christians) enjoyed a much higher standard of living, owned more land, and had larger incomes.

21 Sanal P. Mohan, 'Religion, Social Space and Identity: Construction of Boundary in Colonial Keralam'. Paper presented at the *Conference of Subaltern Historians*, Lucknow, 3-8 January 1998.

22 The habit of referring to the unconverted fisher folk as 'Hindu' goes as far back as the writings of Francis Day in 1863, who distinguished between 'Hindu' and Christian Mukkuvas: Francis Day, *The Land of the Perumauls or Cochin and Its Past and Its Present* (New Delhi: Asia Educational Services, 1863 (1990)), 325. The debates among Araya reformers over the choice of the Sanskritized name 'Dheevara Mahajanasabha' over 'All-Kerala Fishermen's Association' also reflect this: Ettumanoor Gopalan, *Dewer Enna Karmadheeran* (Kochi: Dewer Smaraka Samiti, 1993) 151. Udayabhanu defines Dheevaras as 'Hindus who had accepted fishing as their traditional occupation': 'The Dheevara Community and Social Change in Kerala', 25.

23 Edgar Thurston and K. Rangachari, *Castes and Tribes of South India Vol. 7* (New Delhi: Asia Educational Services, 1909/1987), 285; *Report on the Census of Travancore* 1931, 380; Udayabhanu, 'The Dheevara Community and Social Change in Kerala', 37-41.

24 Thurston and Rangachari, *Castes and Tribes of South India,* vol. 7, 281-82; *Report on the Census of Travancore*, 1931, 380-81; Gopalan *Dewer Enna Karmadheeran*, 20-22.

25 Udayabhanu, 'The Dheevara Community and Social Change in Kerala', 106-7.

26 Arne Martin Klausen, *Kerala Fishermen and the Indo-Norwegian Pilot Project* (Oslo: International Peace Research Institute, 1968), 104-5.

27 P. S. Velayudhan, '*Adhunika Mataprasthanangal*' (Modern Religious Movements) in P. S.Velayudhan (ed.), *Kerala Charitram,* vol. II (Kochi: Kerala History Association, 1974), 561-62.

28 Filippo Osella and Caroline Osella, *Social Mobility in Kerala: Modernity and Identity in Conflict* (London: Pluto Press, 2000); Menon, *Caste, Nationalism and Communism*.

29 Klausen, *Kerala Fishermen*, 113; Udayabhanu, 'The Dheevara Community and Social Change in Kerala', 211.

30 Klausen, *Kerala Fishermen*, 176-77.

31 The *Report on the Census of Travancore*, 1931, mentions the Araya attempts as 'partially successful', more among the Mukkuvas and the

Marakkans, but not among the Valas (365). The *Report on the Census of Travancore* (1941), 132. The Araya reformers were engaged in intense efforts to bring them under the common umbrella of 'Araya'. See Chapter XII, pp. 383-4. Also see *Report on the Census of Travancore*, 1941, 132; Gopalan, *Dewer Enna Karmadheeran*; Udayabhanu, 'The Dheevara Community and Social Change in Kerala'.

32 Udayabhanu, 'The Dheevara Community and Social Change in Kerala', 224.

33 For instance the Jnanodyaya Sabha website still actively addresses the issues of the Valas, while identifying broadly with the Dheevara identity.

34 J. Devika, *En-Gendering Individuals: The Language of Re-forming in Early 20th Century Keralam* (Hyderabad: Orient Longman, forthcoming).

35 Gopalan, *Dewer Enna Karmadheeran,* 42-45.

36 Araya women at Marad do not work as fish vendors. Yet stereotypes persist. Araya women, generally, have engaged in productive work, particularly so in many southern areas. See Leela Gulati, *Fisherwomen on the Kerala Coast: Demographic and Socio-economic Impact of a Fisheries Development Project* (Geneva: ILO, 1984).

37 It is reported that the Muslim Mahal committee at Marad mobilized resources from Gulf migrants to give out interest-free loans to Muslims; this may have heightened Araya insecurities. K. N. Ganesh, Priyamol Dhanya, V. Srividya, Srilatha Rajani, T. K. Anandi, Ramadas. '*Marad Kalapam—Oranveshanam*' (Marad Riot: An Enquiry), mimeo, 2004; G. Dietrich and N. Nayak, *Transition or Transformation? A Study of the Mobilisation, Organisation and the Emergence of Consciousness among the Fishworkers of Kerala* (Madurai: Tamilnadu Theological Seminary, 2002), 147-8.

38 G.T. Mackenzie, *Christianity in Travancore* (Thiruvananthapuram: Government Press, 1881), 14; Day, *The Land of the Perumauls,* 325.

39 Klausen, *Kerala Fishermen,* 113; Udayabhanu, 'The Dheevara Community and Social Change in Kerala'.

40 Another local-level explanation has to do with the history of conflict over fishing resources among coastal communities. See Dietrich and Nayak, *Transition or Transformation?* 65; P. R. G. Mathur, *The Mappila Fisherfolk of Kerala* (Thiruvananthapuram, 1978), 220-22; Udayabhanu 'The Dheevara Community and Social Change in Kerala', 111, 149.

41 Kalpana Ram, *Mukkuvar Women: Gender, Hegemony and Capitalist Transformation in a South Indian Fishing Community* (New Delhi: Kali for Women, 1992), 4.

42 'Spreading Tentacles of the ISI in Kerala: RSS,' 9 May 2003. http://www.hvk.org/articles/0503/111.html

43 See Zacharias, 'Intelligible Violence', 181-82 for a fuller account.

44 Gyanendra Pandey, *Remembering Partition: Violence, Nationalism, and History in India* (Cambridge: Cambridge University Press, 2001), 178-81.

45 Tanika Sarkar, 'The Woman as Communal Subject: Rastrasevika Samiti and the Ram Janmabhoomi Movement', *Economic and Political Weekly*, 26: 35 (1991), 2057-62.

46 Teesta Setalvad, 'The Woman Shiv Sainik and Her Sister Swayamsevika,' in Sarkar and Butalia, *Women and the Hindu Right,* 233-44; Tanika Sarkar, *Hindu Wife, Hindu Nation: Community, Religion and Cultural Nationalism* (New Delhi: Permanent Black, 2001); Paola Bachhetta, *Gender in the Hindu Nation: RSS Women as Ideologues* (New Delhi: Women Unlimited, 2004).

47 Anuradha Chenoy, Gujarat Carnage: The Politics of Gender in the Politics of Hate. *Aman Ekta Manch Digest*, 3 June 2002. http://www.onlinevolunteers.org/gujarat/news/articles/gender-politics.htm

Once, in Rangdum: Formations of Violence and Peace in Ladakh

RAVINA AGGARWAL[1]

The separatist insurgency which has raged in Kashmir since 1990 had—until that moment—not affected the predominantly Buddhist region of Ladakh.

(*The Guardian* 25 July 2000)

On 11 July 2000, three Buddhist monks from Rangdum monastery in the Kargil district of Ladakh were killed by unidentified assailants. The incident transpired just a few days before *sbyar-gnas*, the annual summer fair held on the fifteenth day of the sixth lunar month of the Buddhist calendar, for which villagers from the region gather to celebrate and feast at the monastery. Located at a considerable distance of almost 130 mountain kilometres southeast of the town centre of Kargil, past the glacier of Parkachig and the twin peaks of Nun and Kun, the monastery stands on a hillock surrounded by streams and meadows. According to oral accounts by villagers from an adjoining village, just after twilight on that fateful day, assuming that expected supplies of barley and other goods had been sent from the Zangskar area for the fair, monks from the monastery raced down the hillock when they heard the persistent honking of a truck horn.[1] One junior and three senior monks reached the road first, whereupon the assailants emerged from the truck, lined the monks up and sprayed them with bullets. The junior monk, Stanzin Tsering, dove into a nearby stream and escaped.

No arrests have been made until today, although the widely circulated verdict is that 'militants' and 'enemy fundamentalists' are responsible for the killings. Such an ascription of culpability is echoed in many of the narratives memorializing the incident, in which Ladakh is portrayed as an inherently peaceful place threatened by looming violence from external agents. In the Special Mentions segment of the Rajya Sabha debates, for example, the Member of Parliament and Ambedkarite leader, Mr R. S. Gavai, stated that 'three innocent Buddhist monks were brutally killed by gun-toting anti-national elements outside Rangdum Monastery in Zanskar Valley.'[2] Similarly, in an interview for rediff.com, a monk from Zangskar was quoted as saying, 'We are a peace-loving people and do not involve ourselves in activities that lead to bloodshed. We are scared that the militants might strike again and kill more lamas.'[3]

In this essay, I critically investigate the attribution of violence and homicide to external factors that stand outside the historical and social locus of Ladakh. In so doing, I seek not to produce an authentic culprit but rather to illustrate the structural agendas through which a naturalized and idealized Ladakhi subject of violence becomes articulated. By examining how cartographies of the nation-state are played out within the parameters of Ladakh's geopolitical landscape and social body, I expand upon Allen Feldman's argument that 'political violence is no longer fully anchored in ideological codes and conditions external to the situation of enactment and transaction. Political enactment becomes sedimented with its own local histories that are mapped out on the template of the body.'[4]

The classification of the assailants as 'enemy agents' is a reference to those engaged in the cause of Kashmiri independence. Ladakh, which is the largest territorial region of the State of Jammu and Kashmir in India, constituting about 60% of the area, has undoubtedly witnessed several transformations since the civil resistance movement began in Kashmir in 1989. Yet Rangdum has often been earmarked as a distinct episode in Ladakhi history. Treating Rangdum as an isolated episode may counter a tendency to fetishize violence as the dominant means of interaction in Ladakh but it also prevents existing modes of violence from being addressed with gravity and concrete investment in the future. Consequently, this essay moves away from discussing the Rangdum incident as an exceptional slippage from a prevailing norm of non-violence or as a typical example of existing

The Rangdum Monastery.
Photograph by Ravina Aggarwal

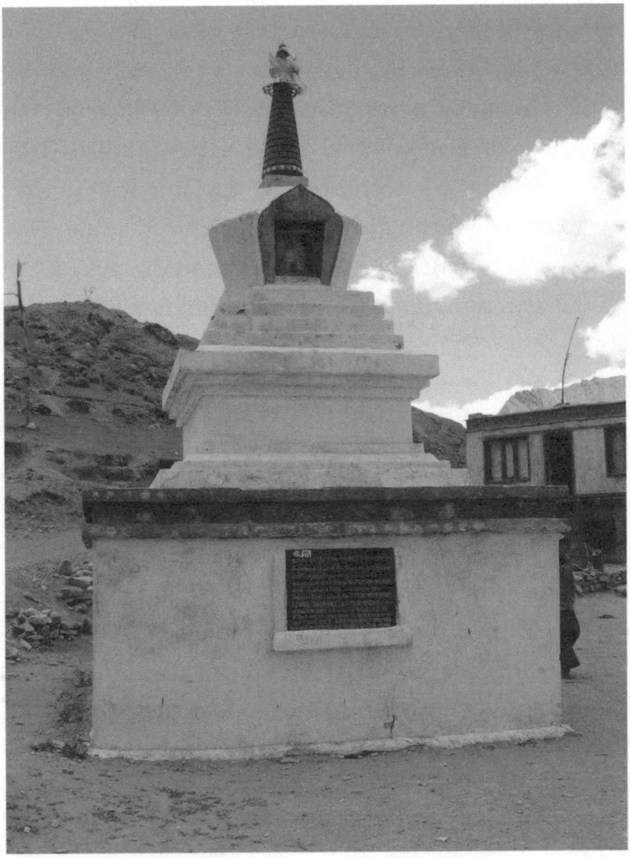

The *mchod-brten* commemorating the murdered monks at the entrance of Rangdum monastery.
Photograph by Ravina Aggarwal

violence and explores instead the socio-political conditions and manifestations of both violence and peace that intersected with this event.

FORMATIONS OF VIOLENCE

In this section, I examine how the Rangdum episode is inflected with histories and structures of violence that frame the political economy and inter-religious interactions in the region. Violence is not restricted to 'enemies' of the state and non-state actors. Instead, violence has been actively sanctioned by the state as a criterion that defines citizenship and belonging in minority ethnic and religious communities on the borders of post-colonial India.[5] According to Hansen and Stepputat, 'To become a normal sovereign state with normal citizens continues to be a powerful ideal, releasing considerable creative energy, and even more repressive force, precisely because its realization presupposed the disciplining and subordination of other forms of authority.'[6]

Furthermore, given the state's placement of violence in the body of the marginalized, discourses of suffering and terror have also become vital to the act of self-representation in Ladakh. For instance, the following words are inscribed on a plaque on a *mchod-brten* built at the entrance of Rangdum monastery:

> Foundation stone of this Stupa was laid, Museum and Rangdum Preparatory School were inaugurated on 11-7-2001 by Shri THUPSTAN CCHEWANG, Hon'ble Chairman, L.A.H.D.C. in memory of three innocent monks namely Rev Tsering Motup (Khanpo) 2. Zotpa Stanzin (Umzet) & 3. Tashi Konchog (Gyeskos) of RANGDUM GONPA who attained MARTYRDOM at the hands of cruel fundamentalist enemy agents on 11-7-2000. THESE SACRED MEMORIALS ARRANGED BY RANGDUM GONPA WELFARE SOCIETY, (ZANSKAR-KARGIL)

A *mchod-brten* (pronounced chor-ten) is a memorial shrine containing the relics of the deceased, usually a venerated member of the ecclesiastical order or a person of high status and affluence. In this case, the enshrined and violated body becomes the site through which patriotism and martyrdom, nation and religion are conflated and legitimated.[7] For citizens of the Ladakhi border who belong to racial and religious minorities, escape from a national stigma of treason and violence leads them to ascribing violence to those 'outlaws' who are believed to place the fundamentals of religion over the ideals of the secular nation.

What follows is an analysis of how the ideologies and material manifestations of violence, both episodic and structural, state and non-state, persist in shaping the life of Ladakhis.

CROSS-BORDER VIOLENCE

Violence in Ladakh is linked to its positioning as a highly strategic border zone that is frequently subjected to direct military action. Additionally, as Catherine Lutz argues, 'the capillaries of militarization fed and molded social institutions little connected to battle.[8] The assassination of the three monks at Rangdum took place barely a year after a ceasefire had been declared in what has been called a 'limited' war fought between India and Pakistan in 1999 in Kargil, one of the two districts of the Ladakh region. The Kargil war was the fourth war between India and Pakistan, three of which were fought over the Kashmir issue and all of which were partially fought on Ladakh's land. During the course of the war, the Indian army recaptured around 70 positions from approximately 800 *mujahideen* and Pakistani militia who had infiltrated the LOC into sectors of Kargil district along the Srinagar-Leh highway. Of the 1,000 officially estimated casualties, twenty-five Ladakhi soldiers and at least three civilians were killed. In addition to the loss of lives, Kargilis were displaced from their homes and had to take refuge in camps set up in villages away from the direct line of fire. These camps were plagued by overcrowding and unsanitary conditions.[9] As fields had to be abandoned, agricultural activity was adversely affected, leading to shortages in grain. There was a substantial cost to livestock that perished in starvation in the absence of people to tend for them. Deserted houses became targets for robbery and several families lost their possessions. The war disrupted the tourist economy which had already been affected by the violence in Kashmir and drastically slowed down progress on various developmental projects.

Besides the actual occurrence of war itself, Kargil continues to be constantly faced with warlike conditions, which are lightly labelled as 'routine shelling'. Such routinization of violence affected the social and economic functioning of the town and had damaging psychological consequences on Kargilis, as accounts by Kargili residents have attested.[10] As a result of wars and security considerations, there is a disproportionately large military presence in Ladakh. The militarization of the region intensified after the Sino-Indian war of 1961-62 when large numbers of troops were stationed in the border areas. Ladakhis could find employment largely in its paramilitary forces (such as the Ladakh Scouts, Indo-Tibetan Border Security Forces) and as porters and cooks. From the nineties onward, Ladakhis were increasingly involved in counter-insurgency operations in the Kashmir valley. Villagers residing along the Line of Control had to compulsorily serve as porters for transporting ammunition during the Kargil war. Following the war, diplomatic ties between India and Pakistan deteriorated, resulting in increased defence expenditures and combat-ready military positions along the border areas. The number of troops stationed in the region rose from 3,000 in the 3 Infantry Division to 20, 000 and as the paramilitary Ladakh Scouts was given regiment status, admission to the army was opened up to such an extent that in some cases, the entire working-age male population of a village left to join the army. An accompanying ideology of patriotism, distinguishing border subjects who defended state violence as a means of controlling 'outlaw terrorists,' became the dominant mode through which Ladakhis could assert citizenship and press claims for development funds. Thus, war and its related discourses of violence, surveillance and interrogation framed the territorial and political interaction between the state and its subjects in the wider border zone of Ladakh and in places located in Kargil district, such as Rangdum.

VIOLENCE WITHIN JAMMU AND KASHMIR

Cultural and political struggles in Ladakh: Among the primary suspects in the Rangdum killing was the Lashkar-e-Toiba ('army of the pure'), an extremist group that came into existence during the Soviet occupation of Afghanistan and then extended its mission to advocating statehood for Kashmir and the imposition of pan-Islamic law. This group was known for its highly publicized tactics of violent resistance against security forces and civilians through its suicide squads (*fidayeen*). Although Ladakh did not fall under the usual target area of groups such as the Lashkar-e-Toiba, nonetheless, Ladakhis have frequently pointed out that their inclusion in the State of Jammu and Kashmir has not spared them from violent occurrences in the Kashmir valley ever since Ladakh was invaded by the Dogras in the mid-19th century and annexed to the maharaja's princely state of Jammu and Kashmir.

The international boundary dispute between Pakistan and India over the status of Kashmir has had serious consequences internally on the relations between Ladakh's two major religious communities, resulting in over a decade of communal tensions that were further brought to light by the Rangdum episode. Of Ladakh's estimated population of 300,000 (about 3% of the population of the state), Kargil district is about 80% Muslim and about 18% Buddhist, whereas an overwhelming proportion of Leh, the other district of Ladakh, is Buddhist, with about 16% of Muslims. In Kargil, Buddhists are clustered around the Wakha-Mulbeg area and the sub-region of Zangskar; Rangdum lies mid-way between the village of Padum in Zangskar and the capital town of Kargil district, also called Kargil.

The assassination of the monks occurred a few days after protestors in Kargil had virtually closed down the town over a comment they perceived as blasphemous. The comment was made by Sonam Gombo, a leader of the Ladakh Buddhist Association (LBA) in Leh who had questioned the judgment skills of Muslim organizations, alleging that they refused to support the campaign for Union Territory status for Ladakh but were willing to put their faith in a holy text they erroneously thought had descended from the skies.

The subject of Union Territory status for Ladakh has a long and fluctuating history post-independence. The demand for regional autonomy from the state of Jammu and Kashmir had been articulated by Ladakhi leaders even prior to the ceasefire line with Pakistan, drawn after the United Nations declaration in 1949, and then reiterated in 1968 and 1972. In 1989, relations between Buddhists and Muslims reached an all time low when the separatist movement began in the Kashmir valley. A series of rallies were organized by the LBA to renew the demand for Union Territory and call for an end to Ladakh's placement in the State of Jammu and Kashmir. The LBA alleged that state-sanctioned conversions to Islam, corruption, embezzlement, unfair allocation of funds to the region, and disproportionate employment patterns in government offices had threatened the survival of the Buddhist community and of Ladakh's distinct cultural heritage.[11]

The Agitation, as the period from 1989-1992 came to be designated, was first directed against the Kashmiri government by the LBA but it was soon levied on sunni Muslims within Ladakh, who were criticized for being opportunistic agents of the state. The LBA argued that Buddhism's 'leniency, liberalism, and patience' had prevented its youth from adopting Kashmir's 'Pro-Pak culture of the gun', to which 'the indoctrinated' sunni youth were more susceptible.[12] They imposed a 'social boycott' (*me len chu len chad pyes*), preventing Buddhists from inter-dining, inter-marrying, and interacting with Muslims. Initially, shi'a communities were not targeted for boycott but the LBA's rhetoric of impending Islamic peril soon caused friction and when the shi'a leadership displayed its reluctance to join in the Union Territory movement, the Boycott eventually extended to them too. Cases of arson and rioting were common during this period. Scuffles broke out, bombs were hurled at automobiles and cargo trucks on the Leh-Srinagar highway, and government-owned properties were damaged.[13] The Kashmir Armed Police fired bullets to subdue unarmed demonstrators on 7 and 27 August but its action resulted in the death of four civilians, heightening the LBA's distrust of the state's authority.

Dissatisfaction against Ladakh's marginalization in India was verbalized by the LBA in religious terms, a move that was partially a response to the growing communal sentiment of Indian nationalism. Violence against minorities was increasing in other parts of India, spurred by the political dominance of Hindu nationalist groups that attempted to reformulate Indian identity on the basis of cultural purity and territorial nationalism. In Ladakh, Hindutva presence was gaining a foothold through cultural festivals such as the Sindhu Darshan, sponsored by the BJP government. The region had come to the notice of Hindu extremists more so after the Kargil war, and the

LBA was increasingly in conversation with the RSS and other right-wing groups.[15]

The LBA made use of the term, '*phyi-pa*' (outsiders) for Muslims so as to differentiate Islam from what it argued was 'indigenous' Buddhist culture. The image of endangered cultural purity was liberally used even as most of the measures taken by the LBA against the sunni Muslim community in fact revolved around their prominence in Ladakh's modern economy, which had registered a shift from subsistence agriculture to cash labour resulting in the fragmentation and reformulation of existing structures of control over economic resources. At this time, a younger generation of leaders educated in private schools and universities outside Ladakh replaced the religious clergy in positions of political authority. It may be assumed that a leadership with a modern education would have less interest in religious rivalry as compared to religious clerics, but in actuality the new leadership was less invested in mutual dependency between religions that held together the peasant economy in the countryside and looked more toward obtaining parity or higher economic standards in economic sectors such as tourism that had become more profitable in recent years. Additionally, following the Iranian revolution, an emphasis on canonical Islam and stricter prohibitions against dance, music, and alcohol consumption espoused by shi'a clerics in Kargil adversely affected the pluralistic social customs practised there.[15]

While upholding the social boycott for three years, the LBA simultaneously kept up its agitation for Union Territory status. It reached a compromise with the Indian government and accepted the provision for a Ladakh Autonomous Hill Development Council (LAHDC) in order to obtain greater control over developmental and social affairs. Even though the formation of the LAHDC did accommodate the political aspirations of local leaders who could now serve as councillors, it did not automatically solve problems related to religious and regional differences. As far as relations between Leh and Kargil were concerned, the LBA was bitter that Kargilis had not raised their voices for Scheduled Tribe Status but when it was granted in 1989, they had been equal beneficiaries along with the Buddhists of Leh. The LBA also accused the Kargili leadership of violating the rights of Buddhists to build a religious shrine in the marketplace for the convenience of those who were stationed in Kargil for work. Kargil had refrained from availing of the Hill Council even though the Council Act of 1995 made a provision for two such Councils. The LBA accused Kargili politicians of siding with Kashmir and acting in an obscurantist manner whenever there was a protest that involved speaking up against the Srinagar government. Kargilis, for their part, acted in a circumspect fashion in order to keep their options open because they saw Srinagar as an important link for communication and access to the world outside. Yet, especially after the Kargil war, officials from Kargil were quick to distance themselves from militancy in the Kashmir valley and to insist that they were loyal and peace-loving patriots who had resisted the pressures to engage in violent anti-India activities.

By the year 2000, the Councillors had begun to express their discontentment over the Council's ineffectiveness, which they linked to the misuse of power by the Jammu and Kashmir state government. As a report demanding regional autonomy for Jammu and Kashmir was forwarded to the centre by the state government, the LBA renewed its demand for Union Territory status for Ladakh and began organizing in earnest. The aggressive anti-Kashmir government language used by the LBA, as well as its lack of a clear strategy for political power sharing with minorities in Leh, did not win it the support of the Muslim groups at the time. This was the situation when the Rangdum incident occurred. Ripples from the violence at Rangdum were felt in various parts of Ladakh. In the town of Leh, capital of Ladakh region, the news of this assassination was accompanied by the imposition of strict curfew and Section 144, prohibiting the public gathering of more than four individuals at a time, to prevent communal clashes between Buddhists and Muslims. In Zangskar's Padum village, a breach of customary grazing rules escalated into a boycott-like situation as Buddhist and Muslim groups stopped attending each other's weddings.[16]

Despite its depiction as a unique and external incident, Rangdum occurred in a milieu of tension and inter-religious protest. Such violence was not inherent to the religious communities on the Ladakhi border but was instead located in their historical and contemporary struggles over political and cultural power.

Disputes over land: Religious difference was ranked significantly high as a motive for the murders by the Rangdum villagers but such allegations were concretely rooted in socio-economic conditions rather than merely in abstract definitions of cultural and religious identity. That monasteries are land-owning institutions is a key factor in understanding the social background of the Rangdum incident, a material aspect of organized Buddhist practice in Ladakh that is often neglected in depictions of the religion as essentially spiritual and other-worldly. The importance of Rangdum's materiality is attested in the commemorative literature produced after the year 2000 that stakes claim to the monastery's cultural and territorial heritage. The monastery's museum, inaugurated at the same time as the mchod-brten shrine for the dead monks, has on display these auspicious symbols—shells of two tortoise, two conch shells, and three small statues, two representing the Buddha and the third Milaraspa, the poet-saint revered by Buddhists—that are believed to have been discovered at the site when the monastery was founded by the 8th Ngari Rimpochey, Gelegs Tagspa, in 1785 on land granted by the Ladakhi king, Tshewang Namgyal. At the time of its establishment, three lay households were also settled in the area to assist the monastery. These houses continued to multiply and now there are two major villages, Yuldo and Tashi Thonggzes, that have grown on land belonging to the monastery. In return for permission to live on and use the land and its resources, the households are expected to pay a portion of their produce for the upkeep of the monastery.

Visitors to the monastery are handed a petition generated at the Rangdum Labrang in Leh for aid to the Rangdum Save Committee, according to which 'the entire un-inhabited area with all the content of pasture, water, woods, and herbs' stretching from Pentsela to Kanjila had been donated tax-free by the king to Ngari Rimpoche, abbot of the monastery. In considerably legalistic language, the petition goes on to defend the monastery's rights, dating from monarchic times until the present, to the property in the area:

> The said proclamation were again authenticated by the subsequent rulers of Ladakh including Tsetan Dorjer Namgyal and King Dorjay Tsepal Tondup Migyar Nambargynlva etc through their separate proclamation. After the Dogra rulers, the said proclamation was not withdrawn and the said area continues to be in the possession of the Rangdum Gonpa and the people till date.

Having used historical records to legitimize the monastery's claim over the land, the petition outlines the sequence of boundary violations perpetuated by the Gujjar Bakkarwals of the Doda district of Jammu, who are accused of encroaching upon the Rangdum vicinity since 1975 despite both direct orders to vacate after criminal and civil lawsuits filed by the monastery's management as well as negotiated agreements permitting them to graze their horses and flocks of sheep and goats only in a delimited space near the outer boundaries of Rangdum village on the other side of the river Suru. The Bakkarwals are blamed for conspiring with 'militant groups' in the murder of the monks so that they could terrorize local villagers into migrating away from their land and then usurp it for pasture. Also indicted is the state government of Jammu and Kashmir for failing to maintain secularism or implement the law in light of the power wielded by the influential and relatively affluent Bakkarwals.

Produced in Leh and intended for an audience of sympathizers and donors from outside Ladakh, the petition adopted some of the rhetoric of religious discrimination and militancy that was generated in Leh during the Agitation. Interviews with residents of the Rangdum villages confirmed some of the views expressed in the petition but did not explicitly connect the incident to religious bigotry. One middle-aged householder from Yuldo recalled that the dispute with the Bakkarwals for pasture had been ongoing since the second half of his father's life. Pasture is an invaluable resource for the extended village of Yuldo, comprising 24 households, which is economically dependent on animal husbandry. With temperatures too cold for agriculture, villagers in Rangdum exchange butter and other dairy products for grain with farmers in the Zangskar region and also from the villages of Panikhar and Parkachig in Kargil. Quarrels over pasture become more acute in Autumn, when the waters of the river subside, and it is possible for animals belonging to Bakkarwals to trespass over into Rangdum land. According to Praveen Swami, the increase in the number of sheep from approximately 5,000 to 35,000 that the Bakkarwals bring for grazing in the Rangdum area every summer also increased the pressure on pasture resources.[17]

Villagers pointed out to me that Bakkarwals had a history of violence and hostility in the region. They alleged that people in Rangdum were frequently attacked by Bakkarwal shotguns and that a few years ago the headman of Panikhar had been shot to death when the village had collectively protested against Bakkarwal encroachment. In another instance, two butchers and their two servants had gone to purchase sheep from their Bakkarwal trading partners but had never returned. I was told that Bakkarwals would often steal top quality horses and cattle and take them to Doda, and that once they had drowned almost twenty-five horses from Parkachig so that their own horses could have more access to pasture. In the opinion of those I interviewed, the murders of the monks were premeditated acts involving Bakkarwals rather than random militants because Bakkarwals were intimately aware of the details of everyday life in Rangdum, including such matters as preparations for the annual festival. They held the shootings responsible for frightening the fourth surviving monk into giving up his monastic robes and settling down to a married life in Leh, and for the reduced number of monks in Rangdum monastery that had dwindled from thirty to twenty-five because potential recruits to the ecclesiastical order were now too discouraged to stay on. Protecting against future occurrences of violence, Tibetan security commandoes, popularly known as 'Establishment 22,' were stationed at the monastery by the current Ngari Tshang, the incarnate abbot who holds ownership of the monastery and its lands and is the younger sibling of the current Dalai Lama.[18]

Instead of clearly revealing the guilt of anti-state agents or religious fundamentalists in perpetrating violence, the killings in Rangdum also exposed the failure of the state to provide protection to remote areas and implement justice for their residents. According to Praveen Swami, 'rather than address the issue with modern livestock management practices or the introduction of an ecologically sustainable land use regime, communal politicians have cashed in on the conflict.' In the winter of 2000, the predominantly shi'a Muslim villagers of Parkachig and the Buddhist villagers of Rangdum teamed together and convinced the army and police to tighten security to prevent Bakkarwals from returning to the region.[19] Rangdum villagers gave access to their grazing land to horses belonging to people from Parkachig, a measure that contradicts assumptions of alliance-building strictly on the basis of religious affinity.

The formations of violence implicated in the Rangdum episode demonstrate that violence can manifest itself in spectacular episodes mediated by large political bodies but it can also gain ground in intimate community experience, its origins can lie in politics and history as much as religious differences, and its agents can be state institutions as well as representatives who actively challenge the nation-state. Therefore, violence, as Nancy Schepher-Hughes and Philippe Bourgois suggest, has to also be understood in the context of peacetime activities and everyday politics so that the conditions that enhance the possibility of violence can be assessed more comprehensively.[20] As far as Ladakh is concerned, where the discourse around peace refers to more than a time marked by the cessation of hostility, studying the processes and practices of representing and producing peace become as critical as analysing violence.

FORMATIONS OF PEACE

Peace, as Richard Fox has argued, has been treated as a 'residual' category of violence in academic scholarship.[21] Most of the literature that deals with Kashmir too revolves around explanations for the origin of anti-state violence there. The explanations range from one-sided nationalist justifications of India's or Pakistan's claim over Kashmir to more nuanced estimates that locate violence in excessive central control and the resulting failure of the state to guarantee the effective functioning of the democratic process. Based on problems identified, numerous proposals have been laid out for the resolution of the Kashmir dispute. A majority of these proposals, however, centre on issues of territoriality and sovereign control.[22] In the Introduction to one of the first volumes to address the ground realities for understanding violence and peace in Kashmir, Urvashi Butalia asks, 'How will peace return to Kashmir?'[23] Narrowing the scope of that question to apply to Ladakh, I critically assess the potential of movements for peace across religious lines in a place which has commonalities with the Kashmir valley but also diverges from it in the sense that Ladakh has not been concertedly involved in a move to carve a separate nation-state from India. I contend that in order to be effective, peace-building efforts must be evaluated in accordance with their ability to accommodate specific contexts relevant to Ladakh's social and political universe.Such an approach can be useful for thinking toward a programme for peace that is sensitive in affecting institutional and ideological reform more broadly, but is also adaptable to the distinct histories and cultural particularities that distinguish Ladakh.

The State as an Agent of Peace: Although the success and sincerity of its actions remains open to debate, the Indian state has been involved in mediating initiatives for peace in the region, through direct diplomatic and trade-based relations with Pakistan and through developmental, political, and cultural policies internally. Rather than dismissing these policies on account of the continuation of violence in Jammu and Kashmir, it is important to uncover the potential opportunities and limitations they provide for resolving violence. In Ladakh, a year after the Rangdum killings and two years following the Kargil war, a vigorous mission to win the cooperation of Ladakhis with Operation Sadbhavna (Operation Goodwill) was launched by Lieutenant-General Arjun Ray, who assumed leadership of the 14th Corps in the Northern command of the Indian army, created specially for the Ladakh region.[24] This initiative, which took on a development/welfare shape, was advertised as an example of the commitment to peace championed by the state's military sector. Operation Sadbhavna aimed to transform the alienated relationship between Ladakhi civilians and the military into one of mutual trust by building schools, hospitals, vocational centres offering training in carpet weaving, knitting and sewing and even computer training. The plan encompassed 190 villages over an area of 1200 kilometres along the Line of Control with a total target population of 100,000 citizens. Self-described as a social healer and by others as a soldier-scholar, Arjun Ray explained the reasoning behind Sadbhavna, declaring 'coercive diplomacy' to be a losing battle which had been politically motivated and yielded no resolution.

Ladakhi leaders initially hailed Sadbhavna as a revolutionary and progressive initiative that would bridge the existing gap between the missions and objectives of the armed forces and the lifestyles and expectations of the civilians they were deployed to protect. A promotional video made on Operation Sadbhavna shows school children singing to the tune of *When You're Happy and You Know It*, students composing their names and poems about their village on computers, villagers, volunteers, and local leaders testifying to the benefits of its various schemes. In a state where the image of the army conjured torture, brutality, rape and hopelessness, Ray's vision of a military engaged in peace activities and humanitarian work seemed like a benign solution.

But even as it aimed to rectify problems that the civil government had neglected, Sadbhavna often ended up duplicating and undermining civil-state functions, a glaring reminder that under neo-liberal conditions the state had not receded but was increasingly surrendering its civil-developmental functions to militaristic ones. The programme's attempts to elicit participation from civil society organizations by using both development-saturated campaigns to attract corporate actors and grassroots-sensitive promotion techniques to generate community support were ultimately undercut by the military's own assignment of security and surveillance. Finally, Operation Sadbhavna claimed to benefit Buddhist and Muslim communities equally and without bias but it still constructed Ladakh's Muslim population as a potential threat and eventually failed to generate goodwill between Buddhists and Muslims.

What was learned from Operation Sadbhavna too was that decades of militarization and resistance in the valley, where members of one area and religion of the state were cast as patriots and others as militants, meant that for Ladakhis, any settlement of the Kashmir issue would require a regionally-sensitive plan. Due to the heavy dependency on the army in Ladakh, militarization had become both the symbol of violence and the condition of prosperity and economic security. Demilitarization, in that case, would have to be accompanied by taking such structural adjustments into account and finding alternative economic strategies in order to bring about an acceptable peace in the region.

Transnational Connections, Sustainability and Peace: Besides the Indian army's use of 'peace' as a condition that can preclude war in Ladakh, the term 'peace' is also invoked in transnational discourse but as an intrinsic and timeless characteristic of Ladakh's environment and culture, so much so that such discourses rarely allude to the various wars fought in the region or to the fairly visible degree of militarization.

At Rangdum, together with the monks who were murdered was another victim, a German tourist named Harfurth Wolf who was reported to be hitching a ride on the truck on which the militants had boarded. He was allegedly abducted after the militants killed the monks and a few weeks later his body was discovered shot to death. Wolf was among a growing body of travellers who were able to visit Ladakh after tourists were officially permitted to enter it in 1974. In recent years, tourism has become the largest of private enterprises in Ladakh. Besides travellers looking for adventure and spiritual peace in what is often advertised as a Shangrila, students from the West pour in to earn school credit or work experience from volunteering in one of the several non-governmental organizations that have mushroomed there. The emergence of neo-Buddhist interests on the global scene has been instrumental in harnessing aid and funds for grassroots organizations in Ladakh that stress sustainable development and cultural preservation but in such a manner that sustainability and environmental harmony are equated with the essence of Buddhism.

In contrast, a substantial portion of Ladakh's Muslim areas have been left out of the picture. For example, following the Kargil war, barring the distribution of food packages, blankets and firewood by Oxfam and Save the Children's Fund, there was very little participation by non-state agencies in either providing immediate relief measures or in assisting in refugee rehabilitation, sanitation, health, and social reconstruction of Kargil. The demonizing of Islam as a terrorist religion in the West has had severe implications for South Asia in general and Jammu and Kashmir in particular.[25] In Ladakh, the selective investment brought about by such ideological underpinnings has exacerbated rifts between Buddhists and Muslims and the classification of Buddhism as inherently peaceful has sidetracked the need for interventions that facilitate inter-religious exchange.

Symbolic displays and political coalitions: In addition to peace, for which the Ladakhi word *zhi-ba* is used to refer to a state of calmness and tranquillity, a recurring signifier is *gcig-gril* or 'unity'. Shortly after the Rangdum incident, the curfew imposed in the town of Leh by security forces was lifted when a procession of political leaders, community elders and religious heads of organizations such as the Gompa Association, LBA, LMA, Anjuman Moin-ul-Islam marched through the marketplace in a peace vigil, many attired in secular or religious Ladakhi garb. It was only after this gesture of unity that the tension between Buddhists and Muslims relaxed and the curfew was lifted. Marching through the streets of Ladakh is a public form of persuasion and information dispersal in a small society where personal access to politicians is important. Another instance of such a public demonstration across religious lines was a march to register a collective condemnation of the United States' invasion of Iraq in 2002. Of the leaders who marched together after Rangdum, several of the younger generation had at one time participated in the Agitation that aggravated the cleavage between religious groups in Ladakh.

The end of the Agitation in 1992 and the changing climate in Kashmir heralded the return of electoral politics in Ladakh. Elections were tense affairs and campaigns frequently made use of religiously inflammatory language, especially in the contest for the sole parliamentary seat for the Lok Sabha that is shared between Kargil and Leh. Although the unhealed fissures between the regions of Kargil and Leh and between Ladakh's diverse religions often made voting a communal process accompanied by threats and a few instances of physical violence, voting patterns revealed that electoral decisions were by no means made solely on account of religious alliances. In a sudden move during the Jammu and Kashmir State Assembly elections in 2002, political parties in Leh were dissolved and a new party, the Ladakh Union Territory Front (LUTF) formed, to renew the demand for Union Territory status and to put regional interests at the forefront. Leh's Muslim groups joined LUTF and in return, an executive post in the cabinet of the LAHDC was given to the Muslim councillor.

Coalition parties have often been criticized as weakening the democratic process and making it unstable, yet as political scientists such as Pranab Bardhan have argued, they can function to curb excesses and serve as important catalysts for negotiation.[26] In the Lok Sabha election during 2004, Thupstan Tshewang, the candidate fielded by LUTF, was victorious with the help of a faction in Kargil, which agreed to refrain from supporting the National Conference candidate who was a very strong competitor rather than become a part of LUTF. Thupstan Tshewang's victory also met with some destruction of property and protests in Kargil. With the Congress coming in to power at the centre in 2004, the LUTF was ridden by serious rifts from within the Buddhist leadership itself. In defiance of the spirit of LUTF, Tsering Samphel, President of the LBA and a Congress veteran, re-established the Congress party in Leh.

Although not free from contradictions and disagreements, symbolic gestures of unity such as the vigil after Rangdum as well as strategies for forming political alliances to arrive at a regional rather than religious platform, reflect the need for inter-religious cooperation in Ladakh to avoid disrupting the tourist economy and achieving long-term political goals, respectively.

Civil society initiatives for unity: On 5 July 2000, six days before the Rangdum incident, an unusual conference called Youthnet 2000 was coordinated by a non-profit organization called Rural Development and You and various other youth associations in the Conference Hall in Leh. It was unusual because it was the first forum I had seen that specifically and consciously addressed the problems of identity and difference among Ladakhi youth. Among the participants were youth groups from both rural and urban areas in Leh, and from organizations concerned with youth welfare from different regions and religions of Leh and Kargil districts. The invited participants also included Thusptan Tshewang, then the Chief Executive Councillor of the LAHDC, and Maulvi Omar, who was on the board of the Islamiya School in Leh. The morning session was organized as a series of talks by various political, administrative, and education representatives. Speaking in languages that ranged from Ladakhi, Urdu, English, to Hindi, participants expressed their hopes for unity and social justice in Ladakh. In his opening address, Stanzin Dawa, President of Rural Development and You, said, 'Youthnet was convened to promote networking, integration, and unity among various organizations working on youth issues so that we may face the challenges, problems and opportunities of the 21st century. Unfortunately, we are divided and isolated in our own associations and societies. There is a lot of discord and fragmentation in society. Our objective is to arrive at a common vision and common platform across boundaries of religion, political groups and region. We must work together to enhance Ladakh's culture and name in the future. The seeds we sow in the fields will determine the harvests we reap. We hope to sow the seeds of unity today so that youth may work collectively for the culture and development of Ladakh.'

Most of the speakers left after lunch and the workshop that followed was attended primarily by youth groups brainstorming together to outline a course of action for overcoming social problems. It was recognized that the experience of Ladakhi youth was different from their parents' generation, having grown up in a social milieu of changing ties of kinship and neighbourliness where prescriptive behaviours generated by the Agitation were still extant and there were severe prohibitions on inter-religious intermarriage. Migration to towns, education and a reduced dependency on agriculture had created new religious and economic affiliations that were not adequately represented by the current political and social patterns of power distribution.

Proposals for ending religious fragmentation between the youth that were forwarded during the conference can be grouped into two models:

1. Shared economic goals: Finding a common platform, such as youth unemployment, for which religious differences could be

put aside. Besides cooperative efforts around economic and political issues at the village and town levels, this category also included efforts at promoting sports and other forms of entertainment and education that did not specifically pertain to religion.

2. Religious Interdependence: Highlighting and celebrating religious syncretism and emphasizing friendship and historical convergences in identity rather than differences in religion. After the Agitation ended in 1992, attending festivals and ritual celebrations of other religious groups had resumed in Ladakh, but even though this was seen as an important step, people I interviewed attested that it felt more like a symbolic gesture rather than a return to communal harmony.[27] Without arriving at a solution on how to cultivate a forum for completely bridging the religious divide that had set in, the youth at this conference nonetheless acknowledged publicly for the first time that the Agitation had not necessarily led to social justice and increased opportunities for them.

At the end of the conference, participants decided to make the event an annual affair and hold the next Youthnet session in Kargil. But with the Rangdum incident that transpired less than a week later, the momentum was largely lost and has not been recovered yet.

Five years after Rangdum, the shadow of violence that expelled itself on the bodies of three monks is mostly perceived to be the doing of outsider militants by Ladakhis, a strategy that has worked to foster a partial truce across diverse religions within Ladakh. But violence, as this article has consistently argued, has to be situated at the intersection between the international and episodic and the immediate and everyday. Relegating it solely to essentialized religious differences or to external and undemocratic outbursts masks the routinized practices of repression that also subject Ladakhis. Refusing to locate violence within Ladakhi history and society diverts attention away from the difficult and painful process of analysis, reconciliation and unification that had begun to materialize just before Rangdum.

Notes

I am grateful to Haley Duschinski for inviting me to participate on a panel on peace-building in Kashmir at the Kroc Institute at Notre Dame University, where an earlier draft of this paper was presented. In her role as discussant, Urvashi Butalia offered valuable comments to the panelists. For helping me with gathering information in Rangdum, I am grateful to Sonam Phuntsog, Raza Abbasi and various monks and villagers for their hospitality and responses to my questions. I thank Srirupa Roy and Amrita Basu for their editorial suggestions.

1 There are some differences in the series of events reported. While Praveen Swami ('Murder in Leh.,' *Frontline* 2004, 17 (15), July 22-August 04) reports that the monks were awakened from their sleep and ran towards the truck thinking that a traveller was in distress or the truck had lost its way, people I interviewed focused on the monks' presumption that ritual materials had arrived from Zangskar, a version of the events also corroborated in an interview by Onkar Singh ('We are Scared More Lamas may be Killed,' *rediff.com*. http://203.199.83.75/news/2000/jul/18leh.htm, 2000).

2 http://164.100.24.167/rsdebate/synopsis/190/sy22082000.html

3 Onkar Singh ('We are Scared More Lamas may be Killed'.

4 Allen Feldman, *Formations of Violence: The Narratives of the Body and Political Terror in Northern Ireland* (Chicago: University of Chicago Press, 1991), 4.

5 See also Veena Das and Deborah Poole, 'State and its Margins: Comparative Ethnographies,' in Veena Das and Deborah Poole (eds.), *Anthropology in the Margins of the State* (Delhi: Oxford University Press, 2004), 3-33.

6 Thomas Blom Hansen and Finn Stepputat, 'Introduction', in Thomas Blom Hansen and Finn Stepputat (eds.), *Sovereign Bodies: Citizens, Migrants and States in the Postcolonial World* (Princeton: Princeton University Press, 2005), 3.

7 See Allen Feldman, *Formations of Violence,* for a good discussion of the body as a site of state control and resistance.

8 Catherine Lutz, 'Making War at Home in the United States: Militarization and the Current Crisis,' *American Anthropologist* 104: 3 (2002), 724.

9 See Pamela Bhagat, 'Reclaiming Lives: The Health of Women in Kargil District,' in Urvashi Butalia (ed.), *Speaking Peace: Women's Voices from Kashmir* (New Delhi: Kali for Women, 2002), 96-112.

10 Lecture presentations by Kaneez Fatima and Raza Abbasi at the conferences of the International Association for Ladakh Studies held at Oxford, England in 2001 and Leh in 2003 respectively.

11 See Martijn van Beek and Kristoffer Bertelsen, 'No Present Without Past: The 1989 Agitation in Ladakh,' in Thierry Dodin and Heinz Rather (eds.), *Recent Research on Ladakh* 7 (Bonn: Ulmer Kulturanthropologische Schriften, 1997), 43-65; and Ravina Aggarwal, *Beyond Lines of Control: Performance and Politics on the Disputed Borders of Ladakh, India* (Durham: Duke University Press, 2004) for greater details on these events.

12 Ladakh People's Movement for Union Territory Status, *A Brief Information Booklet* (Leh: Publicity Division, LPMUT, 1989).

13 Aggarwal, *Beyond Lines of Control.*

14 Martijn van Beek ("Dangerous Liaisons: Hindu Nationalism and Buddhist Radicalism in Ladakh." In *Religious Radicalism and Security in South Asia*. S. Limaye, M. Malik, and R. Wirsing, eds. Honolulu: Asia-Pacific Center for Security Studies, 2004, pp. 193-218).

15 Nicky Grist, *Local Politics in the Kargil District of North India*. Ph. D. Dissertation, Goldsmiths College, London, 1996.

16 Kim Gutschow, *Being a Buddhist Nun: The Struggle for Enlightenment in the Himalayas* (Cambridge: Harvard University Press, 2004), 33.

17 Praveen Swami, 'Kargil Realities', *Frontline* 2001, 18: 16, 4-17 August.

18 A brief and rather laudatory history of 'Establishment 22' can be found on http://www.chushigangdruk.org/history/history11.html.

19 While revelling in the banishment of Bakkarwals from Rangdum, a Rangdum resident who I interviewed also told me of a similar situation in Padar in Jammu, where Bakkarwals had been prohibited from grazing by the local Hindu landholders, but he also noted that their absence had led the Padar villagers to rue the loss of fertilizer they had previously been able to obtain from the manure of Bakkarwal animals. Such admissions point to a more complicated nexus of transactions and recognition of interdependency rather than exclusion between various religious communities in Jammu and Kashmir.

20 Nancy Schepher-Hughes and Philippe Bourgois, 'Introduction: Making Sense of Violence,' in Nancy Schepher-Hughes and Philippe Bourgois (eds.), *Violence in War and Peace* (Blackwell Publishing, 2004), 1-31.

21 Richard Fox, 'Cultural Dis-Integration and the Invention of the New Peace Fares,' in Jane Schneider and Rayna Rapp (eds.),

Articulating Hidden Histories: Exploring the Influence of Eric Wolf (Berkeley: University of California Press, 1995), 275.

22 For a fairly complex and multi-tiered set of propositions for bringing about inter-regional and international peace in Jammu and Kashmir, see Sumantra Bose, *Kashmir: Roots of Conflict, Paths to Peace* (New Delhi: Vistaar Publications, 2003).

23 Urvashi Butalia (ed.), *Speaking Peace: Women's Voices from Kashmir* (New Delhi: Kali for Women, 2002), xxi.

24 Further details on the possibilities and limitations of Operation Sadbhavna can be found in Ravina Aggarwal and Mona Bhan, 'Disarming Violence: Democracy, Development, and Security on the Borders of India' (n.d.).

25 See Sumantra Bose, *The Challenge in Kashmir: Democracy, Self-determination and a Just Peace* (New Delhi: Sage Publications, 1997) and Robert Wirsing, 'Introduction: Religion, Radicalism and Security in South Asia,' in S. Limaye, M. Malik, and R. Wirsing (eds.), *Religious Radicalism and Security in South Asia* (Honolulu: Asia-Pacific Center for Security Studies, 2004), 1-14.

26 Pranab Bardhan, *The Political Economy of Development in India* (New Delhi: Oxford University Press, 1998).

27 Aggarwal, *Beyond Lines of Control*.

Media, Terror and Islam
The Shifting Media Landscape and Culture Talk in India

PAULA CHAKRAVARTTY AND SRINIVAS LANKALA

The strategic role of the media in waging and representing extreme violence was 'globalized' with the First Gulf War in 1991.[1] Patrons of India's finest five-star hotels were, for the first time, able to watch the 'video-game' real-time bombings of Baghdad, beamed courtesy an unregulated CNN, setting the stage for the rapid proliferation of cable television across most of urban and much of rural India by the turn of the new century. Today, there are some 30 million cable television subscribers in India, among the estimated 80 million households with access to television. Adding to this dramatic expansion in television access, India witnessed an equally significant boom in the print media, with the daily circulation of the vernacular press increasing by some 500% between the 1980s and end of the 1990s.[2] In this hypermediated environment, it becomes necessary to trace the shift in discourses that rationalize as well as to challenge the legitimacy of terrorism versus state-sanctioned violence.

Most obviously, many in the Indian media drew instant links between the 11 September attacks on the World Trade Center (WTC) and the terrorist violence that 'India had endured for too long'. This discourse was heightened with the 13 December 2001 terrorist attack on the Parliament building, which took place literally in front of live television camera crews. As *Times of India* political editor, Manoj Joshi explains:

> Though there was a huge disparity in the casualties, the attack

> on the Parliament, the primary symbol of the Indian state, was seen by Indians as a grave provocation. In the Indian mind, there is a continuum of sorts in the two events, especially since they were separated by just three months.[3]

In what follows we contrast the symmetry of media coverage of these two events with what has been assessed as the national Indian print media's heroic response to the massacres of Muslim citizens by a Hindu nationalist administration in Gujarat in 2002. The central question that we pose in our essay is: what accounts for the divergence in coverage of these events?

We draw from Mahmood Mamdani's argument about a new variation of Orientalist 'culture talk', equating political beliefs with Islamic cultural essence originating in the US in the post-Cold War period, to see how this might be rearticulated through the Indian media's coverage of 'terror' and 'Islam' in the shadow of the events of 11 September. Mamdani has argued that the Bush administration's conflation of Islam with terrorism singles out 'bad Muslims' as those responsible for terrorism, while acknowledging 'good Muslims' who are 'anxious to clear their names and consciences of this horrible crime and would undoubtedly support "us" in a war against "them."'[4]

In making sense of how this peculiar US or at least Western formulation becomes part of Indian media discourse, it is important to firstly acknowledge that the conflation of 'terrorism' with Islam is not novel in the modern historical context of India. For instance, scholars have examined how Doordarshan, the state-owned national television network monopoly, played a pivotal role in normalizing Hindutva political discourse in the 1980s and 1990s.[5] Journalists and scholars have also examined the new importance of the media during periods of crisis; for instance the role of the print media in the aftermath of the destruction of the Babri Masjid and the subsequent violence in Bombay in 1993, or the role of the electronic media in 'the first TV war fought by the Indian armed forces' in Kargil in 1999.[6]

We analyse the discourse on terrorism by focusing on the English-language national print media—newspapers and magazines—because of their role as representatives of liberal modernity against the encroachment of communalism in the public sphere. The relative autonomy of the print press from institutions of state power and commercial pressures has historically distinguished the national press from other media outlets. Most of today's national newspapers were founded by British entrepreneurs for a largely British-Indian readership, while some newspapers, notably the *Hindu,* the *Indian Express* and the *Hindustan Times* began as responses to the colonial press by the English-speaking liberal Indian nationalist elite. Large business houses with corresponding web-based publications today, own all the major English language newspapers and magazines, and direct and indirect linkages to the expanding field of privately owned national news channels.[7] These media outlets reach a small but influential sliver of the nation's vast media-literate public. Whether in print or electronic form, we extend Arvind Rajagopal's claim that the cultural dominance of this genre of national journalism is reflected in the perceived neutrality of the English language and its identification with a pan-Indian elite in contrast to the limited reach and representational claims of a regional language. This identification of the English language press with the Indian nation rather than with a language-community allows it a claim on the Nehruvian discourses of modernity and secularism.[8] Thus while a few national publications articulate right-wing views, the majority of English-language national newspapers and magazines tend to be harshly critical of the BJP and its affiliates, while stopping short of any harsh scrutiny of Indian military action in Kashmir and elsewhere, or the state's suppression of civil liberties.

Our analysis begins by locating the similarities and differences between the US and Indian variants of majoritarian nationalism in relation to Islam. We then look at Indian national media coverage of the 11 September attacks as a starting point to examine this trajectory, punctuated by two major incidents in whose coverage the articulation of Hindutva and American discourses is most apparent: the attack on the Indian Parliament in December 2001 and the massacre of Muslims in Gujarat in March 2002.

FRIENDS AND ENEMIES IN THE 'WAR ON TERROR'

The origins of 'terrorist' in Indian media discourse have had a long and changing history, not exclusively associated with Islam, but always cast as the Other of the moderate mainstream. The colonial media identified socialist and anarchist nationalists who used violent means as 'terrorists', in contrast to the more acceptable mainstream represented by Gandhi's Congress. After independence, the words 'terrorist' or 'militant' were primarily used to refer to Sikh separatists in Indian Punjab—the words still retaining the sense of a violent agent provocateur engaged in destabilizing the status quo, now represented by the post-colonial nation-state. The identification of Muslims with terrorists emerged only in the context of the conflict in Kashmir. The current violent phase of the conflict, which began in the early 1990s, coincided both with the crisis in foreign exchange reserves and the 'opening up' of the Indian economy and with the rise of a fundamentalist Hindu nationalist political movement around the Babri Masjid issue. While the Kashmiri separatists were originally understood as 'militants' fighting the Indian state, the changing relationship in the 1990s between India, the Palestinian struggle and the post-colonial Arab world in general also saw the gradual identification of the Kashmiri 'militant' with the global 'Islamic terrorist'.

While rooted in 19th-century Orientalizing discourses and their construction of a 'Hindu' religious and philosophical corpus—and also in early 20th-century fascism—the current phase of Hindu nationalism begins with the rise to political power of the BJP. The BJP is itself an affiliate of the RSS which also has several other 'daughter' organizations such as the Vishwa Hindu Parishad (VHP, or the World Hindu Council), the Bajrang Dal and the Shiv Sena, among many others. The RSS, founded in 1922, operates through this elaborate network of affiliates as well as through its own local branches called shakhas.[9] The idea of Muslim terrorists enacting violence against the putative Hindu nation-state was a necessary construct for the emergence of the BJP's discourses around the need to protect the nation from Muslim enemies. This militaristic discourse also shaped the violent campaign against Indian Muslims and other religious minorities as the 'enemy within'.

The Muslim as terrorist has also had a strong and varied existence in the American popular imagination owing to a diverse range of xenophobic influences, most notably that of Hollywood. While the genealogy of the 'Arab' in Hollywood films has been discussed in depth elsewhere,[10] the current conflation of Arab, Muslim and terrorist also owes a great deal to the mediated construction of the 1979 Iranian revolution and the ensuing hostage crisis on the one hand and the 1987 Palestinian uprising on the other, along with the many instances of Arab support to the Palestine Liberation Organization (PLO) and Arab stands against the state of Israel and the US. The efforts of Anti-Arab organizations such as the Anti-Defamation League to intimidate Arabs and Muslims in the United States, coupled with the extensive influence of such organizations on the top levels of the US administration has also been instrumental in generating official sanction for this construction of the Arab as 'Islamic' terrorist. As Susan Akram and Kevin Johnson argue, 'Since at least the 1970s, US laws and policies have been founded on the assumption that Arab and Muslim noncitizens are potential terrorists and have targeted this group for special treatment under the law. The post-September 11 targeting of Muslims and Arabs is simply the latest chapter in this history.'[11]

Mamdani traces the origins of the modern discourse of religious fundamentalism to the 1920s American protestant political movements, which after a long spell in the wilderness returned to take over the US state beginning with the Carter presidency and culminating in the current administration of George W. Bush.[12] The attacks on the World Trade Center (WTC) in New York and on the Pentagon in September 2001, led to the creation of a quasi-religious nationalist fervour, the categorization of 'terror' as the enemy in the shape of Arab Muslims, and calls for an unending war against such enemies couched in the apocalyptic language of millennial Christianity. These were the immediate precursors to the US bombing of Afghanistan and its subsequent invasion of Iraq.

The articulation of the discourses around this American patriotism with the Hindu nationalism of the BJP and its ideological affiliates is most evident in the Indian media's characterization of terrorism filtered through both frameworks. Once American sources began to assert that attacks on the WTC and the Pentagon could be linked to Islamic groups with bases in Afghanistan, much of the Indian English-language media rushed to frame the devastating tragedy in terms of the ongoing domestic campaigns against 'terrorists' in India. On 12 September, alongside pictures of the airplanes exploding into the twin towers with lead stories documenting the attacks, national English-language dailies such as the *Indian Express* featured cover stories with headlines such as 'Terror Strikes India; Airfields on Alert, Vigil Up on Border.'[13] Similar to the right-wing Israeli government, the BJP administration moved quickly in its attempt to equate terrorism in America with 'Islamic' terrorism. Within twenty-four hours of the WTC attacks, Prime Minister Atal Bihari Vajpayee gave a televized address to the nation asserting India's support of any US military action. He asked Indians 'to be part of this global war on terrorism . . . Terrorism respects no logic, as India which has had to pay a horrific price for it knows only too well.'[14]

While the articulation of these distinct discourses of nationalism might appear forced, it depends on two shared assumptions: the construction and demonization of a violent and medievalist Islam on the one hand, and the modernist discourses of nationalism and patriotism on the other. These parallels can be drawn not in terms of the religious beliefs of the victims, but in terms of the common discourses of 'Islamic terrorism' that run through them. Overall, the Indian government and its Hindu fundamentalist supporters have tried to frame the American crisis as an opportunity to target a common enemy of civilization, and most television coverage reinforced the government's position, along with the more conservative newspapers. Experts and journalists flooded the print and electronic media, speculating about the connection between the terrorists who had attacked the US and the so-called 'freedom fighters' or jehadis responsible for attacks in Kashmir and other Indian cities and the hijacking of flight IC-814 on 31 December 1999. A telling newspaper headline reads 'Mumbai to New York, the Road Passed through Kandahar.'[15]

India's diverse national print media, however, were far from monolithic in their support of this belligerent vision. Most papers provided a context for the attacks, drawing on the paradoxical history of the US and its political and military support of the most conservative forces in Afghanistan, Pakistan, and Saudi Arabia. Moreover, writers drew parallels between the rise of conservative fundamentalist regimes throughout Asia and the Middle East, including the rise of the BJP in India.[16] A series of articles and editorials from the *Times of India*, the *Hindu*, the *Indian Express*, *Frontline* magazine, *Outlook* magazine, and others vehemently criticized the government's strategic 'war-mongering' against Islamic 'terrorists' and condemned the administration's escalation of an already volatile situation. These articles pressed Indian television programmes to represent views from moderate and liberal Indian Muslims and warned of the dangers of allowing the debate to shift between two poles of religious fundamentalism.

Although clearly a much broader debate existed in Indian media culture over the relationship between terror and Islam than did in the United States,[17] there is no doubt that the dominant discourse reproduced the American narrative of a war against 'civilization' reformulated through a Hindu fundamentalist framework. Apart from offers of solidarity and help, a significant refrain from that first week of reporting is the constant drawing of parallels between the events in New York and Washington and the conflicts in Kashmir and terrorist incidents in Mumbai and other cities. The primary response of the English language press was to equate the 9/11 attacks with the militant separatist movement in Kashmir. This equation consisted primarily of drawing ideological parallels between Al Qaeda's alleged role in the 9/11 incidents and Pakistan's 'sponsorship' of militant groups in Kashmir. The mediated spectacle of the attacks and the immediacy of the tragedy meant that no parallel or comparison could be drawn in terms of the acts themselves. The equations that were made therefore had to be those of ideology and political classification. The ideology was already at hand in the form of 'Islamic' fundamentalism, and the political classification of 'terrorism' was also in currency as a name to identify Kashmiri separatists. George W. Bush's much quoted 'either . . . with us or with the terrorists' speech also made the elision in India much easier.

The US responded to the events of 11 September by closely allying itself with Pakistan, and the Indian government's initial outpouring of support was replaced with accusations of betrayal. Not only was the US betraying its 'natural' non-Islamic ally in the 'war against civilization', it was also supporting a military dictatorship over a market-friendly democracy that had offered airspace, intelligence, and even military support. The US decision to lift sanctions against Pakistan in exchange for General Pervez Musharraf's cooperation in the war against the Taliban was assessed by *India Today* as an instance where 'America can't see its true friend in the fog of war.'[18]

The Indian government's precarious relationship with Washington gave the Indian media much more room to uniformly criticize US foreign policy. On this issue we see an aggressive critique of American 'bullying' from both the left and, perhaps more interestingly, the Hindu Right. This critique of US foreign policy became resonant once again when 38 people were killed by a car bomb in Srinagar, the capital of Jammu and Kashmir province, on 1 October of that year. The Indian government demanded that the US include the organization allegedly responsible for the bomb—a group linked by the Indian administration to Pakistan—on the official 'list' of terrorist organizations. Prime Minister Vajpayee issued a statement to President Bush 'telling him there was a limit to India's patience'.[19] Following the US' own course of action in combating terror, Indian news programmes and magazines provocatively asked 'Should India Attack?'[20] The point of contention for the Indian right was America's flawed response to terrorism defined by its own 'narrow self-interest' and 'double standards'. They argued that the international community's disinterest in terrorism in India—be it the Liberation Tigers of Tamil Eelam (LTTE) in Sri Lanka, Sikhs fighting for Khalistan, the ongoing violent insurrections in the Northeast and Bihar, or most significantly the violence in Kashmir—translated to the sanction of military attack only when the West, specifically the United States, was the target of violence.[21]

13 DECEMBER: TERROR AND TRIAL BY MEDIA

Differences in the national media coverage over the correlation between Islam and terror seemed to disappear following the attacks of 13 December and the subsequent legal drama to find those responsible. On 13 December 2001, a group of militants drove into the heavily guarded Indian Parliament complex with the alleged intention of blowing up the building and killing the assembled members. The resulting shootout, which took place in front of live television cameras, left all the militants and six security personnel dead. This incident was instantly compared to the 9/11 attacks, in intent and ideological context, if not in political magnitude or effect. A high-profile target (the 'symbol of Indian nationhood' was the phrase in several newspapers and in the Union cabinet's resolution on the attack),[22] a group of 'fidayeen' or suicide bombers and the intent of crashing an explosive-laden vehicle into a crowded building were common elements in both instances. The looming context of Islam as a terrorist ideology was also the unsaid common thread that ran through both events.

Most newspapers were quick to draw the parallel, and point to the restraint shown by the Indian state in not engaging in a full-scale military conflict with those who 'harboured' the terrorists (i. e. Pakistan) as the American state had threatened to do. *The Hindu* noted in its report: 'There has been a marked note of restraint in the government's reaction, for now. Its response was conditioned by the fact that so far it has not been possible to identify any group responsible for the daring attack',[23] although its editorial page echoed the government's view of the incident: 'The cataclysmic potential of an attack such as this is mind-boggling and it is only for this reason that the shock and the tragedy of the incident have been accompanied by an undercurrent of relief. At the same time, the act of brutality committed within the walls of the Parliament complex is an ugly reminder of the extreme vulnerability of India—even its most secure and fortified places—to the menace of terrorism, particularly to suicide attacks.'[24]

The *Outlook* cover story that week drew the inevitable comparison: 'It may not have been quite on the scale of 9/11, but the family resemblance was there for all to see. The targeting of a central symbol of a nation, the willingness on the part of the assailants to sacrifice their lives to attain their objectives, the careful planning that must have preceded the event, the political climate that makes possible such extreme acts—the analogies to the attack on WTC and Pentagon in December 13's assault on Parliament are plenty. What is up for debate now is the ways of reacting to the event: the question of a military option.'[25] The Indian Cabinet's hawkish resolution, adopted the same day and quoted in all the reports, uses language strikingly similar to that of the Bush administration after 11 September: 'We will liquidate the terrorists and their sponsors, wherever they are, whoever they are.'[26]

Another striking parallel was in the state's response to civil liberties and the rule of law. The Indian state saw the 13 December incident primarily as a window of opportunity to pass a more 'draconian' Prevention of Terrorism Ordinance (POTO) similar in content, context and intent to the American state's USA-PATRIOT Act. Indeed some of the features of the two laws were almost identical, especially in terms of their provisions for indefinite detention without charges, the admissibility of unauthorized telephone tapping as legal evidence and the increased scope for unauthorized surveillance of individual citizens. Strong opposition to POTO from the parliamentary left (the CPI and CPI-M, which opposed the ordinance's specific targeting of Muslims) and from the Congress party (which felt that the existing anti-terrorism law, TADA, was adequate) had ensured the failure of the ordinance to pass in an earlier session of parliament, but that opposition was muted in the aftermath of the Parliament attack.[27]

December 13 also saw the emergence of a common nationalist viewpoint against the terrorist attack irrespective of party or ideology; although the opposition still criticized the government's 'handling' of the crisis and the security lapses in the Parliament complex. All the parties in the parliamentary opposition, from the Congress to the two main communist parties, viewed the incident in terms of a security failure, criticizing the government for not having done enough by way of protecting the Parliament building. They also echoed the government's rhetoric about the attack on India's 'nationhood' and 'democracy'. While they might have differing viewpoints on the issue of attacking Pakistan, as *Outlook* noted, '(e)verybody—both the ruling alliance and the Opposition parties—are unanimous in their tough-talking against those responsible for the dastardly attack on India's Parliament.'[28] It also quoted senior CPI-M member Somnath Chatterjee's response: 'What we need is a more alert government with a better administrative will . . . (h)ad adequate precautions been taken, this incident wouldn't have occurred.'[29]

For our purpose, the most significant outcome was the almost immediate arrest and prosecution of the alleged perpetrators. In a case that also served to demonstrate the influence of Hindutva on even the highest levels of the Indian judiciary, Syed Abdur Rahman Geelani, a Kashmiri Muslim lecturer in the University of Delhi, and three other 'accomplices', were arrested and charged with treason and conspiracy scarcely two days after the incident. The Delhi police on the basis of an intercepted two-minute telephone conversation arrested Geelani with his stepbrother in Srinagar. The other three 'accomplices' were Mohammed Afzal the alleged coordinator of a Kashmiri separatist organization called the Jaish-e-Mohammed and Shaukat Husain Guru, a fruit merchant (who were both arrested in Srinagar), and Shaukat Husain's wife Afsan Guru, arrested from her apartment in Delhi.

The English-language media's response to this instantaneous resolution of what appeared to be a complex conspiracy was, with few exceptions, celebratory and full of praise for the investigating agencies. The Jaish-e-Mohammed's links to the Pakistani intelligence agency and the Kashmiri ethnicity of the accused seemed to provide irrefutable proof of their guilt. The fact that Afzal, a former militant with the separatist Jammu and Kashmir Liberation Front had subsequently *surrendered* to Indian security forces in 1993 was never mentioned, nor were the actual contents of the incriminating telephone conversation, which apart from Afzal's 'confession', was the only material evidence in the case. The case against Geelani wove its way through a Special Court, where he was pronounced guilty by a visibly hostile judge and sentenced to death, to the Delhi High Court where he was eventually acquitted.[30]

On 20 December 2001, five days after Geelani's arrest, the Delhi police arranged a press conference, which turned out to be a trial-by-media with Afzal admitting to his guilt and complicity with the five slain 'terrorists' who stormed the parliament building, and also exonerating Geelani of any involvement. At this the officer in charge, Additional Commissioner Rajbir Singh, ordered Afzal to stop and asked the assembled journalists not to mention Afzals' assertion of Geelani's innocence. Astonishingly, all the journalists complied. This incident came to light when Geelani's case was appealed in the Delhi High Court. Geelani's counsel called two of the journalists—from television news channel *Aaj Tak*, and the *Times of India*—as witnesses to testify to Afzal's statement and subsequent censorship by the police. This stage of the trial also heard an independent translation of the intercepted cell phone conversation, which contradicted the police translation of the same conversation almost entirely, and was found to have nothing to do with the 13 December attack. Moreover, since the POTO law was applied to Geelani only five days *after* his arrest, the interception of the conversation was ruled illegal and therefore inadmissible as evidence.

The allegedly incriminating phone conversation had been the only material evidence produced against Geelani, and without it the case against him could not be sustained. The analysis in the media however focused on the *inadmissibility* of the evidence rather than on the fact that it was a fabrication to begin with; implying that Geelani had been acquitted on a technicality. The trial against Geelani also directed public and media attention away from the actual attack on the parliament building. All five 'terrorists' had been shot dead. They were immediately assumed to be Pakistani nationals despite the lack of any substantial evidence. The 'mastermind' behind the attack was believed to be a shadowy Pakistani 'terrorist' called Ghazi Baba, later claimed to have been killed in an 'encounter' with Indian security forces in Kashmir.[31]

Immediately after his acquittal, the Delhi Police appealed to the Supreme Court, even as Geelani filed an affidavit with the High Court affirming that Special Branch police was shadowing him, and he feared that he would be made the victim of an 'encounter'. On 8 February 2005, even as the appeal was pending before the Supreme Court, Geelani was shot and seriously injured while leaving his lawyer's house in South Delhi.

The Supreme Court finally upheld the acquittal in August 2005, but with a rejoinder by the presiding judge that he was not entirely convinced of Geelani's innocence, that a 'needle of suspicion' still pointed to him, but that he would give him 'the benefit of the doubt'.[32] By this time, the campaign for Geelani's release was well known and widely reported, and the prosecution's lack of evidence was finally being exposed three years after the original sentence. In keeping with the refusal to question the state in larger questions of 'national security', the trials of Shaukat Husain Guru, Afsan Guru and Mohammed Afzal, the other three accused, remained uninvestigated and unreported. Even the left-liberal *Hindu* editorialized the day after the Supreme Court decision that while it was opposed to capital punishment in general, 'there is no warrant for any special sympathy for Mohammed Afzal whose role as a conspirator in the Parliament attack case—which has been detailed by the prosecution and confirmed by three courts of law—has been established beyond a shadow of doubt.'[33] As things stand, Geelani and Afsan Guru have been acquitted, Shaukat Husain sentenced to life in prison and Mohammed Afzal awaits his death sentence.

While the language and tenor of the reportage has been discussed exhaustively elsewhere,[34] what concerns us here is its place in the discursive continuum of the process of constructing an 'Islamic' enemy. The news reports were either fabrications or misrepresentations of facts, or they were verbatim repetitions of the police versions of the case. The editorials and op-ed commentaries followed this pattern, with even secular liberal commentators echoing nationalist arguments for attacking Pakistan or ensuring punishment for the 'accused'. The undercurrent of the Muslim Other, while never overtly acknowledged was obvious through the reports. This was apparent in the reporters' assumptions about the 'accused's' motives, a television reconstruction of the police version of the incident broadcast on the satellite channel Zee TV, and the judges' own statements about what they thought of the accused. The entire tragedy played out against the BJP government's successful attempts to pass POTO through Parliament, and the RSS' increasingly shrill and violent rhetoric against the Muslim enemy within and without. The Kashmiri origins of all of the accused served to only emphasize this undercurrent, since the state of Jammu and Kashmir was already alienated from the Indian mainstream, and its separatist movement—and the conflict between India and Pakistan over the state's territory—was one of the main justifications for the RSS' campaign against Muslims in the rest of India.

In retrospect, the media's coverage of the 'Geelani case' seems an attempt to achieve a respectability of sorts for the Parliament attack by equating it with the 11 September attacks. This was apparent in the first reactions by the Indian government to the incident, when the home minister L.K. Advani said, 'Had the terrorists managed to enter Parliament House, the magnitude of the devastation would have eclipsed the September 11 incidents',[35] before immediately going on to compare the attack with the 1999 hijacking incident. In a further attempt to draw parallels, his speech also unfavourably contrasted the vocal opposition to the government in India with the lack of any political opposition to the Bush administration's own response following the 11 September attacks.[36] *The Hindu* on 16 December also reported the Indian Prime Minister's remarks on religious fanaticism: 'we saw it on September 11 and we have seen it again on December 13'.[37] *Outlook*, in an 'investigation' titled 'WTC Could Have Been Repeated Here: Al Qaeda is probably the source of even December 13 and IC-814' quotes 'highly placed police sources' as indicating that 'Al Qaeda and other ISI-backed terrorist groups are possibly using the same pool of operatives and the same training grounds.' It also quotes the Delhi police commissioner M. N. Singh: 'There is a strong possibility of linkages between the IC-814 hijacking, the September 11 strikes in the US and the December 13 attack on Parliament House.'[38]

REPORTING A GENOCIDE: THE LIMITS OF NEHRUVIAN CULTURE TALK

Three months after the attack on the Parliament complex, in an atmosphere of increasing communal polarization, a train carrying Hindu nationalist volunteers from Ayodhya was stopped outside Godhra station in Gujarat. One of the coaches was set on fire, killing 57 passengers on board. While the circumstances surrounding this incident are still unclear and the official explanation ultimately tended toward the conclusion that the fire was set inside the coach, and seemed more accident than arson, the immediate explanation given was that the coach had been burned by Muslims in Godhra in revenge for the 'pilgrims' recent *kar seva* (literally 'service through work', a euphemism for activist work with the Sangh's organizations, primarily the VHP) in Ayodhya. As other chapters in this book have shown, the incident at Godhra faded into insignificance in comparison to its violent aftermath.

Immediately following the incident the VHP released a video showing the funerals of the dead passengers, with brief sketches of their lives and interviews with their families. The RSS and its affiliate organizations mobilizing Hindutva activists and sympathizers across the state of Gujarat to 'avenge Godhra'. The RSS campaign against Muslims was incorporated into official state discourse, with Chief Minister Narendra Modi himself responsible for the most vitriolic speeches. Many of his speeches from this period, mainly in the urban centres of Ahmedabad and Gandhinagar but also in several small towns, harp on the 'foreignness' of the Muslim in India and are replete with references to '*Mian* Musharraf', a pejorative reference to the Pakistani President, General Pervez Musharraf. The process of Othering the Muslim was also accomplished by a constant public repetition of derogatory stereotypes, of the Muslim male as a circumcised, polygamous, parasitical, disloyal and unpatriotic Other; or by mocking Muslim practices of prayer and ritual.[39]

While this kind of hate-speech had been part of the RSS' repertoire for decades, what was unusual in Gujarat was the appropriation of this discourse of the Muslim as foreigner by the state administration, and by the head of the government himself. This not only legitimized the discourse to other functionaries of the administration, but also secularized it in the eyes of the national citizen-subject by bringing the legitimizing power of the Indian state to uphold the virulent hate-speech. The state's legitimacy which derived partly from its colonial predecessor's self-presentation as an entity divorced from, and above, the petty politics of religious rioting, normally enabled it to exercise its authority in the form of enforcing curfews, declaring emergencies, and deploying the military in earlier instances of religious conflict. In Gujarat however, while Modi depended on this legitimizing power of the state to undergird his authority over the administration and citizens, he utilized it not merely as a reason for deploying force, but as a platform for the rhetoric of the RSS.

The cadres of the RSS, the VHP, the BJP, the Bajrang Dal and other allied organizations went on a spree of violence in the next three days, marked by a complete absence of the state police or other administrative machinery. Cadres targeted Muslim homes, businesses, educational institutions, graves and mosques. A terrorized Muslim population in the cities and countryside was forced to flee to other states, or—if they were fortunate—find a place in one of the refugee camps in Ahmedabad. Faced with no resistance, and supported and encouraged by the state administration, most of the RSS cadres were supplied with detailed census data and municipal records which had Muslim homes and businesses pinpointed with efficient accuracy. An investigative report from *Outlook* magazine details the complicity of the police in the massacres: 'In Ahmedabad, for instance, one official recalled how for the last few months, there had been concerted attempts to get lists of Muslim business establishments from the Ahmedabad municipal corporation . . . VHP volunteers have also been making the rounds of professional institutions and universities, seeking the names and addresses of Muslim students. Some government sources say VHP members have drawn up lists of government departments . . . and identified "undesirables" and their addresses.'[40]

The ensuing weeks also revealed the near-total polarization of the state with cities like Ahmedabad and Gandhinagar physically divided along religious lines. While the vast majority of the refugees were poor Muslims (in a community already impoverished through systematic discrimination) the class-blind nature of the massacres was most tellingly revealed in the way Ehsan Jafri, a former Member of Parliament, a senior Muslim leader from the Congress party and a resident of an elite 'housing society' (apartment complex) was burned to death along with several members of his family. This was despite his frantic phone calls to the state police headquarters and to the national leadership of his party. The targeting of Muslim businesses also occurred in a highly efficient and matter-of-fact fashion, irrespective of the class and social position of the business owners. Class and caste however did play a role in the hierarchy of their attackers. As in previous such attacks by the RSS family of organizations, the leadership consisted of wealthy high-caste Hindus, while the actual mobs that committed the massacres were poor and from backward castes. This was however the highest Hindutva mobilization of Dalits, and several of the mobs were composed of and led by Dalit and adivasi members.[41] However, several reports mentioned middle-class Hindu women as active in the looting of Muslim shops. In Ahmedabad for instance, in a macabre yet literal intersection of the post-1990s consumerist boom and its parallel rise of the virulent hatred of Muslims, middle-class Hindu families were seen driving down to the city's commercial areas to loot clothes and consumer goods from Muslim-owned shops, even coordinating with each other for the best 'bargains' over their cellular phones.

On 24 September 2002, almost seven months after the massacres in Gujarat, in an attack on a prominent Hindu temple in the Gujarati capital city of Gandhinagar, two men threw hand grenades and opened machine-gun fire, killing 26 people and injuring 74. Paramilitary forces in a televized gun-battle killed both men. Letters recovered from their person said that the attack was in revenge for the violence against Muslims in the incidents seven months earlier. The men were also said to belong to a newly floated Muslim organization called the Tehreek-e-Kasas, or the Movement for Revenge. The temple in question was in a highly guarded elite section of the capital, and belonged to the large and extremely wealthy Swaminarayan sect. The incident also occurred in the midst of Narendra Modi's violent re-election campaign, which had been planned as a series of *gaurav yatras* or 'journeys of pride' in a motorized chariot throughout Gujarat. The incident is also significant, since it preceded two watershed events: POTO was passed through Parliament to become the Prevention of Terrorism Act (POTA) and Narendra Modi was re-elected chief minister of Gujarat, in an election which saw a large swing in the votes of the state's adivasis and Dalits in favor of the BJP. The campaign rhetoric leading up to the election—in which 'terrorism' was a major issue—saw even more blatant anti-Muslim statements from Modi. On the last day of the campaign, in an uncanny foretaste of George W. Bush's own re-election campaign two years later, *Outlook* reported him saying, 'If the BJP wins, the entire country will burst [fire-] crackers. But if the Congress wins, crackers will be burst in Pakistan. Pakistan wants a government of its own convenience in Gujarat so that it can carry out its sinister terrorist attacks here.'[42]

The role of the English-language print media in reporting the genocide was held by the BJP government in power as demonstrating an 'Anti-Hindu bias' but seen by most of the government's critics as crucial in holding the state accountable.[43] Most of the publications we have been looking at throughout this chapter define themselves as liberal and strongly secularist. During the Gujarat massacres, all the publications with the exception of *India Today* and the *Pioneer* were strongly anti-RSS and made their editorial opposition to the Sangh Parivar very clear. The previous comparison of the 13 December attacks with the Gujarat massacre begs the question driving this essay: why would a secular, liberal, privately-owned media industry with a long tradition of press freedom, convert itself so easily into a mouthpiece of a xenophobic, war-mongering, Hindu nationalist government? What would explain the complete lack of investigative reporting even when faced with what were obviously forced confessions and fake evidence? The anti-Muslim tenor of the government's statements after the Parliament attacks and during the Geelani case is clear enough, yet the otherwise secular English-language press simply echoed the government's positions.

We find parallels in similar situations concerning 'national security' and the armed forces: the Kargil conflict of 1999, bomb blasts in Srinagar, Kashmir earlier in 2001, the attack on a temple in Gandhinagar, Gujarat in September 2002 and a police shootout in a Delhi shopping mall in November 2002. In all these cases (the first a major armed conflict between the Indian Army and Pakistani 'infiltrators'; and the others all incidents that occurred in densely populated areas) the English language press was content to toe the government line, raising doubts only when human rights advocates or alert activist judges did so. This disconnect, between Hindu nationalism framed as patriotism and Hindu nationalism framed as religious hatred, is all the more surprising when we consider the increasing Hinduization of the Indian nation-state since the recent rise to political power of the BJP.

This disconnects takes us back to Mamdani's notion of 'culture talk', in this case inflected through Nehruvian secular nationalism. We have tried to locate the ways in which the Indian national print media recognizes a distinction between 'our' Muslims in India and 'their' Muslims in Pakistan. While the same covert and overt undercurrent of Hindu nationalist ideology is responsible for the construction of both these 'enemies' as the Other of mainstream Hindu India, this process of 'othering' the Muslim takes place at different registers: the 'enemy within' of the RSS is an 'othering' that occurs at the level of Indian political discourse and is part of what is understood and defined as Hindu communalism, while the demonizing of the Pakistani Muslim 'terrorist' is a process rooted deeply within a secular post-colonial nationalism. The national English-language print press can therefore be seen as operating within the constraints of Indian secular nationalism, always distinguishing between the 'good Muslim' Other who is the victim of Hindu communalism, and the 'bad Muslim' who is the Pakistani terrorist 'infiltrating' Indian territory to attack (Hindu) temples, shopping malls and government buildings.

THE MEDIA AND DOUBLE-HEADED NATIONALISM

Mamdani argues that religious fundamentalism in this sense is unique to Christianity since it has a definite hierarchy of religious leadership that runs parallel to the political structure of modern Christian states, while Islam has always been engaged with politics and has not really produced a distinct religious hierarchy except in the case of the Shi'a imams in Iran and Iraq. Hinduism however, in so far as such a distinct and discrete religion can be identified, has no overarching religious hierarchy whatsoever. But the political movement of Hindutva created by the RSS and its affiliates owes a great deal to the violent and exclusionary cultural nationalisms of the early 20th century, rather than to religious fundamentals. The BJP's triumph in the closing years of the last century can be understood thus as the fruition of a modernist project of ultra-nationalism. Its similarities with fundamentalist Christianity lie in the necessity of the demonization of Islam and the 'othering' of Muslims as an essential characteristic of their self-definitions.

However, the response from the liberal factions of the Indian intelligentsia, as represented by the English-language news media, also falls into the trap of what Mamdani calls the 'culture talk' of 'Good Muslim, Bad Muslim'. While the English-language media responded almost heroically to investigate and condemn the instigators and perpetrators of the massacres in Gujarat, the same newspapers and magazines stayed silent or deliberately falsified reports in dealing with the Geelani case and the attack on Parliament. The blind spot of 'national security' won over any commitment to truth seeking and truth-telling. The connections between a Hindu nationalist government's attacks on the rights and freedoms of Muslims in the name of fighting terrorism and the same government's genocidal killing of Muslims in the name of a Hindu nationhood were not drawn. The submission of privately controlled news media to government diktats is similar to the ultra-nationalist responses and the embedded journalism seen in the US media following the 11 September attacks. These similarities are what enable our comparisons between developments in India and the attacks on New York and Washington. They also allowed the use of the American invasion of Afghanistan and Iraq as justificatory discourses in reference to the conflict in Kashmir or the intensification of violent campaigns against Muslims. Or, as in the case of Geelani, the American state's denial of basic civil liberties and liberal human rights to citizens both enabled and justified a similar curtailment of rights in India.

The English-language media's contradictory responses to the 11 September attacks, the Parliament attacks and the genocidal violence in Gujarat can now be seen as part of its location within the Nehruvian framework of a post-colonial secular nationalist ideology. Rather than being seen as inconsistent, they have to be understood within the continuum of the media's relationship to the Indian nation-state. The media's reactions to 9/11 can be understood on two different but related planes: first, as part of the nationalist-patriotic project of the mainstream (Hindu) Indian state, the media opposed the US' allying itself with its Other, Islamic Pakistan; and secondly, representing its elite secular liberal constituency, the media also articulated a post-colonial, formerly non-aligned nation's opposition to US hegemony and the demonization of Islam. In practice however, the distinction between these two levels is not as clear, and is a reflection of the intertwined nature of Hindu communalism and liberal secularism in India, where communalism is 'neither a "pathology", nor an antithesis of nationalism, but merely its dark underside that refuses to go away.'[44] The coverage of the 13 December attack and the Gujarat violence illustrates this conflicted nationalism of the English-language press. The Parliament attack and other incidents involving 'terrorism' called forth the nationalist patriotic sentiment of the media, and this nationalism was, consciously or unconsciously, coded as Hindu, just as the 'terrorism' was always coded as Muslim. The fact that this both echoed and reinforced the essentialist binary oppositions of the Sangh Parivar was not acknowledged, or perhaps not yet completely understood. The genocide in Gujarat, on the other hand, brought out the secular liberal traditions of the same media institutions: in the new opposition between Hindu communalism and secularism, played out within the broad parameters of post-colonial nationalism, they vigorously defended the secular Nehruvian institutional and ideological framework from the onslaught of its Hindu nationalist variant. However, they remained, and still remain, unaware of the duplicity of their contradictory roles. Within a broad discourse of Indian nationalism, they still posit a clear opposition between 'communalism' and 'secularism', while in the everyday practice of reporting that discourse, the two coalesce into a double-headed, inadvertently Hindu, nationalism. In this, perhaps, they simply reflect the complex articulation of the many nationalisms that characterize the modern Indian nation-state.

Notes

1 Armand Mattelart, *Mapping World Communication: War, Progress, Culture* (Minneapolis: University of Minnesota Press, 1994) and Paul Virilio, *Desert Screen: War at the Speed of Light* (London: Continuum, 2000).

2 Robin Jeffrey, *India's Newspaper Revolution: Capitalism, Technology and the Indian Language Press, 1977-1997* (London: C. Hurst and Co., 2000).

3 Manoj Joshi, 'September 11 and After: Pressure for Regulation and Self-regulation in the Indian Media' in Peter van der Veer and Shoma Munshi (eds.), *Media, War, and Terrorism: Responses from the Middle East and Asia* (New York: Routledge, 2004), 129.

4 Mahmood Mamdani, *Good Muslim, Bad Muslim: Islam, the USA and the Global War Against Terror* (Delhi: Permanent Black, 2004), 15.

5 See Purnima Mankekar, *Screening Culture, Viewing Politics: An*

Ethnography of Television, Womanhood and the Nation in Postcolonial India (Durham, NC: Duke University Press, 1999) and Arvind Rajagopal, *Politics After Television: Hindu Nationalism and the Reshaping of the Public in India* (Cambridge: Cambridge University Press, 2001).

6 See Subarno Chatterji's interesting comparison of the media coverage of the Kargil conflict and the Gujarat violence: Subarno Chatterji, 'Media Representations of the Kargil War and the Gujarat Riots', *Sarai Reader 04: Crisis/Media* (New Delhi: CSDS, 2004), 110-17. For background see Thomas Blom Hansen *The Saffron Wave* (Princeton: Princeton University Press, 2001).

7 It is beyond the scope of this paper to discuss in detail comparable television news coverage of these events, although we recognize that television news coverage reaches a much wider audience and will only grow in the years to come. Although there are few research studies of television news at this time, Manoj Joshi cites an industry study that shows that television news viewership overall increased significantly following both the 11 September and 13 December attacks. See Joshi, 'September 11 and After', 129.

8 For a discussion of the 'split public'—the divisions between the readership of English language newspapers and the regional language press and the ways in which this division intersects with the conflict between Indian secularism and Hindutva—see Rajagopal, *Politics After Television,* 156-71.

9 The history and recent rise of the RSS as an Indian political phenomenon has been painstakingly traced in several excellent works, both popular and academic. These include Christophe Jaffrelot's exhaustive *The Hindu Nationalist Movement and Indian Politics* (New Delhi: Penguin Books, 1996); A. G. Noorani's *RSS and the BJP: A Division of Labour* (New Delhi: Leftword Books, 2001); Thomas Blom Hansen's *The Saffron Wave: Democracy and Hindu Nationalism in Modern India* (New Delhi: Oxford University Press, 1999); and Tapan Basu et al's *Khaki Shorts and Saffron Flags: A Critique of the Hindu Right* (Hyderabad: Orient Longman, 1993).

10 See Jack Shaheen's *Reel Bad Arabs: How Hollywood Vilifies a People* (New York: Olive Branch Press, 2001) and *Arab and Muslim Stereotyping in American Popular Culture* (Washington DC: Georgetown University Press,1997); and Edward Said's seminal *Covering Islam: How the Media and the Experts Determine How We See the Rest of the World* (New York: Vintage Books, 1997). Also see the American-Arab Anti-Defamation Committee's exhaustive Bibliography of Anti-Arab

Discrimination, Stereotyping, and Media Bias online at http://www.adc.org/index.php?id=505 (10/01/2005).

11 Susan M. Akram and Kevin R. Johnson, 'Race and Civil Rights Pre-September 11, 2001: The Targeting of Arabs and Muslims' in Elaine Hagopian (ed.), *Civil Rights in Peril: The Targeting of Arabs and Muslims* (Chicago: Haymarket Books, 2004).

12 Mamdani, *Good Muslim, Bad Muslim,* 38-44.

13 Gaurav Sawant, 'Terror Strikes India', *The Indian Express,* 12 September 2001.

14 For a more specific analysis of transnational Indian media coverage following the 11 September attacks see: Paula Chakravartty, 'Translating Terror in India' *Television and New Media,* 3: 2 (2002), 205-12.

15 J. Dey. 'Mumbai to New York, the Road Passed through Kandahar'. *The Indian Express,* 24 September 2001.

16 P. Radhakrishnan, 'The Taliban Tangle', *The Hindu,* 24 September 2001.

17 For a fuller discussion of the Anti-Arab bias in the mainstream American news media's response to the 11 September attacks, see Robert Morlino's '"Our Enemies Among Us": The Portrayal of Arab and Muslim Americans in Post-9/11 American Media', in Elaine Hagopian (ed.), *Civil Rights in Peril.*

18 'The Natural Ally', *India Today,* 29 October 2001.

19 Balraj Puri, 'India, Kashmir and War against Terrorism', *Economic and Political Weekly,* 27 October 2001.

20 'Should India Attack?' was the headline on the cover for the issue dated 29 October, which had the image of a missile heading towards a Pakistani flag in the background. An earlier cover, from 15 October of that year had the picture of Kashmiri separatist leader Masood Azhar, exchanged for the hostages of the Indian Airlines flight hijacked by the Taliban militia in 1999. The headline beneath the picture read: 'Wanted—India's Bin Laden.'

21 Mani Shankar Aiyar, 'Lighting Bush Fires: Whose War against Terrorism Is It Anyway?' *The Indian Express,* 2 October 2001.

22 Harish Khare, 'A Decisive Battle has to Take Place: PM', *The Hindu* 14 December 2001.

23 Ibid.

24 Editorial: 'Ugly Terror Strikes Again.' *The Hindu* 14 December 2001.

25 Ranjit Bhushan, 'Shock Therapy', *Outlook,* 24 December 2001.

26 Rahul Datta, 'Take the Battle to Enemy Camp, Forces Tell CCS', *The Pioneer* 14 December 2001

27 Manoj Joshi provides more on the specific impact in terms of regulating media and its parallels with the US and the UK. See Joshi, 'September 11 and After'.

28 '"Attack on Parliament:" Revenge will be our only Compensation"', *Outlook,* 24 December 2001.

29 Ibid.

30 For a detailed account of the attack and Geelani's ordeal see Nandita Haksar, and K. Sanjay Singh, 'December 13'. *Seminar*, 521 (January 2003); and for Nandita Haksar's reflections on the trial, 'The Many Faces of Nationalism', *Seminar* 533 (January 2004).

31 See Nirmalangshu Mukherjee's 'Who Attacked Parliament?' in *Revolutionary Democracy*, 10: 2 (September 2004) at http://www.revolutionarydemocracy.org/rdv10n2/index.htm

32 J. Venkatesan, 'Apex Court Upholds Geelani's Acquittal', *The Hindu*, 5 August 2005.

33 'Just Acquittal, Unjust Suspicion', *The Hindu,* 6 August 2005.

34 See Nandita Haksar's essay 'Tried by the Media: The SAR Geelani Trial' in *Sarai Reader 04: Crisis/Media* (pp.158-164). Haksar, a noted human rights advocate, was also Geelani's counsel. Also see Nirmalangshu Mukherjee's comprehensive enumeration of newspaper headlines from the period: 'The Media and December 13' published online in *Revolutionary Democracy* http://www.revolutionarydemocracy.org/miscl/dec13.htm . The website for the *All India Defense Committee for Syed Abdul Rehman Geelani* at http://www20.brinkster.com/sargeelani/ has more details of the case itself and its numerous retrials.

35 Pioneer News Service: 'Nation Should Prepare: Advani' *The Pioneer*. 18 December 2001.

36 The report continues: '(Advani) also ridiculed those raising questions about security failure, saying nothing of that sort was witnessed in the US after September 11 terror strikes. "Questions could have been raised over how four planes were hijacked in a single day in the US and how Pentagon, the seat of American defense, could be attacked," Mr. Advani said. "It demonstrated resolve of the people of the US," he said, regretting that things on the contrary were witnessed here' (ibid.).

37 Malabika Bhattacharya, '"We'll Respond to Terrorism on Many Fronts:" PM', *The Hindu* 16 December 2001.

38 Priyanka Kakodkar, 'WTC Could Have Been Repeated Here: Al Qaeda is probably the source of even December 13 and IC-814', *Outlook* 31 December 2001.

39 Rakesh Sharma's independent documentary film on the Gujarat massacres, *Final Solution* has extensive footage of the campaign speeches by Narendra Modi and other BJP and VHP activists. The film was banned in India for several months until the BJP's defeat in the October 2004 general election.

40 Ranjit Bhushan, 'Thy Hand Great Anarch', *Outlook* 18 March 2002. Also see Darshan Desai and Joydeep Ray, 'Dial M for Modi, Murder', *Indian Express* 24 March 2002 for another investigation into the state-sponsored nature of the genocide.

41 Human Rights Watch in its report on the Gujarat carnage concluded, 'Much like attacks against Christians in Gujarat and other parts of the country, the recruitment and targeting of Dalits and tribals is aimed in part at consolidating the Hindu vote bank and encouraging voters to defect from the opposition Congress(I) party. Many Dalits and tribals were actively involved in the violence against Muslims. While Dalits were deployed in urban centers, towns and villages, far-flung districts saw tribals taking part in the anti-Muslim pogrom. Dalit and tribal participation in the violence has also made them the scapegoat in police arrests while those that orchestrated the violence roam free' in 'Compounding Injustice: The Government's Failure to Redress Massacres in Gujarat', *Human Rights Watch* 15: 3(C). Also see Davinder Kumar, 'Poisoned Edge' *Outlook,* 2 July 2002.

42 Darshan Desai and Saba Naqvi Bhaumik, 'The Fear Factory', *Outlook*, 23 December 2002.

43 See Joshi, 'September 11 and After'.

44 Hansen, *The Saffron Wave*, 217.

MASS VIOLENCE AND THE WHEELS OF INDIAN (IN)JUSTICE

Zoya Hasan

The mass killings of Sikhs in New Delhi in 1984 and the 2002 pogrom in Gujarat have rightfully acquired a place in public and political discourse as two horrific episodes of extreme violence in post-colonial India.[1] But they do not stand alone. In the years between the violence of Delhi (1984) and Gujarat (2002), several major episodes of communal violence took place in Meerut-Malliana (Uttar Pradesh) in 1987, where Provincial Armed Constabulary *jawans* lined up and shot dead in cold blood fifty-three Muslim youth; the Bhagalpur massacre of 1989 during which an overnight slaughter of the Muslim minority took place (nearly 1,000 were killed); and the mass violence in Bombay in 1992-93.

Each of these major cases of mass violence has called forth investigations by numerous commissions of inquiry and civil society groups. Despite these inquiries, there has been no systematic effort to prevent the recurrence of violence and no fair or impartial administration of justice to punish the guilty. Indeed, the tragedy is not just that mass violence happened but that successive governments are not prepared to do anything to prevent it or to provide justice to the victims. Instead of those responsible being punished, they are frequently elected to national and state legislatures and become ministers and chief ministers. As a result, the Indian state has acquired a reputation for not being able to cope with communal violence fairly or to protect the minorities who are the main victims of it. Both state and courts have repeatedly shown their incapacity to deal with communal issues, even more than other social atrocities such as caste violence.

Most accounts of Hindu-Muslim violence tend to focus on the event of violence, on how and why violence occurs, what factors account for its outbreak and the agents involved. This essay, in contrast, is focused squarely on the post-violence situation. Drawing upon comparative material from the mass violence of Mumbai and Gujarat, it focuses attention on the hitherto only partly examined aftermath of violence.

On the issue of securing justice, relief and rehabilitation for victims of communal mass violence, it poses the question as to why there is no conviction and prosecution of individuals involved in organized violence in India even when there is evidence of the active or passive involvement of influential people and personnel from the administration and police. In fact, allegations of state connivance in mass violence have been strengthed by the failure of the criminal justice system to bring those responsible to justice—a fact highlighted by the Supreme Court in a recent order which reportedly referred to 'connivance' between the government and prosecution service in Gujarat.[2] What are the limitations of the state's role in the post-violence period, especially the inquiry commission approach or the judicial process? The question is, are we perhaps using obsolete legal concepts to deal with mass killings that have state backing? What about the issue of the constitutional responsibility of the state to prevent such mass killings? And the larger question is, what does the post-conflict situation tell us about equality of citizenship and justice in India's democracy?

Many social scientists, civil society groups, bureaucrats and policemen link the state response to riots, and the overall problems of prevention of riots, to the politicization, corruption and institutional weakness of governments. Many argue that political interference in law and order decisions has incapacitated the police force and it does not have the independence to take action against rioters.[3] There is no doubt that the problem of political interference is serious and has grown worse in the past two decades. However, as Steven Wilkinson points out, state capacity alone cannot account for variations in Hindu-Muslim violence across time and space, because most state governments in India possess the minimal capacity required to prevent communal conflict if political leaders treat this as a priority.[4] The issue is not that state capacity is inconsequential, rather that governments can prevent violence if there is the political will to do so. Therefore, the key issue is the political will to protect or not protect minorities. The most notable examples of this are West Bengal and Bihar in the 1990s, which have had low levels of riots and deaths because political leaders have made the prevention of communal violence a priority. At the other extreme is Gujarat and Maharashtra, that have had high levels of communal violence and a complete absence of political will to prevent mass violence. Partly this is due the intensification of communal politics and prejudice against minorities in these two states and partly because of the low rates of conviction and prosecution. While there may no direct connection between riot prevention and prosecution, prosecuting the guilty even after the fact can prove to be a deterrent in the continuation of violence or the outbreak of fresh violence in the most violent states of Gujarat and Maharashtra.

For those concerned about the fairness of Indian democracy, examining the aftermath of violence is crucial because it gives us important insights into the lasting consequences of the politics of religious division and the resultant threat to processes of pluralism and equality. We need to understand the post-conflict situation in order to form an adequate conception of the challenges of religious nationalism and ethnic politics and the problem it poses for non-discrimination and equal respect for all groups. Democracy combines the rule of law and constitutional governance to ensure democratic and secular justice. Without justice governance itself is unjust and inequitable. Failure to protect the life and property of individuals belonging to the minority communities is a powerful site of discrimination in Indian society and threatens democracy in the long run. The claim to be the world's largest democracy and a Great Power will be considerably diminished if mass-level crimes and barbaric forms of collective victimization of vulnerable groups go unpunished. If India is to live up to its acclaimed status as a strong and vibrant democracy, it must establish and affirm the rule of law impartially. Punishing the guilty is therefore necessary not only from the viewpoint of humanism and compassion; it is imperative for strengthening the secular foundations of our democracy.

TWO MAJOR EPISODES OF MASS VIOLENCE: MUMBAI (1992-93) AND GUJARAT (2002)

These two major episodes of mass violence in independent India are associated with political movements and actions of the Hindutva organizations linked to the Sangh Parivar.[5] Starting in the late 1980s, the BJP, VHP and RSS collaborated in a militant religious mobilization to 'liberate' the Ram Janmabhoomi site in Ayodhya. In October 1990, L. K. Advani personally led the temple campaign, which took him through eight states, stoking religious emotions, leaving communal conflict and violence in its trail. The agitation provoked huge incidents of rural and urban violence, of which the Mumbai violence was the worst instance. Even states where communal violence was uncommon were unable to escape the violence engendered by the agitation. The religious fervour aroused by the *rath yatra* was a key factor in increasing the violence, which was clearly the product of sustained mass mobilization and derived from a broader discourse of communalism that was the driving force behind the spurt in violence. For the BJP-RSS combine the Ayodhya campaign combined with an appeal to Hindutva offered a strategy to mobilize popular support to replace the Congress as the dominant party. This period was witness to a continuous pattern of violence that culminated in the destruction of the Babri Masjid by Hindu mobs, claiming that it was built on the remains of a Hindu temple.

Riots followed shortly after this in Mumbai. Muslim demonstrators protesting against the demolition and Hindus leading victory processions sparked the riots. The riots took place in two phases—the December 1992 phase, lasting for five days to a week, and the January 1993 phase, which occurred between January 6 and 20.[6] The first was mainly a Muslim backlash as a result of the Babri Masjid demolition in the week immediately succeeding demolition. The second phase was by and large a Hindu backlash occurring as a result of the widely reported killings of four Hindu Mathadi Kamdar, allegedly by Muslims, in Dongri (an area of South Mumbai). Over 1,500 people were killed in the riots and thousands were displaced.[7]

The second major episode of mass violence occurred in Gujarat in March 2002.[8] As other essays in this volume have documented as well, more than 2,000 Muslims were killed, over 150,000 displaced and scores of women raped in one of the most brutal instances of carnage in the history of independent India. There is copious evidence that the violence was planned before the horrific burning of the Sabarmati Express at Godhra station killing fifty-nine Hindus, and that the post-Godhra carnage was aided and abetted both by the police and by local BJP/RSS politicians. In the days and weeks that followed, further waves of violence swept the state. The attackers were mainly highly politicized Hindus shouting slogans such as *Jai Sri Ram* and *Jai Hanuman* and the victims were almost all Muslims. Official information furnished to the Election Commission of India indicated that only 12 of the 25 districts in the state were affected; however, relief was distributed in 20 districts which means 20 districts had been affected.[9] The Additional Director General of Police, R. B. Sreekumar, further informed the Commission that 151 towns and 993 villages covering 154 out of 182 assembly constituencies in the state were affected by the violence.[10] Violence was directed against all Muslims regardless of social class. One former chief justice of the Rajasthan High Court, living in retirement in Gujarat, fled, later commenting to an investigative tribunal that there was 'a deliberate conspiracy to stifle criminal law'.

The Gujarat violence and the state response have been extensively examined in the press and by human rights organizations.[11] It cannot strictly be called a communal riot in the conventional sense. It was a carnage aided and abetted both by the police and local politicians.[12] The National Human Rights Commission's (NHRC) investigation into the violence reported evidence of a complete breakdown of law and order in Gujarat. It found irrefutable evidence of the government's unwillingness to control violence.[13] It is clear from all the evidence placed before the Concerned Citizens' Tribunal that what began in Godhra, could have, given the political will, been controlled promptly at Godhra itself.[14]

Instead, the state government under chief minister Narendra Modi took an active part in leading and sponsoring the violence against minorities all over Gujarat.[15] His words and actions throughout the developments in Gujarat show that he was openly defying the constitution and indulging in actions directed against Muslims.

According to press accounts and human rights investigations the Modi regime facilitated the violence in many ways: police received orders not to intervene in the carnage, and those who disobeyed were punished by demotions and transfers. In this regard, the most damaging was the testimony of the Director General of Police who headed the CID (Intelligence).[16] R. B. Sreekumar said that political leaders had pressured the police force into not registering riot offences. He observed that: '[He] instructed that I should not concentrate on the Sangh Parivar as they are not doing anything illegal.' Other features of police behavior include the registration of FIRs not naming the accused, the refusal to take action against VHP activists who participated in the violence, and the non-use of the Disturbed Areas (Special Courts) Act, 1976 and the Prevention of Damage to Public Property Act, 1984. Even after the arson attack at Godhra no preventive arrests were made under Section 144 of Criminal Procedure Code.

These patterns of state complicity continued even after the cessation of violence. State authorities discriminated against Muslims in payment of compensation and rehabilitation of the victims.[17] The relief and rehabilitation was inadequate, failing to provide food, shelter or security. Shelter and rations were scarce. Four years later, the majority of the family members of those killed in the Gujarat violence have yet to receive their compensation disbursements.

State agencies even obstructed other agencies that were attempting to step in with relief and rehabilitation, and forced closure of relief camps after giving people a pittance to compensate for their losses.[18] In the makeshift camps established by the Muslim community, the state government refused even to provide basic facilities, security or a survival stipend.[19] The compensation to be paid was unfair. At first, more compensation was paid to the Godhra (Hindu) victims than the Muslims. Later, it was equalized.[20] The conditions of proof for obtaining compensation required proofs of identity, which victims of arson could scarcely provide. As the International Initiative for Justice in Gujarat has pointed out, the state used the term 'assistance' rather than 'compensation', indicating that the state considered these payments not as a right or entitlement of the victims but as charitable measures.

Prior to Gujarat 2002, state authorities in India were not always efficient in the task of rehabilitation of internal refugees created by ethnic conflicts, but they did not deliberately discriminate in compensation and resettlement.[21] State obligation, though not specifically spelt out is implied in the fundamental right to life and equality. The state's liability to pay compensation for tortuous actions has been well established in a number of cases.[22] The failure of the state in this regard is therefore even graver than its complicity in the violence. As a result, privatized relief and rehabilitation dominated the post-conflict situation in both Gujarat and Bombay.[23] Muslim NGOs and relief organizations provided relief for the mostly Muslim victims—leading to a dangerous irony that post-conflict reconstruction efforts furthered rather than mitigated the communal divide.[24] The government took hardly any step to dispel the notion that they are hostile to minorities and their rights as equal citizens of India. Moreover, the Gujarat violence and suffering were a direct result of either calculated state disregard or state collusion and complicity. In the circumstances, the liability and responsibility of rehabilitation falls squarely on the government, and the NGOs cannot and should not be expected to deal with the crisis; the NGOs can at best support and supplement state efforts.

POST-VIOLENCE INVESTIGATION AND THE ILLUSION OF JUSTICE

In India, an official commission of inquiry is usually set up to inquire into riots and prepare reports on the causes of tension. A commission of inquiry appears to be a body constituted in the aftermath of a controversial event of public importance through the supreme legislative body of the country or state. Different countries recruit members to these commissions differently. In India, inquiry commissions are set up under the Commissions of Inquiry Act, 1952.[25] It is customary to appoint an ex-judge of the Supreme Court as the head of the commission. It is to be noted that these commissions are only recommendatory and do not have the power to prosecute. Nonetheless they help focus public opinion on a concrete set of 'facts' (outlined in the commission's report) when there are a number of interpretations of the same controversial event.

Commissions of Inquiry perhaps perform some vital tasks in the orientation of public opinion. There does seem to be a direct correlation between the rise of parliamentary democracy and the setting up of official investigations into matters of public importance. This could perhaps be due to the pressures of mass democracy and the growng importance of public opinion, which seeks answers from and holds the state accountable. Among the most well-known commissions are: Jagmohan Reddy on Ahmedabad (1969), Raghubir Dayal Commission (1967), D. P. Madan on Bhiwandi (1970), Vithayathil on Tellicherry (1971), Jitendra Narain on Jamshedpur (1979), Venugopal on Kanyakumari (1982), the Srikrishna Commission on Bombay (1998), and the Ranganath Mishra Commission inquiring into the 1984 anti-Sikh violence (1985).

The failings of the state administration in dealing with the violence are clear from these reports. All inquiries bring out some of the common elements in riots: planning and organization, political involvement, clear targeting, absence of state prevention, and precipitating events etc. Each has, more or less, drawn the same conclusions: the police failed to act with impartiality in every case; the top brass rarely acted on its own and almost always looked to the political leadership for direction; the miscreants exploited every such delay in action by indulging in looting and arson. These reports provide a basis for prosecuting a number of people against whom 'credible evidence' exists. Although these reports have immense relevance to the system of governance the importance accorded to them is minimal. The government, state officials and law enforcement agencies never take seriously the recommendations regarding responsibility even of leading policemen. None of the reports have resulted in convictions.

Nevertheless, governments continue to favour the commission formula to deal with outbreaks of communal violence or any type of mass violence. In keeping with this approach the Congress-led government of Maharashtra on 23 January 1993, appointed Justice B. N. Srikrishna, then a sitting Judge of the Bombay High Court, to head a one-man commission to investigate the riots. It is important to remember that the Srikrishna Commission was initially set up in 1993 and could submit its report only in 1998, after its Terms of Reference were expanded to include the Mumbai bomb blasts at the Bombay Stock Exchange and subsequent riots of early1993.

The 800-page report is a detailed investigation of the violent rioting that occurred in the state capital of Mumbai following the 1992 destruction of the Babri Masjid in northern India. The Commission cited the immediate causes of the riots as (i) the demolition of the Babri Masjid, (ii) aggravation of Muslim sentiments by Hindus due to their celebration rallies and, (iii) the insensitive and harsh handling of the protesting mobs—which initially were not violent—by the police. There is plenty of evidence of the Shiv Sena's complicity in the riots. For example, the Commission found that Shiv Sena leaders led a mob, which 'attacked Chacha Nagar Masjid and the Muslims in the vicinity'. They stated, 'There is no doubt the Sena took the lead in organizing attacks on Muslims under the guidance of several leaders,' specifically naming Sena chief Balasaheb Thackeray as the driving force behind the riots. The Report clearly blamed the Shiv Sena for the preplanned targeting of Muslim life and property in Mumbai. In a searing indictment of the well-organized violence, the Report stated that the measures taken by the police were inadequate and the curfews and the statutory ban on an assembly of five were not effectively implemented. The police force was hopelessly inadequate to deal with the extraordinary situation that arose in the wake of the destruction of the Babri Masjid. Further, the Report held that the police responded unsympathetically to calls for help by individual members of the Muslim community, and sections of the police remained inactive or even participated in the violence.[26] The police were indicted for being biased and harsh in their treatment of Muslims during the span of the riots and the Commission documented the fact that there were several incidents of unnecessary police firing.

The Srikrishna Report thus exposed the partiality of the state and the collusion of the Shiv Sena, which it emphatically condemned. The Report points to a 'built-in-bias against Muslims, which became pronounced with murderous attacks by the Constabulary and officers'. According to the Report this bias was manifest in their reluctance to firmly put down incidents of violence and arson. 'On occasion the attitude was that one Muslim killed was one Muslim less'.[27]

The Srikrishna Report remains unimplemented even eight years after its submission. As we have seen already, the Commission was categorical in fixing responsibility and in criticizing politicians and the government. It was unsparing in its censure of the Shiv Sena's role in the instigation of riots and that of the police which did nothing to stop the rampaging mobs. However, the legal process did not take any action against the persons accused in the Commission's report. Not a single member of the Sena was brought to justice, and no action was taken against the erring officials or police. The Maharashtra chief minister Manohar Joshi condemned the report as 'anti-Hindu and pro-Muslim'. His government rejected the Report in the legislative assembly owing to its bias in favour of one community. In short, the inquiry commission proved meaningless because of inaction by successive governments.

The Congress, which was in power when the riots broke out, and had set up the Commission in response to public pressure, had welcomed the Report and initially demanded the arrest of Bal Thackeray, but later retracted, demanding just 'stern action against the guilty'. After saying this it fell silent. With an eye on the elections, it wanted to win back the Muslim votes, but did not want to alienate the Hindus. While the Shiv Sena openly defended its role, the BJP maintained a studied silence. For both the Sena-BJP government and the Congress-NCP, the report was best buried. The former rejected it because it indicted both parties for their role in the riots; the latter was reluctant to alienate the Hindu voters and the influential police force. The government found a way out of implementing the report by filing an affidavit in the Supreme Court in January 2000 that it plans to refer the report to the Crime Branch. Over 200,000 people had to flee the city and many of them have not returned. Yet, not one of the culprits has been convicted. Though cases had been registered against some of them, instead of prosecuting them, the government just decided to quietly close the cases. Nearly 3,000 cases were thus dropped.[28] The Commission indicted thirty-one police personnel from the rank of Deputy Commissioner of Police to Constable. The Shiv Sena-BJP government promoted ten of these indicted police officers.[29] Of the indicted police personnel, the government has suspended five constables. It is always easy to take some symbolic action against the lower ranks. But the higher ranks go scot-free or are even rewarded. The government decided to exonerate twelve police officers indicted by the Srikrishna Commission as stated in the affidavit submitted to the Supreme Court.

A similar pattern can be observed in the case of the Gujarat violence. On the surface at least, a different kind of resolution appeared to be in order since a different mechanism of inquiry was activated. In the immediate post-conflict period, Justice Nanavati, a retired judge of the Supreme Court, was asked to head a commission of inquiry, which is yet to submit its report four years later. However, unlike the case of the Mumbai violence and the seemingly infinite countenancing of delay, matters were not left to stand. For a variety of reasons, not the least of which have to do with considerable activism on the part of the civil society inquiry commissions and citizens' tribunals convened by diverse sets of local, national, and international actors, the central government announced a new institutional measure. The National Human Rights Commission (NHRC) was authorized to carry out the major investigation, which it did with relative speed, submitting its Final Report and recommending, amongst other things, a CBI inquiry.[30] It was clear from all the reports, most notably the NHRC'S, that the police force in Gujarat could not be trusted with the investigation and prosecution of the case.

The NHRC's investigation was repeatedly checked and countered by the Gujarat state government. For instance, in the initial months, the government confronted the NHRC with a dilution of issues by showing that the 'riots' were just another part of Gujarat's long history of communal riots, pointing to the earlier Commissions of Inquiry by Justice Reddy in 1969 and Justice Dave in 1985. If the Modi government had been left to its own devices, they would have followed the usual pattern of 'riot as explosion' to bypass addressing the issues of responsibility and accountability. The BJP government was keen to portray the violence as an unfortunate explosion in which, despite the administration's efforts, there was bedlam and death. The projection of 'riots as explosion' has the effect of saying that nobody was really culpable, that unfortunately the rule of law yielded to mob passions.[31]

The final Report of the NHRC did not take cognizance of these claims. Instead, the NHRC indicted the state government on multiple counts, citing its active role in different stages of the violence. Thus, the state government's handling of the Godhra affair in light of the advance information available was singled out. The Commission felt that 'the facts indicate that the response was often abysmal, or even non-existent, pointing to gross negligence in certain instances or, worse still, as widely believed, to a complicity that was tacit if not explicit.'

The Report also directed its attention to the post-conflict justice and rehabilitation process. Expressing deep concern about the criminal justice delivery system and the negation of human rights of victims, the NHRC Report spoke of the massive breakdown of law and order. It pointed to violations of numerous fundamental rights set out in the Constitution of India, including: equality before the law (Article 14); prohibition against discrimination (Article 15); protection of life and personal liberty (Article 21); and protection against arrest and detention in certain cases (Article 22). On this basis, the NHRC reiterated its submission that the Central Bureau of Investigation (CBI) and not the state agencies should carry out the investigation of the various crimes, and that significant criminal trials should likewise be removed from the purview of the state courts.

Despite the NHRC's plea, neither the state nor, as it turns out, the central government wanted an independent investigation by the CBI. On encountering resistance from Modi's government in the form of dismissal of this recommendation, the NHRC asked the central government to direct the state government under Article 355 of the Constitution. In the end, the investigation of the cases was not handed over to the CBI or supervised by a national monitoring committee. It was left entirely to the Gujarat police. Those suspected of transgression were effectively put in charge of investigative justice.

In the case of criminal trials, the approach was different. The NHRC filed a Special Leave Petition in the Supreme Court seeking orders for five key cases in which individuals were accused of perpetrating communal violence, to be tried outside the state.[32] Seeking retrial of the cases in courts outside the state was consistent with the active role that the Commission had played in the 'trial of justice'-post-Godhra. Among these was the Best Bakery case in which fourteen people were burnt to death on 1 March 2002, in a bakery in Baroda city.[33] Despite the fact that this was among the worst cases of violence in the aftermath of Godhra, and that this was the first to come up for hearing (and therefore of considerable importance as a precedent setting case), the state court acquitted all the accused. Of the 120 witnesses listed by the prosecution, more than a third never made it to the box. Of the seventy-three who did, more than half turned hostile. The prosecution's prime witness and main complainant—Zahira Shaikh—who was escorted to the trial by the local BJP legislator, told the court that she'd neither seen nor heard anything about the incident. The judgment provoked a storm of protest and a spate of critical editorials and commentary in leading newspapers.[34]

The NHRC's plea to move the case outside the state did not go unheard.[35] In a historic verdict the Supreme Court on 12 April 2004 quashed the acquittal of all the twenty-one accused in the Best Bakery. It took the unprecedented step of ordering re-investigation and retrial of the case after both the trial court and high court had acquitted the accused. Not only this, the Court transferred the case to Maharashtra. There are very few cases in the past where the Supreme Court has ordered a retrial of a criminal case in another state. 'The justice delivery system was being taken for a ride and was allowed to be abused, misused and mutilated by subterfuge', noted the Supreme Court. Indeed, never before has the highest Court so strongly expressed its lack of confidence in the administration and the justice system of the state. The bias of the state is highlighted from the Court's view that: 'The modern day Neros were looking elsewhere when Best Bakery and innocent children and helpless women were burning, and were probably deliberating how the perpetrators of the crime could be protected.'[36] By ordering the retrial the apex court touched on the heart of the matter: the failure of the state administration to discharge its constitutional responsibilities of providing protection of life and liberty of all citizens without discrimination on the basis of religion.

The Gujarat state government applied for a modification of the apex court's order in a review petition to which the Court gave a fitting reply. Thereafter, the stage was set for a special court to be designated and the trial to begin. Despite several hurdles to block the trial in Mumbai, charges were framed and the re-trial began on 4 October 2004. However, less than a month after the commencement of the retrial in the premises of Mazgaon Court in the formerly working-class locality of south central Mumbai, on 3 November 2004, Zahira Sheikh, the young face of this tragedy who had somehow come to symbolize this struggle, in a press conference held in the presence of two lawyers in Vadodara, actually declared herself as a hostile witness. Sheikh, in effect, reaffirmed the testimony she had given before the fast track trial court in Vadodara on 17 May 2003. This was clearly a bid to not simply derail the ongoing Best Bakery retrial in Mumbai, but to seriously discredit the judicial and constitutional processes that had made history by ordering retrial and transfer in the first place.[37]

In sum, the NHRC report represented a departure from the standard 'ritual of inquiry' in two ways. The first was at the level of the report itself, or the kinds of indictments, analyses, and recommendations that were offered in the context of the Gujarat violence of 2002. One major outcome of the NHRC intervention in the Supreme Court was that the Gujarat government was now under compulsion to reveal to the court the specific steps taken it had taken to ensure protection of witnesses in the Best Bakery and other pending cases.

Overall, both the Srikrishna Commission and the NHRC indict the state machineries of Maharashtra and Gujarat respectively for their failure to prevent violence and their active complicity in the violence. But there are significant differences that stem from the mandate of these commissions, and from their divergent constitutions as national (NHRC) and state (regional) level bodies (Srikrishna Commission). For instance, the NHRC did not restrict itself to collecting evidence and suggesting reforms for the administrative machinery of the state. Therefore its indictment of the state is stronger than that of the Srikrishna Report. Moreover, the Srikrishna Commission did not make any recommendations in the area of relief and rehabilitation of the victims, which significantly the NHRC does, in detail. The NHRC also recommended payment of compensation to the victims, which the Srikrishna Report did not take into account. In another significant difference, the NHRC Report directed the state government to rebuild places of Muslim worship destroyed in the violence. It gave a detailed list of all destroyed mosques and madrassas and emphasized the importance of this measure in rebuilding the lost confidence of the Muslim community. The Srikrishna Report was clinical in its assessment of casualties, reducing them to statistics, whereas the NHRC stresses the need for post-trauma counselling of victims and the provision of better facilities at relief camps.

The second difference was at the level of implementation or concrete outcome. The Srikrishna Report had merely confined itself to a statement about the need for speedy trials. In this context, it is interesting to consider Thomas Hansen's argument with regard to the role of the Srikrishna Commission in legitimating the state. He argues that the appointment of the Commission helps to sustain the 'myth of the state' as sublimely sovereign and an impartial arbiter between social factions. The Commission is thus a mechanism as also a site for the state to legitimize itself as the guarantor of security and justice for its citizens.[38] He argues that the commission and the court proceedings can be seen as 'state spectacles', 'public displays of the state as a producer of impartial and universal justice' as well the 'profane sides of state power in the form of brutality and misconduct by politicians, officials and police.'

To overstate the case, the implementation of recommendations was never really the mandate, or the intention, of the Srikrishna commission. This statement can be extended to cover all other commissions of inquiry as well. Usually, by the time reports come to written after overcoming the various procedural hurdles in the way, they are far from useful. Very often commissions are appointed by the government in power to buy time and evade responsibility.

In this regard, the NHRC report seemed to chart out a different path. As we have seen, the NHRC Report both recognized the need for speedy and fair trials to enable the healing of community wounds, and pursued avenues for their implementation. In the end however, implementation was confined to the singular issue of transferring (a discrete number of) cases outside the state of Gujarat. And with the dramatic turnaround of the Best Bakery case documented earlier, the 'wheels of justice' have once again ground to an all-too-familiar halt. In the absence of any wide-ranging restructuring of political, judicial— indeed constitutional—orders, and without a transformation in political will, the NHRC inquiry remains an isolated, 'exceptional' intervention.

CONCLUSION

From the Mumbai violence in 1992-93 to the Gujarat pogrom in 2002, Hindu-Muslim riot cases have invariably *not* resulted in conviction and prosecution of the communally guilty. Over the past fifteen years the reluctance of the party in power and unwillingness of the administration to make timely interventions to prevent violence has become a central concern for minorities and their relationship to the state. Hindu-Muslim violence is of course not new. As we can see from the two major episodes of violence, what is new is the active (or passive) involvement of government and administration in the riots against minority communities. In the post-violence phase—from the registration of cases, to the gathering of evidence, to the prosecution of the accused, to the delivery of justice in courts—the judicial process has been allowed to become a casualty to political processes, or executive fiat. Since the episodes of large-scale communal violence are usually fomented by political elites to advance their own political agenda, shielding the guilty is an accepted part of the post-conflict political process. Not only has this alienated minorities; it signals to the public at large that immunity for grave crimes is the rule in India; the powerful cannot be brought to book; the law is only applied against the underprivileged and powerless.

Four years after the Gujarat killings justice has not been done.[39] The acquittal of the accused in the Best Bakery case raised serious questions about the capacity of the state government and legal system to punish the guilty. The tragic twists and turns in this high profile case underscore the complexity of winning a court case against mass crimes, especially when these crimes are well organized and enjoy the support of local and powerful political organizations. In the case of the Bombay riots, a similar pattern can be observed. Thus despite the considerable evidence of the Shiv Sena's involvement in mass crimes, legal intervention has been conspicuous by its absence. The failure to dispense justice in such cases is not an instance of justice being denied or derailed; rather it involves a deeper, more complex pattern of inaction and the incapacity of the political and legal system to deal with large-scale communal violence.[40] This is not because things go wrong in one individual case, such as the Best Bakery case. Instead, the recurrent breakdown of prosecutions indicates a pattern of institutional bias against minorities that may well be responsible for the lack of justice.

There are at least three major reasons for the abysmal record of justice in cases of mass violence against minorities. The foremost is the lack of political will to stop the violence, and later, to punish its perpetrators. Comparative evidence clearly shows that large-scale rioting does not take place when there is a political will to stop it and the police force is ordered to do so. The complicity of political and administrative personnel remains the primary issue and this needs to be addressed frontally, for without it justice has no chance.

Independent inquiries and newspaper investigations have found that local administration and law and order agencies had the capacity to prevent violence but failed to take preventive action, because of direct orders from the top or because they feared retribution if they acted without seeking political approval.[41] A. S. Samra, Bombay's former police commissioner, observed: 'Our penal code and our idea of justice revolves around the idea that individuals commit crimes and are punished, whereas political parties as a whole do politics. There might be individuals within these parties who commit crimes, even leaders, but they must be punished as individuals. What can we do to an organization? Ban it? This is difficult to do more permanently in a democracy?'[42] The contention that it is difficult to convict murderers in riot cases is debatable. There is something wrong in suggesting that cold-blooded murders committed in front of a large number of people by known locals are impossible to detect and prosecute.

Both the Srikrishna and NHRC Reports indicted incumbent governments for inaction during the periods of violence. Both cases make it amply clear that violence was not just an act of failure but part of a design.[43] Yet, the political will to uphold the rule of law was simply not there. The Bombay and Gujarat violence and their aftermath epitomize the irresponsibility of political parties and the broader inadequacies of their engagement in the justice process. Even parties who oppose communal politics have not had the courage to propose any specific reform, systemic or otherwise, to deal with the legal and political aspects of riots and to discourage parties from engineering mass violence for the sake of electoral advantage. This is despite the fact that the scale of death and destruction wrought by communal violence is greater than any single instance of terrorism or caste atrocities, the two recurring problems for which India has for years had special laws.[44] The principle of adopting stringent laws and provisions to deal with the scourge of terrorism and caste violence should apply to communal violence as well. But this requires a consensus that the perpetrators of violence against minorities should be brought to book in the same way as persons responsible for caste atrocities. Such a consensus is clearly not there, which is hardly surprising given the position of communal violence as an acceptable form of political violence in modern India. As other essays in this volume have established, communal politics and discourse have been a central plank of the BJP/RSS for the past several decades; one that the Congress has repeatedly shown it is not above using for its own advantage either.

The second difficulty arises from the infiltration of communalism into state structures, immobilizing the state and preventing it from being able to provide justice. Adding to the problem is that unlike caste violence, communal violence is not a structural problem, it is an institutional problem which often stems from communal biases and prejudices within society towards religious minorities. Communal prejudice is hard to identify and pinpoint and even harder to deal with. Even though communal violence is one-sided, there is a common perception that it is two-sided; hence, apportioning of blame against any group or set of individuals or pinning responsibility is extremely difficult. Thus, individuals indulging in such violence can resort to group mobilization to cover up their actions.[45] Perpetrators of communal violence can indulge in atrocities knowing fully well that their actions will go unpunished.

This should compel us to take cognizance of a pattern of 'institutional communalism' along the lines of the 'institutional racism' that is now widely acknowledged and addressed in the United Kingdom. Such an approach is urgently needed in India because the formal right to equality before the law can have substantive meaning only if we can find ways to neutralize the legal effects of discrimination in dealing with mass violence against minorities. There are very few Muslims in positions of authority in the police force, bureaucracy and political parties at the national or state level. Although there is no direct relationship between minority proportionality in the administration and levels of communal violence,[46] the presence of minorities in office and allocation of political positions provides opportunities to incorporate the concerns and interests of minority groups in the calculations of politicians belonging to a variety of groups.[47]

The third difficulty relates squarely to the incapacity of a legal system that simply does not work in cases of mass violence.[48] The complication might arise from using obsolete legal concepts to deal with mass killings which have the backing of the state. Injustice is recognized, but a 'nobody-can-really-be-blamed' in mob violence formula disguises the failure of the rule of law, and everyone is let off.[49]

One basic problem here is with regard to the definition of a 'riot'. For one, the definition is usually ambiguous; thus trying to prove a rioting case is very difficult. Next is the issue of criminal punishment and responsibility. The view of a 'riot as a mob explosion' resulting in a legal breakdown has dominated political thinking on communal riots. The most important task is taken to be the restoration of peace without controversy and without blaming anyone, rather than the carriage of justice.[50] Implicit in this approach of shunning controversy has been a repeated reluctance to use criminal law against named agents, particularly 'important people'. As Dhavan argues, 'in India political governance seeks to generalize the problem of riots out of existence in the name of peace; and legal governance, no less exactingly, seeks to individuate the problem out of existence by insisting on rigorous proof of individual complicity.'[51] Thus, the law punishes only those who give provocation for a riot (Section 153), provide the land for unlawful assemblies (Section 154), benefit from the riot (Section 155) or harbour those who participate in such unlawful acts (Section 156-7).[52] This partly explains the low conviction rate in India, because proving that individuals are guilty of the crime of rioting has always been difficult, especially given the laws of evidence of hostile groups in such cases.[53] It has also encouraged the myth that no one can really be punished for what happens in a riot because riots are political acts. This is the kind of deliberately created ambiguity through which L. K. Advani and others seek to escape both moral and legal blame arising out of their presence at the demolition of the Babri Masjid.

The Supreme Court Best Bakery judgment and the resignation of Jagdish Tytler from the Union Cabinet in 2005 over his alleged involvement in the 1984 violence mark the beginning of an attempt by the judicial and political process to deal with mass violence. This is a small but significant step, which has set a new benchmark for the pursuit of justice in India's democracy. For the first time since independence a politician who appears to be complicit in the violence has had to pay the political price for his involvement. It is a triumph of the rule of law and secular politics over moral indifference and communal injustice. No doubt, much more remains to be done to bring the guilty to book and deliver justice to the victims. Yet, the sacking of a minister from the union council of ministers is a positive gesture. Prime Minister Manmohan Singh's apology to the Sikh community in Parliament also will force the Congress and political parties to look at communal violence and post-conflict justice issues in way that has not been done before.[54] Political authorities cannot, as they have done in the past, sweep all questions under the debris or get away by expressing helplessness in dealing with communal violence.

In the end, however, justice is not the only issue at stake. Of equal importance is the issue of the state's responsibility to defend the citizen's fundamental right to life against communal depredations. Thus radical reform and corrective measures that include both police and judicial reform,[55] and witness protection schemes are necessary.[56] To ensure that such mass violence does not recur in future the government may need to introduce a law to deal with communal violence of the kind experienced in Bombay and Gujarat. Overall, stringent laws and preventive action on the lines of the Scheduled Castes/Scheduled Tribes Atrocities Act are in order.

With the tabling of the Communal Violence (Prevention, Control and Rehabilitation of Victims) Bill in the Indian Parliament in 2005, it would appear that the United Progressive Alliance government is demonstrating an unusual willingness to undertake such transformative measures. However, the Bill has been widely criticized by anti-communal groups, human rights organizations and women's groups. These citizen groups had also rejected earlier drafts of this bill, but few of their concerns have been addressed in the version of the Bill that was hurriedly tabled in the Rajya Sabha on 5 December 2005.

According to one commentator the basic flaw in the draft is that it cannot be invoked even when communal crimes take place unless the state or the central government decides to declare an area as communally disturbed. Therefore if a state has the support of the centre, it can engage in the worst kind of communal crimes and get away with it. The Act can only be invoked in the most extreme circumstances where there is criminal violence resulting in death or destruction of property and there is danger to the unity of the country. The most controversial provisions relate to granting immunity to the police and the army despite the fact that various Commissions of Inquiry have found the police and civil authorities either passive or partisan.[57]

It could be said, then, that the Communal Violence Bill continues to exceptionalize violence. Whether through the reservation of indictments for the most 'extreme' cases or the granting of immunity or exemption to civil and police authorities, the dislocation of violence from normal political processes of governance is the main thrust of the Bill. This is in part a reflection of the structure of law itself. And so, although it is offered as an investigation of the workings of law, government, and justice in the aftermath of mass violence, this essay concludes with a call to interrogate the limits of legal solutions to the problem of violence in India. While this does not mean that the quest for justice must be abandoned, it requires an engagement with the wider political arena of post-colonial India, and the unexceptional, yet enduring, social, political, and economic inequities and discrimination that continue to endure long after the fires of Gujarat, Bombay, Delhi, Bhagalpur, or Meerut have faded from our line of sight.

Notes

1 I most grateful to Rajeev Dhavan, Senior Advocate in the Supreme Court for discussions on the criminal justice system and for making available legal materials on riots and the criminal justice system, Amrita Basu and Srirupa Roy for editorial support, and Vasundhara Sirnate, Adnan Faruqui and Manzur Ali for providing research support for this article.

2 *India: Abuse of the law in Gujarat: Muslims detained illegally in Ahmedabad*, Report of the Amnesty International, 2003.

3 See chapter on 'State Capacity Explanations' in Steven Wilkinson, *Votes and Violence: Electoral Competition and Communal Riots in India* (Cambridge: Cambridge University Press, 2005).

4 Ibid., 85.

5 The data released by the Home Ministry affirms that prior to the Babri Masjid demolition, the percentage of Muslim victims in communal riots was 80%. Post-Babri demolition the ratio might have become more adverse to Muslims. Cited in Ram Punyani, 'Is Riot Free India a Possibility, *Counter Currents*, 15 September 2005.

6 Thomas Blom Hansen, *Urban Violence in India: Identity Politics, 'Mumbai', and the Post-Colonial City* (Delhi: Permanent Black, 2002).

7 According to the Amnesty International, 1,788 people were killed in Mumbai.

8 Gujarat violence has been documented in many reports: *Concerned Citizen's Tribunal Report*, 2002, *Gujarat Carnage 2002: A Report to the Nation*, April 2002; *State-Sponsored Carnage in Gujarat, March 2002; Communalism Combat*, 2002.

9 *General Elections to the Gujarat Legislative Assembly*, Election Commission of India Press Note, 16 August 2002. No. ECI/PN/35/2002/MCPS, 15.

10 Ibid., 15.

11 See especially the NHRC Report, 2002.

12 On this aspect see cover story 'Communal Fascism in Gujarat: Appeasing the Hindu Right on Ayodhya', *Frontline*, 29 March 2002.

13 Established in 1993 under statute—The Protection of Human Rights 1993—the NHRC is an important institution for defending human rights. Headed by an ex-Chief Justice of India and including judges from the Supreme Court and High Court and others, it is a distinguished body which has to date made significant interventions despite its limited powers.

14 For details of the Gujarat government's response to the riots see

27 Ibid.

28 Hosbet Suresh, 'And Justice For All', *The Little Magazine* (New Delhi), 25 July 2003.

29 'India's Dismal Record in Riot Convictions', *The Times of India*, 12 May 2005.

30 *NHRC Final Report*, 21 May 2002

31 Rajeev Dhavan, 'Criminal (In)Justice System', *Journal of the NHRC*, 2 (2003).

32 V. Venkatesan, 'For a Fair Trial', *Frontline*, 29 August 2003.

33 'Most Wanted: Gujarat Best Bakery Case Shows the Criminal Justice System at Its Worst', *The Indian Express*, 30 June 2003; 'Speedy Injustice', *The Times of India*, 30 June 2003.

34 'Charred Justice', *The Statesman*, 1 July 2003, 'Fixing Witnesses', *The Hindu*, 1 July 2003, 'Justice Blindfolded', *The Hindustan Times*, 30 June 2003, 'Half Baked Justice, *The Hindustan Times*, 4 July 2003.

35 The NHRC in its SLP pointed out that even though the principal witnesses turned hostile, the Fast Track Trial court judge Justice Mahida made no attempt to ascertain why this was happening, the cross-examination was perfunctory, trial was reduced to a farce by doing away with a detailed cross-examination by the investigating officer who took the witness stand. For details see V. Venkatesan, 'For a Fair Trial'.

36 *The Times of India*, 14 April 2004.

37 Teesta Setalvad, 'Long Wait for Justice', *Communalism Combat*, October 2003.

38 Thomas Blom Hansen, 'Governance and Myths of State in Mumbai', in C. J. Fuller and Veronique Benei (eds.), *The Everyday State and Society in Modern India* (Delhi: Social Science Press, 2000).

39 Teesta Setalvad, Gujarat Genocide Victims: Waiting for Justice', *Communalism Combat*, June 2005.

40 Rajeev Dhavan, 'Justice, Justice and the Best Bakery Case', *India International Quarterly*, New Delhi, Monsoon 2003; and 'Riots as Murder: Re-examining the Best Bakery Case'. Available online at http:// www.sabrang.com/spaper/rajivdhavan.pdf

41 Dhavan, 'Justice, Justice and the Best Bakery Case', 94-95.

42 Quoted in Hansen, *Urban Violence in India*, 140.

43 Indira Jaising, '1984 in the Life of a Nation', *The Indian Express*, 1 November 2004.

44 Manoj Mitta, 'In 2004, a Response to Gujarat', *The Indian Express*, 20 February 2004.

'"We Have No Orders to Save You", State Participation and Complicity in Communal Violence in Gujarat', *Human Rights Watch* 14:3 (2002).

15 See for example 'Modi Ties Hands of Cops Who put Their Foot Down', *The Indian Express*, 26 March 2003.

16 Details in R. B. Sreekumar, 'Diary of a Police Officer', *The Indian Express*, 16-17 April 2004.

17 Harsh Mander, 'State Subversion: Gujarat Victims Completely Isolated', *The Times of India*, 22 November 2003.

18 In *R. Gandhi v. Union of India*, the Madras High Court held the state liable to pay compensation to victims of anti-Sikh riots in the wake of Mrs Indira Gandhi's assassination. AIR 1989 Madras 205

19 Harsh Mander, *Cry, My Beloved Country: Reflections on the Gujarat Carnage* (Delhi: Rainbow Publishers 2004), 80-2.

20 *The Hindustan Times*, 21 March 2002.

21 *Amnesty International*, 'A memorandum to the government of Gujarat on its duties in the aftermath of violence', 28 January 2005.

22 The State's liability to pay compensation for tortuous actions has been well established in a number of recent cases. *Union Carbide v. Union of India* (1991) 4 SCC 82; *D.K. Basu v. State of West Bengal* (1997) 1 SCC 584; *Nilabati Behera v. State of Orissa*, (1993) 2 SCC 746; *Chairman Railway Board v. Chandrima Das* (2000) 2 SCC 465.

23 Report of Delhi-based Forum for Fraternity and Reconciliation, published in *The Hindu*, 29 July 2002. In *Challa Ramkonda Reddy v. State of AP*, the Andhra Pradesh High Court held the state liable for constitutional tort even for inaction of its officials. AIR 1989 AP 235.

24 *The Indian Express*, 22 August 2003.

25 Rules regarding these commissions are outlined in the Commissions of Inquiry Act, 1952. The 1952 Act has this to say about what a commission of inquiry is: 'The appropriate Government may, if it is of opinion that it is necessary so to do, and shall, if resolution in this behalf is passed by each House of Parliament or, as the case may be, the Legislature of the State, by notification in the Official Gazette, appoint a Commission of Inquiry for the purpose of making an inquiry into a matter of public importance and performing such functions and within such time as may be specified in the notification and the Commission so appointed shall make the inquiry and perform the functions accordingly.'

26 Srikrishna Report findings cited in Praveen Swami, 'A Searing Indictment', *Frontline*, 11 September 1998.

45 The classic example of such group solidarity was Modi's repeated invocation of Gujarat's *asmita* (pride) in the post-violence situation, hence implicit protection for the perpetrators of criminal violence.

46 Wilkinson, *Votes and Violence*, 129-32.

47 Wilkinson develops an important argument along these lines. Ibid.

48 Rajeev Dhavan, 'Is India's 'Best' Justice Good Enough?' *The Hindu*, 25 July 2003.

49 Ibid.

50 Rajeev Dhavan, 'Criminal (In)Justice System', Journal of the NHRC, 2 (2003).

51 Ibid.

52 Wilkinson, *Votes and Violence*, 89-90.

53 Ibid.

54 The Prime Minister in the Rajya Sabha on 11 August 2005: 'Sir, I have no hesitation in saying that what took place after Indira ji's death was a great national shame, a great national tragedy,' *The Indian Express*, 13 August 2005.

55 For instance, the failure of a policeman, bureaucrat or minister to take all necessary and reasonable measures within his/her power to prevent or control mass violence must render him/her liable for punishment.

56 See Siddharth Varadarajan, 'Moral Indifference as the Form of Modern Evil', *The Hindu*, 14 August 2005.

57 There is also the concern that it would encroach on state rights and it has the potential of misuse against any state governments. On some of these aspects see Colin Gonsalves, 'The Contours of a Communal Violence Law', *The Indian Express*, 12 August 2005.

COMMUNALIZING THE CRIMINAL OR CRIMINALIZING THE COMMUNAL?
Locating Minority Politics in Bangladesh

DINA M. SIDDIQI

In this essay, I critically analyse the 'place' of the minority Hindu population in contemporary Bangladesh, especially as it is reflected in competing discourses on violence against minorities. I locate contested understandings of such violence in local, national and international contexts, keeping in mind the mutually constitutive and fluid nature of such frames of reference. I ask what discursive spaces are available for public discussions of minority politics. Drawing on a particularly symbolic moment of crisis—targeted violence against minorities following Parliamentary elections in October 2001—I trace the possibilities, silences and slippages embedded in representations of the event. I use the 'critical event'[1] of post-election violence, taken as a signpost for the future by many, to interrogate popular understandings of the place of minorities in the nation and the underlying gendered politics of representation. I argue that majoritarian imaginations tend to exhibit a fundamental 'misrecognition'[2] of the historical and structural factors that render minority communities—especially Hindus—susceptible to state and non-state violence. By the same token, misrecognition of a different order can be found in the discursive strategies of those who are the most vocal in protecting minority interests.

OUTSIDER GENEALOGIES: THE AMBIVALENT PLACE OF HINDUS AS CITIZENS

In Bangladesh, public discourse on the 'minority problem'[3] tends to veer between ostrich-like denial and a call to arms that verges on rhetorical excess in moments of crisis. This 'excess' can be understood as a fall-out of the syndrome of misrecognition, a subject to which I will return. Silence, denial and a not-so benign neglect are hallmarks of majoritarian responses to reports of discrimination and violence faced by ethnic or religious minorities. Ask any Muslim Bangladeshi about communalism, nine times out of ten, s/he will tell you it doesn't exist, that communal riots happen in India, not in Bangladesh. Indeed, there is a great deal of pride that the pogrom against Muslims in Gujarat in 2002 did not result in retaliatory violence against Hindus in Bangladesh. Suffice it to say, the absence of 'riots' does not necessarily indicate the absence of all forms of violence. Among other things, riots require two relatively equal sides to battle it out.[4]

The actual number of non-Muslims in Bangladesh remains a subject of contestation. Religious and ethnic minorities constitute close to 15% of the , if unofficial estimates are to be believed. Official statistics place the figure at 11.7%.[5] Ethnic communities have long insisted that their numbers are underestimated in official census figures—a move they claim is calculated to diminish their significance as a group and highlight their numerical minority status. For the most part minorities are conspicuous by their absence in the public sphere, in the judiciary, in the administration as well as in academic institutions, business and entertainment. At present, there is no cabinet minister, no ambassador, no Supreme Court judge, no vice-chancellor and no senior armed forces officers from a minority community.[6]

In his essay in this volume, Willem van Schendel notes the territorial ambiguity of processes of state formation in post-Partition South Asia. He argues that the 'rough edges' inherited by post-colonial states have engendered specific forms of violence, territoriality and sovereignty. Van Schendel's argument throws light on the 'awkward place' of Hindu-Bengalis in the new nation of East Pakistan. As I will argue, the structural embeddedness of Hindu-Bengalis as the Other in the foundational narrative of (East) Pakistan was to have repercussions well beyond Partition. The messiness and territorial uncertainties of post-Partition East Pakistan/Bangladesh are deeply implicated in the production of violence against groups that do not easily fit into the foundational narratives of the nation. The latent 'Othering' of Hindus has been recuperated by successive incarnations of the East Pakistani and Bangladeshi states at specific moments of crisis.

From the outset, the cultural practices of the East Pakistani state attempted to construct Pakistani national identity as fundamentally incompatible with existing Bengali culture, which itself was cast as Hindu in essence. The putative opposition between the cultural categories of Bengali and Muslim had a much earlier genealogy, however. In the late 19th and early 20th centuries, members of the emergent Muslim-Bengali community were engaged in two simultaneous and seemingly contradictory struggles: to be recognized as authentically *Bengali* and as properly Muslim *at the same time*. On the one hand, in the eyes of the North Indian Urdu-speaking elite, that is, those who claimed to represent all Muslims in the colonial order of things, the credentials of Muslim-Bengalis had always been suspect. They were seen as converts from the lower castes who were much too Hinduized in their cultural and linguistic practices. Such an outlook had earlier provided one impetus for the various Islamic reform movements in Bengal. This perhaps is a reason why in the early definitions of the territories that would constitute Pakistan, Bengal was not considered.

On the other hand, for the majority of Hindu-Bengalis in colonial India, the category of Muslim-Bengali was an oxymoron. Socially, the Muslim-Bengali was dismissed as an inferior Other, again with alien cultural and linguistic practices. In the literary world, the 'chaste' (highly Sanskritized) Bengali used by Muslim writers such as Meer Mosharraf Hossain at best occasioned patronizing surprise from established figures such as Bankim Chandra Chattapadhyay. As a sign of praise, Bankim once said of Meer Mosharraf's writing style, 'many Hindus cannot write such a chaste Bengali as he has written.'[7]

The question of the purity of Bengali Islam resurfaced under Pakistani rule. In 1949, the Pakistan Central Minister for Education proposed replacing the Bengali alphabet with Arabic script in order to nationalize and Islamize the Bengali language. In the dominant state view,

> Not only Bengali literature, even the Bengali alphabet is full of idolatry. Each Bengali letter is associated with this or that god or goddess of Hindu pantheon . . . Pakistan and

> Devanagri script cannot co-exist. It looks like defending the frontier of Pakistan with Bharati soldiers! To ensure a bright and great future for the Bengali language it must be linked up with the Holy Qoran . . . Hence the necessity and importance of Arabic script.[8]

In this instance, religion was certainly 'a tool of domination' as commentators have noted.[9] Further, and critically for our purposes, the proposed 'cleansing' of Bengali culture of its 'Hindu' attributes left no place in the nation for its Hindu citizens.

The spectre of the Hindu as outsider, as not sufficiently Pakistani, and therefore not entitled to the same rights as other Pakistani citizens, was resurrected regularly in moments of state crisis. When such views were institutionalized in state practice or used to justify state appropriation of citizens' property, the long-term consequences could be devastating. The East Pakistan (Emergency) Requisition of Property Act of 1948 accorded the government the power to acquire, temporarily or permanently, any property it considered necessary for the administration of the state. The Act was widely used to appropriate the property of religious minorities. Several years later, the East Bengal Evacuees (Administration of Immovable Property) Act of 1951—allegedly necessitated by the exodus of Hindus to India—authorized the state to take charge of the property of an 'evacuee,' either by request or at its own discretion. The Act limited the power of the courts to question the orders passed or action taken under the Act. Predictably, Hindus living in East Pakistan were perpetually in danger of having their land requisitioned as evacuee property.

Under the provisions of the Defense of Pakistan Ordinance, promulgated in the wake of the Indo-Pakistan war of 1965, the government enacted through executive order The Enemy Property (Custody and Registration) Act of 1965. The Act identified India as an enemy country. It authorized the take-over of all interests of the enemy (nationals/citizens of India) in firms and companies and in lands and buildings for control or management. An accompanying circular specified that Muslims residing in India, including Indian citizens, were excluded from the category of 'enemy' even though the Act explicitly defined citizens or nationals of India as the enemy. The circular assured Muslim owners that their property would be handed over to them or their heirs on demand. In contrast, once the property of a member of a minority community had been taken over, their ownership right would lapse forever.[10]

The 1965 Act quite literally institutionalized the construction of Hindu citizens as the 'enemy within', whose loyalty to the nation was always suspect. Meanwhile the Muslim Indian, by virtue of religion, could always lay claims on the East Pakistani state.

RECASTING NATIONALISM THE ISLAMIC WAY

One could argue that Bangladesh is especially 'sovereignty-challenged' because the messiness of Partition feeds directly into the ambiguity inherent in the nation's existence as an independent *territorial* entity.[11] Secular Bengali nationalism, as originally defined, carried within it the seeds of (or *potential* for) territorial ambivalence that would later be exploited to promote communalized national identities. This is not to imply that the process *necessarily* involved a teleological unfolding in this direction. Events need not have taken a religious turn; had left politics been allowed to flourish for instance, the meanings of citizenship would have been entirely different.

Anxieties generated by the 'rough edges' of the post-Partition condition have been magnified by the unspoken need to justify the nation-state's existence in relation to West Bengal's cultural and geographical borders. For Bengali nationalism as articulated in 1971 was limited to the inhabitants of the territory of East Pakistan; it could not be extended to the Bengalis of India without undermining the essence of the new nation. At particular political conjunctures, this has generated particular kinds of cartographic anxiety.[12] That is to say, latent ruptures in national identity created one of the most critical conditions of possibility for the formation of national identity through a religious idiom and the subsequent production of violent spaces and identities. 'Am I Bengali or am I Muslim first?' was the frequent and agonized refrain of many a progressive intellectual and activist in the 1970s and 1980s. That the apparent contradiction was a historical construct hardly mattered in the heated debates that ensued.

The war in 1971 was formally articulated in terms of a struggle for a secular state based on the unity of Bengali national identity. The implicit 'privatization' of religion following Independence set aside rather than resolved simmering tensions between a secular Bengali identity and its relationship to religion. Between 1975 and 1990, successive military regimes took full advantage of the Bengali/Muslim question, and invoked versions of Islamic nationalism in a bid to secure their power bases. The deletion of the principles of secularism and socialism from the Bangladeshi constitution, the promotion of Islam to official state religion and the removal of a ban on political activity based on religion, marked key moments in state attempts to recast national identity. Other steps followed. For instance, under Generals Zia and Ershad, madrassa education received unprecedented attention; a significant chunk of the total education budget was allocated to the madrassa sector. This has continued to be the case until the present.[13] General Zia set up an Imam Training Academy in order to involve imams in 'development' related issues. In the mean time, the Bangladeshi state itself has been Islamized progressively in everyday representational practices, idioms and discourses. The rituals of the state continue to move toward an overt Islamism (for example prayers in Arabic on state airlines which have increased in duration and complexity in recent times, readings from the Koran to open state-sponsored public events, religious programmes on state-run television for children and the usage of the ostensibly more Arabized greeting *Allah hafiz* instead of *Khuda hafiz* among state functionaries etc.)

Fifteen years of military rule also laid the groundwork for the Islamization of everyday political culture. The restoration of parliamentary democracy in 1990/91 consolidated the process. By the mid 1990s, Islamic symbols and idioms had become part of everyday political vocabulary. Earlier, toward the end of General Ershad's regime, the two major political parties, the Bangladesh Nationalist Party (BNP), and the Awami League (AL), began to draw strategically on Islamic ideology in their bid to challenge the dictator. Ershad had already instituted Islam as a state religion and was actively promoting what he called a 'mosque-based' society. Friday sermons at different mosques attended by the General became high profile events. Ironically, the main Islamist party, the Jamaat-i-Islami (JI)—notorious for its collaboration with the Pakistani army in 1971—was opposed to Ershad's regime.

Thus, the JI also took part in the struggle to reinstate a democratic political system. At different moments both the BNP and the AL sought out potential electoral alliances with the JI, thereby conferring on the party the political respectability it had earlier lacked.[14]

It would be too easy to posit a linear historical progression from secularism to religious fundamentalism in Bangladesh, with the JI as the central actor, which is how conventional narratives would have it. The presence of JI and other Islamists in national politics in the 1980s and 1990s undoubtedly contributed to the broader process of mainstreaming religion in public culture, as scholars have pointed out.[15] However, it is overstating the case that Jamaat's presence in the political arena was the fundamental factor in reshaping public discourse along these lines. The JI's presence was helpful; it enabled the 'transition' to be smoother than would otherwise have been possible. Nevertheless, total focus on the JI overlooks a critical factor and major driving force behind the mainstreaming of Islamic discourse in Bangladesh. This was the consolidation of an 'alternative' national identity proferred by the BNP that had slowly been taking place since 1975. From its inception, the BNP espoused Bangladeshi (as opposed to Bengali) nationalism which is explicitly Islamic in character and which distinguishes between the Bengali-speaking populations of India and Bangladesh. The BNP's ideology is also implicitly anti-Indian.[16] In contrast, the AL has for long been projected in the public imagination as pro-Indian and to a great extent pro-Hindu/anti-Islamic, attributes that have come to be fused with the party's version of secularism. In the circumstances, especially before parliamentary elections in 1996, the AL party leadership was unwilling to take the political risk of being labelled anti-Muslim by sticking to a purely 'secular' agenda. The BNP used the shadow of India, the ostensibly threatening Hindu neighbour and regional bully, to promote its parochial religio-nationalist agenda. The AL did not resist.

No surprise, then, that the AL, which had spearheaded the movement for a secular state, began to position itself as a party that valued Islam as an integral part of national cultural identity. Shortly before parliamentary elections in 1996, the AL leader, Sheikh Hasina performed the Muslim pilgrimage or Haj with much fanfare. Eager to exhibit her personal piety, she emerged in public fully clothed in black headdress, long black-sleeved blouse and prayer beads in hand.[17] Once Hasina 'capitulated,' other women followed suit; it became almost impossible for women holding high political office to leave their heads uncovered. As things stand today, political leaders compete to 'out-Islamicize' one another. The most recent example is the careful staging of the final day of the *Biswa Ijtema*—the largest congregation of Muslims in the world, second to the Haj, that takes place every year outside Dhaka. This once relatively insignificant event has risen in profile. This year, both the Prime Minister and the Leader of the Opposition were conspicuous by their presence at the *Akheri Munajat* or final prayers of this otherwise all-male gathering.

In short, the compulsion on the part of political parties to exhibit Islamic piety was driven as much by latent contradictions in nationalist ideology as by the institutionalization of Islamist politics in the public sphere. The success of the BNP's 'Bangladeshi nationalism' was enabled by its ability to 'fill' the cracks in Bengali nationalist ideology. Rather than contend with the Bengali/Muslim dichotomy Bangladeshi nationalism attempted to cover over the potential contradictions of secular Bengali nationalism. Not the JI but the ambivalent place of Islam in nationalist ideology, which had previously been a spectre, returned to haunt the polity with a vengeance. By acquiescing to—rather than challenging—ever narrowing battles over national identity based on the religious/secular dichotomy, especially in the context of the long-term suppression of left political alternatives, mainstream political parties closed off other available terms of debate. In the process, Bangladeshi Hindus were further marginalized.

COMMUNALIZATION OR CRIMINALIZATION?

Election monitors declared the parliamentary elections of 1 October 2001, in which the incumbent AL was defeated by the BNP and its JI allies, to have been carried out in a free and fair manner. Voter turnout was impressively high, including that of women voters. However, not everyone was able to vote freely. In many places, members of minority religious or ethnic communities were subjected to severe intimidation before the elections, warned to stay away from polling booths or to vote for a specific party.

The period immediately following the elections was marred by systemic violence against AL supporters in general and Hindus—associated in the majoritarian imagination with AL supporters by virtue of their religion—in particular. Although violence during elections is fairly standard for Bangladesh, the backlash after the October elections was exceptionally severe and systematic. Human rights groups have documented forced entry into houses, severe beatings of men and women, and the looting and destruction of property. In addition, the abduction and rape of women occurred in an unprecedented manner across the country. The violence unfolded primarily in rural areas, especially in the southwestern districts that still have a fairly large proportion of Hindu groups. Ain o Salish Kendra (ASK), a human rights organization, characterized the post-election period as a 'reign of terror' and noted in its annual report:

> Though political gangsterism has been identified as one of the most serious threats to democracy in recent years, levels of electoral violence against the minority Hindu community and supporters and workers of the AL were unprecedented in 2001. The newly elected government tended to downplay the incidents and administration, including the police, remained largely ineffective, thus indirectly encouraging the political gangs. The Home Minister acknowledged in Parliament on 18 November 2001 that some 266 murders and 213 rapes were recorded in the first 25 days of October across the country. Higher figures were reported in the newspapers. These exceeded all records of atrocities in previous elections.[18]

The Home Minister did not provide a breakdown of these statistics—which were presumably on the conservative side—by religious or ethnic community. Based on their own investigation and newspaper reports, ASK determined that between 15 September and 27 October, 17 murders, 61 rapes, 666 injuries, 64 assaults of a sexual nature and 13 abductions occurred involving members of the Hindu community.[19] However, signs of post-election violence had been evident since July. It is worth noting that in the fortnight before 1 October, 164 incidents of intimidation or violence, including physical assault, extortion and looting, were highlighted in most major newspapers. Over the next month (between 1 and 27 October) the media recorded 449 more such incidents. The violence peaked during the first two weeks after the BNP-JI victory.[20]

Predictably, the government refused to acknowledge the specificity or extensiveness of minority persecution, discounting human rights reports as exaggerated or manufactured. The new government disregarded appeals by human rights groups to provide protection for minorities, and to initiate proper investigations into these incidents. Local ruling party cadres systematically intimidated and terrorized victims and witnesses, threatening them with further violence if they resisted. Police stations invariably refused to accept cases lodged by the few who dared to turn to law enforcement authorities for protection or justice. In the face of government indifference and disregard, ASK filed a writ petition with the High Court Division of the Supreme Court regarding the failure of the state to protect minority rights. The government responded almost a year later with an appeal. The case is still pending a final hearing.

The violence, instigated primarily by supporters of the victorious BNP-JI combine, appeared to have as its immediate objective the desire to discipline or put in their place those who had dared—or were assumed to have dared—to support the losing party. Post-election events highlighted just how awkward an imputed identity between Hindus and the AL could be in practice. Many Hindus were forewarned that should they venture out to vote, the consequences would be dire: they would be killed or their houses destroyed and they along with their families forced to relocate to India. Paradoxically, the AL allegedly warned minority voters that they would have to answer to local leaders if they refused to vote. Indeed, in the face of electoral loss, Muslim AL political leaders in some cases turned on local Hindus, holding them responsible for the party's defeat. In addition, in many instances 'terrorists[21] took advantage of the situation and indulged in extortion and looting of property.' Indeed, elections appeared to have been yet another opportunity for financial gain for the local criminal-political nexus. Hindu families were frequently compelled to provide substantial *chanda* or protection money in order to save themselves and their property from attacks. As one commentator noted, the reasons behind the violence were not limited to communal factors but were structural and political.[22]

In an effort to understand the severity of election-related targeting of minorities in 2001, Meghna Guhathakurta has traced the implications of recent processes of class formation in Bangladesh.[23] In her analysis, she foregrounds the politics of extortion that typified the AL regime of Sheikh Mujibur Rahman in the immediate post-Independence period. Guhathakurta notes that a change in regime in 1975 did not change the basic extortionist tendencies inherent in the previous regime. In many instances, beneficiaries of the previous regime changed their political affiliations in order to retain their lucrative ties to the state. Under General Zia, 'corruption became institutionalized.' Zia's successor General Ershad took 'state-sanctioned' corruption to new heights. Guhathakurta points out that Ershad's forced resignation in 1990 heralded an unprecedented polarization in party politics between the BNP and the AL, one that affected all levels. Most civil society forums, public universities and even the national Bar Association, are now divided along party lines. Yet, 'it is important to bear in mind that the polarization occurred at a superficial ideological level of Bangali versus Bangladeshi nationalism . . . The polarization did not happen at the level of class. Conflicts between Awami League and BNP were more about power-sharing than anything else . . . '[24] Guhathakurta characterizes the mode of conflict between the two parties as resembling the politics of *char-dokhol* (the occupation of charlands, a typically violent and confrontational process of expropriation). In other words, class formation through extortion, plundering and its attendant culture of violence is not a new phenomenon in Bangladesh. Guhathakurta's line of argument encourages us to understand the phenomenon of minority violence as one in which communalization and criminalization are deeply entangled. Indeed, as should be clear by now, it is difficult to draw lines between communalization and criminalization and between state-sanctioned violence and violent acts perpetrated by non-state actors.

Some scholars have recently argued for the need to recognize the coevality of violence and non-violence, in contrast to more conventional views that understand violence as a moment of rupture in the normal order of things. Writing in the context of North India, Paul Brass states that the boundaries between violence and power, state and society, official and private violence can be fuzzy.

> [. . .] there are sets of forces operating in pursuit of their own interests, which include dacoits, police, villagers who belong to distinct castes and communities, and politicians. These forces do not operate on opposite sides of a dichotomous boundary separating the mechanisms of law and order from those of criminals [. . . In this context, a criminal act] provides the occasion for the testing of relationships and alliances, or for the forming of new ones.[25]

Brass's observations on north India are equally applicable to rural Bangladeshi society, where violence is embedded in everyday social and political relationships, and the lines between state and society are constantly blurred. Those outside the purview of state power, such as religious minorities, are rendered especially vulnerable in this situation.

In short, to understand the particular nature of violence against minorities, we need to understand the specific structure and organization of violence as it functions in and through social practices. We need to locate the emerging cultures of intimidation that have been produced by the state's mode of governance. For an extraordinary 'lawlessness' prevails in Bangladesh, one that bears continuities with past modes of plunder and yet is new and unpredictable in some of its forms. Local modes of governing are now intimately dependent on the promise of violence; fear, intimidation and actual violence are enmeshed in everyday practices of governing. Located in the countryside, these emergent cultures of intimidation are protected, if not always openly supported, by powerful elites who are at the political centre. It would not be an exaggeration to say that the right to extortion and appropriation has become a reward for political loyalty. The structure and operation of political parties, the centralization of power in the capital and the persistence of patronage politics promote and reward criminalization. This process often takes on a communal colour. Members of Parliament locate themselves in Dhaka, leaving local affairs in the hands of party stalwarts who exercise control over local administration as well.[26] Central leaders tend to turn a blind eye toward or even to protect those involved in extortionary practices at the local level, especially if it is in the aftermath of an electoral victory. And, as Guhathakurta notes, it is easier to justify extortion and other criminal practices to political leaders if the targets happen to be political opponents, or those outside the purview of state power.[27]

Moreover, the premium on land as a commodity greatly enhances links between criminalization and communalization. As mentioned in an earlier section of the paper, the Enemy Property Act, of 1965 basically empowered the government to seize the property of anyone who migrated to India, even temporarily, or was considered to have abandoned the country during periods of conflict with India. The newly created Bangladeshi government, instead of abolishing this Act, renamed it the Vested Property Act and used it to take over the property of non-Bengalis or 'Biharis'. In practice and in effect, the Vested Properties Act institutionalized land grabbing and simultaneously challenged the loyalty of those citizens who were not Muslim. It is widely recognized that the Act has been a tool in the hands of rural elites to dispossess and displace Hindus.[28] One study estimates that almost 40% of all Hindu households have been affected by the Vested Property Act; 44% of the individual beneficiaries belong to the AL, 32% to the BNP and the rest to other smaller parties.[29] Clearly, material incentives are a primary driving force in the exploitation of Hindus. By the same token, legalized discrimination in the form of the Vested Property Act, and the constant fear of dispossession of property, works to encourage the exodus of Hindus to India. Of late, fear of material dispossession has been overlaid with anxiety over personal safety, particularly the safety of Hindu women. For many Hindus, fear of being unable to defend the 'chastity' of wives, daughters and sisters has become the dominant trope around which decisions to stay or leave are made.

The institutionalized structures described above have over time produced and enabled silence, complicity and indifference among the majority Muslim population. Meanwhile, the activities and rhetoric of the BNP and JI provide—directly or indirectly—impetus, cover and passion for a newly reconfigured project of spatial and categorical purification. If the AL appeared to extend proprietary rights over the Hindu community, the BNP-Jamaat combine seemed poised to remind Hindus of the fragility of their entitlements as citizens. In the months prior to the election, much of the rhetoric of intimidation drew on the putatively outsider status of Hindus. Reportedly, in one warning to women and minorities to stay away from polling booths, Muslim women were told they would face public disrobing (and its attendant loss of honour, *bey ijjoti*) if they dared to vote. Minorities—men and women—were threatened with eviction from the country (*desh chara kora hobey*) if they exercised their right to vote.[30] The threat of being pushed 'back' into India seemed to have been a predominant theme in the intimidation of minorities. It may have been reinforced by (the generally unsuccessful) attempt of the BNP-Jamaat combine to recast the election as a battle not only between the BNP and the AL but as one between Islam and Hinduism in Bangladesh. So, for instance, prominent JI MP Delwar Hossain Saidee is said to have characterized the elections as a battle between Hindus and Muslims, and warned that voting for Hindu candidates would render a Muslim's prayers unacceptable and make him or her ineligible for a Muslim burial. BNP candidates reportedly called the elections a struggle between the *tupi* (Muslim prayer cap) and the *dhooti* (an item of clothing that in Bangladesh is associated with Hindu men).[31] Ironically, the evidence does not indicate that Hindus vote as a block or uniformly for the AL. In fact, the parents of Purnima, the young girl whose experience is narrated later in the paper, lamented several times that their voting for the BNP in the 2001 election didn't protect them from violence. The idea of an entire religious group as a vote bank turns as much on a monolithic concept of 'the Hindu' as it does on stereotypes about the AL and what it represents.

At the same time, there has been a disturbing demographic decline in the Hindu population over the years. The proportion of Hindus in the total population has gone down from an estimated 28% in 1947, to 13.5 % in 1974, and 10.5% in 1991. In 2001, the census claimed that over 89% of Bangladeshis were Muslim. The accuracy of these figures may be questioned but the trend toward a decline in the Hindu population appears to be real. In the slow bleeding out of the minority population, one can discern echoes of earlier migrations during the Partition.

THE REPRESENTATIONAL POTENCY OF VIOLENCE

Increasingly, in struggles over property and land, and in relation to questions of community identity, women's bodies have become prime sites of contestation and signification. Interestingly, the various parties involved appear to be exceptionally aware of the potential benefits of highlighting or underplaying women's 'plight' as they foreground their particular agendas. Shortly after the parliamentary elections of October 2001, Purnima Rani Sheel, a schoolgirl in Ullapara, Sirajgonj, found herself at the centre of national and international attention. According to Purnima's testimony to a Magistrate, on 8 October, the fourteen-year-old was dragged out of her house, gang-raped for several hours and left unconscious in a nearby field. Earlier, other members of her family had been brutally beaten. Purnima identified several of her attackers as local men belonging to the BNP-JI alliance; like many of their counterparts across Bangladesh, they had been out celebrating their election victory by 'punishing' those they suspected of voting for the opposition party, the AL. The police refused to register a rape case initially, and Purnima's family faced considerable pressure to 'forget' the incident (including a substantial offer of money in exchange for silence). Sustained threats and intimidation from local groups kept the family on the run for several months afterwards.

Partly because urban-based activists took up her cause and partly because her family was willing to (had no option but to?) speak out, Purmina's became the name and the face symbolizing the predicament of religious minorities in Bangladesh. Her youth and innocence made her a perfect victim, so to speak, the violation of whose body could be made to stand for the injustices and violation of the minority community. Just two weeks after her ordeal, Purnima and her family travelled to Dhaka to attend a press conference to narrate their experiences firsthand. At the end of the press conference, convened by the Ekatturer Ghatok Dalal Nirmul Committee (Committee for Resisting the Killers and Collaborators of 1971), the family was presented with a check for 25,000 Taka. The Nirmul Committee, then headed by the journalist Shahriar Kabir, went around the country collecting testimonies about election violence and subsequently published these accounts in a volume. A haunting black-and-white photograph of Purnima, an artfully taken shot, graces the cover of this volume. The young girl is staring out beyond the viewer. A competing volume, sponsored by pro-government forces, came out soon afterward, also with Purnima's face on the cover. This time her face was turned away from the viewer, in shame. Inside, right-wing newspapers reported that Purnima had recanted, that the accusation of rape was a lie she was forced into by 'interested' parties. Many Bangladeshi Muslims chose to believe in the reported recantation. Indeed, one could almost hear a collective sigh of relief at this opportunity for absolution.

The faces and stories of Purnima and others can also be found on the internet, on a variety of sites, usually accompanied by an appeal for donations to help the victim. The rape narrative as the ultimate form of humiliation of the Hindu community has been appropriated by a wide spectrum of political groups. The Awami League's official website under the banner 'Humanity at Stake' carries a gallery of women and girls, Hindu and Muslim, who have been sexually assaulted because of their family's support for the party. Elision and refusal to be accountable on the part of the government was countered with sensationalism by the other side. Prominent intellectuals, some associated with the Awami League, alleged, among other things, that the situation in October was akin to ethnic cleansing and indeed worse than the massacre of Bengalis by the Pakistanis in Bangladesh's War of Liberation in 1971, since the perpetrators were fellow Bengalis this time. In October 2005, a massive three-volume document entitled 'White Paper: 1500 Days of Minority Persecution in Bangladesh' was published by the Committee for Resisting Killers and Collaborators of 1971. Approximately 3,000 pages long, the volumes contain newspaper clippings, articles, field reports and photographs of minority persecution in the 1,500 days between July 2001 and October 2005. The cover of the White Paper is a startling montage of graphic and often bloody photographs of Hindu victims of violence and persecution. The colour snapshots include the bludgeoned and bloodied remains of a man's head, his body intact, another head partially chopped off from the body, and numerous photographs of women and girls covering their faces in shame. The collage includes a shot of Purnima, head turned away, hands partially covering her face. To say the cover is disturbing or provocative would be an understatement. Hindus as a group are rendered into passive and disempowered bodies—the women 'violated' and the men brutalized. The introduction firmly rejects the idea that minority persecution could be 'political' rather than acts of communal aggression.

Rhetorical excess in reporting has serious negative consequences for everyone. The bid to gain attention by comparing October 2001 events with the horrors of 1971 makes it impossible to speak precisely about the violence that actually took place in 2001 without appearing to minimize it. Partisan excess closes down the few spaces left for activism, and silences secular Muslim voices. Over-dramatizing violence against Hindus in Bangladesh provides fodder for dominant conspiracy theories about Indian (read Hindu) efforts to undermine Bangladesh's image and sovereignty. Further, comparing 2001 with 1971 trivializes the deaths of an estimated one to three million Bengalis during the Independence struggle.

When I casually mentioned to a Muslim friend the subject of minority persecution, this is what he told me:

> When they are in Bangladesh, my Hindu friends will report incidents of violence by minimizing them. They may say to me, 'I was shoved in the bazaar yesterday.' But when I meet them in the US, their story expands, sometimes to the point of excess. The same event will be represented completely differently. They will say they were beaten to within an inch of their lives. I never knew that I was considered a threat to their sisters. It was only when we met in America that this came out.

What are the implications of this statement? Is it possible to ever get at the 'truth' of such events? Minorities themselves in Bangladesh have few, if any, safe spaces in which to speak about their predicament. Paradoxically, talk of violence carries great purchase elsewhere. The institutions of the state—the police, the law courts and the administration—discriminate against all marginalized groups, especially minorities. Majoritarian culture invisibilizes them. A few individuals and human rights organizations are the only mouthpieces available. In the circumstances, speech has been rendered a fraught, dangerous and valuable commodity. Location and audience determines what will be said and what must be censored. How does one intervene in the politics of representation ethically in the circumstances?

The figure of the violated Hindu girl/woman (echoing the rape of some 30,000 Bengali women by the Pakistani army in 1971) featured conspicuously in accounts of election-time violence.[32] However, violence against women is constitutive of general political and social disorder in contemporary Bangladesh and in some respects Purnima's experience of being refused protection and justice is not unique. Here, the dilemma for social analysts is a much rehearsed one, of how to represent and analyse the imbrications of gender and community identity, and to address the moral as well as political problems of writing about sexual violence. How do we represent such events *responsibly*, without glossing over a series of complex and evolving relationships, especially between criminalization and communalization, and without minimizing or sensationalizing the actual suffering involved?

Finally, does it make a difference whether we characterize minority violence as either communally or criminally instigated? What difference does it make and to whom? Jonathan Spencer notes the widespread tendency among social theorists to confuse economic explanations with rational ones, rationality with rationalization, or explanation with explaining away, 'as if the murder of a family is somehow more intellectually and morally acceptable if it can be shown to be connected to the pursuit of land or business, and is morally more problematic if it is connected to religious or cultural symbols.'[33] Indeed, most middle class Muslim Bangladeshis, theorists or otherwise, derive considerable comfort from attributing violence against minorities to economic rather than 'cultural/symbolic' causes. This not only renders the violence comprehensible but also absolves the majority community of responsibility and accountability.

GLOBAL CAPITAL AND TRANSNATIONAL TIES

September 11 and its associated after-effects have had a curiously double-edged impact on the space for minorities to make their claims on the majoritarian Muslim state. I would argue that this is directly related to the precarious position of Bangladesh in relation to global capital and politics. It goes without saying that the Bangladeshi state has never been a unitary, autonomously constituted entity. Among other things, transnational institutions and discourses—especially of the Bank-Fund and UN variety—have always been fundamental to its production, self-presentation and its practices. The government has found itself to be peculiarly vulnerable to transnational discourses on the dangers of militant Islam since the so-called war on terrorism was launched.

Bangladeshis have always been anxious about their place in the global order of things (in relation to India as well as to the 'West'). More recently, gender has come to work as a central trope in the construction of the national self-image, in a nation-state that is quite frankly, at this point, obsessed with its image in the international arena. Micro credit, increased female literacy and a successful family planning programme are all matters of national pride. Violence against women is not. The middle-class reaction to the emergence of *fatwa*-related violence several years ago was typical in this regard—the language used to describe the violence as medieval, barbaric, etc. revealed predictable fears of slipping back into a non-modern time and way of living. However, new fears have overtaken older colonial and developmentalist anxieties over modernity and global rankings. Faced with the 'War on Terror', state functionaries are much more concerned about the country's global image as constructed and circulated transnationally, and this has produced a corresponding tendency to silence, suppress, or censor any dissent or criticism—this includes cinematic representations, as well as international media coverage. For instance, the award winning film *Matir Moyna* (*The Clay Bird*, 2002) was reportedly censored not because of its depiction of the Independence struggle but because it had scenes of madrassa students learning to fight with bamboos. Apparently, the government was afraid that foreigners (Americans) would interpret the scene to indicate the presence of Islamic militant camps in Bangladesh. Fear of being labelled fundamentalist is not exactly misplaced, for being blacklisted by the US has direct adverse economic and political consequences both for the nation and for individual interests. The goodwill of the US is very important, so maintaining the image of a moderate Muslim country, with no communalism or fanaticism (not to mention unfailing support for the War on Terror) is just as important.

For minorities, such considerations have led to, on the one hand, some degree of state 'protection' (during major religious festivals, for instance), however reluctant, and on the other the denial and suppression of facts. Of course the state's refusal to recognize crimes against minorities has more than one reason behind it. At the international level, it is about the protection of image. At the level of national politics, those in power are committed to protecting their party cadres at the local level, who are the ones who usually benefit most directly from such violence. Third, specifically in relation to the political party in power, the government wants to maintain good relations with Islamist parties which are often complicit with the violence. Given the general lack of accountability for crimes, those who persecute minorities often literally get away with murder.

Many educated and secular Muslims, in an increasingly defensive mood, refuse to acknowledge the existence of any discrimination against minorities. In other words, there is little dissent from the majoritarian middle classes who feel increasingly besieged in an admittedly difficult global environment for Muslims, and who are also anxious about being excluded from the promises and profits of global capital because of their Muslimness.[34] Imagining themselves as global victims of anti-Islamist practices and rhetoric makes people much less willing to be critical of actual religious extremism and much more accepting of transgressions against minorities.

Paradoxically, the demonization of Islam enables other groups, especially some in the diaspora, to exploit the trope of victimhood themselves. At the same time that the Bangladeshi government was trying to convince the US to allow duty-free access of goods to the US market, the Human Rights Congress for Bangladeshi Minorities (HRCBM), a California-based group which reportedly had ties to the RSS and a very impressive website, was invoking the spectre of minority cleansing to lobby the US government to stop all imports of garments from Bangladesh until the government corrected the minority situation. Two years ago, a prominent Bangladesh-based group (the Hindu Bouddho Christian Oikyo Porishod) held an international meeting in Canada and invited the well-known right-wing commentator Daniel Pipes as the keynote speaker, a move that prompted protests from US-based Bangladeshis. Invariably, anything feeding into the general anti-Muslim vogue only makes the Bangladeshi government more defensive.

The demonization of Islam has also narrowed the discursive spaces available for reclaiming religion, spaces that were squeezed to begin with, so that it is difficult to separate what Ayesha Jalal calls religion as faith from religion as political marker.[35]

CONCLUSION

The Bangladeshi nation-state seems to be in a permanent state of emergency, suspending the 'normal' order of things, so that intimidation and violence have become routinized forms of conflict resolution. What we see is a shifting and hardening of existing cultures of hierarchy and coercion/intimidation, in which minorities form soft targets. At the same time, the *condition* of Hindu communities in the country has come to carry a profound ideological burden. Public discussions on the subject invariably slip into highly polarized party battle lines on nationalism, secularism, the Liberation War and the place of Islam. Only oppositional positions—anti- or pro-Indian, anti- or pro-secular—exist in this discursive universe.

The episodic violence unleashed on Hindu communities in the country, most recently surrounding the general elections in October 2001 during which a large number of Hindu women were reportedly abducted and raped, is neither arbitrary nor exceptional; such episodes are structurally embedded in long-term processes of contestation and expropriation, especially over land and other kinds of property. In the case of religious minorities, institutionalized discrimination (especially the existence of the Enemy/Vested Property Act) and the mainstreaming of Islam in public culture have been exacerbated by what in development-speak is referred to as a crisis in governance. One of the features of this is the widespread criminalization of politics and, in this case, the increasingly blurred lines between communalization and criminalization.

I have argued that the majority Muslim population is fundamentally unwilling to recognize the nature of violence against minorities. The factors that shape such misrecognition have changed over time. From the outset, the legacies and contradictions of Partition and subsequent institutionalized discrimination by the newly formed Pakistani state were critical in signifying the 'awkward' place of Hindus as citizens of the East Pakistani nation. British-colonial and Pakistani discourses conflating the cultural categories of 'Hindu' and 'Bengali', in opposition to 'Muslim', were only partially addressed in subsequent state-building processes. In independent Bangladesh, the *potentially* volatile contradictions of Bengali nationalism underpinning the nation's existence—that is, the fundamentally ambivalent nature of nationhood in relation to the cultural and literal borders of West Bengal—produced nationalist anxieties over territorial sovereignty among a segment of the population as India increasingly came to be perceived as a belligerent and threatening regional hegemonic power. More recently, these anxieties have been recast and refined. They are currently transposed onto questions of economic and cultural sovereignty in relation to India/West Bengal.[36]

Moreover, the state's conscious cultivation of cultural majoritarianism, the rehabilitation of Islamic political parties, including the Jamaat-i-Islami, into democratic political life, and the mainstreaming of Islam in public culture all implicitly promote an (heretofore) unspoken ambivalence toward the 'Hindu' as loyal citizen. The ensuing hardening of all religious identities in Bangladesh has been accompanied by blatantly visible but rising social and economic inequalities. Finally, an emergent siege mentality among the majority population in the wake of the so-called War on Terror further fuels the syndrome of (willing) misrecognition.

The erasure or denial of a distinct identity and the misrecognition of violence is met by what I call an 'excess of rhetoric' on the situation on the ground. This excess, I argue, does not necessarily have salutary effects on the lives of minority communities. Women and their bodies, as the ultimate symbolic site of community well-being and honour are trapped within these two discursive extremes.

Notes

1 See Veena Das *Critical Events: An Anthropological Perspective on Contemporary India* (New York: Oxford University Press, 1995).

2 By using the word misrecognition, I do not mean to imply the existence of a pure version of events that can be recognized with the right lenses. Rather, I am interested in tracing the specific forms of misrecognition produced by histories of cultural majoritarianism in this particular political context.

3 Minority issues are often interchangeable with those of Hindus in popular discourse. This may be in part because Hindus are the largest and most visible minority community. It may also stem from the contradictions of national identity formation that intimately involve questions of Hindu/Bengali/Muslim identity.

4 See Ali Riaz, *God Willing: The Politics of Islamism in Bangladesh* (Lanham: Rowman and Littlefield, 2005).

5 Subir Kumar Bhattacharya, 'Elections in Bangladesh and Minorities', in *The Daily Star*, 11 October 2005, 10

6 Ibid.

7 Quoted in Dhruba Gupta, 'Why Meer Mosharraf Hossain?' in *South Asia Research* 17:1 (1997), 3. The putative opposition between Bengali and Muslim, and the conflation of Hindu and Bengali, has carried over into contemporary historiographic traditions. For the most part, the prolific and much cited literature on colonial Bengal either ignores or marginalizes Bengali speakers who were Muslim. This is symptomatic of the field of gender as well, from Meredith Borthwick's pathbreaking work on the *Bhradramahila* to Mrinalini Sinha's analysis of colonial masculinity. The reinscription in current scholarship of the cultural hegemony of the Hindu *bhadralok* slides over the demographic contours of colonial Bengal, in which the majority—albeit a slim majority—of Bengali speakers were Muslim. In the work of the subaltern studies collective, and Ranajit Guha in particular, the stress on colonial difference leaves little space for the negotiation of local differences, or at least silences some critical differences while privileging others. The suppression of Muslim and

the foregrounding of tribal, for instance, allows uncontested notions of Bengaliness, and of a Hinduized Bengali nationalism to circulate unproblematically, thereby sidestepping the relationship between dominant strands of nationalism and communalism. Such exclusionary moves pushed Muslim-Bengalis outside the orbit of authentic Bengali culture. See Meredith Borthwick *The Changing Role of Women in Bengal, 1849-1905* (Princeton: Princeton University Press, 1984); Mrinalini Sinha *Colonial Masculinity: the 'Manly Englishman' and the 'Effeminate Bengali' in the Late Nineteenth Century*. (Manchester: Manchester University Press, 1995) and Ranajit Guha *Elementary Aspects of Peasant Insurgency in Colonial India* (Delhi: Oxford University Press, 1983). For an insight into the cultural dynamics involved, see Dipesh Chakrabarty, 'Remembered Villages: Representation of Hindu-Bengali Memories in the Aftermath of Partition,' *Economic and Political Weekly* (10 August 1996), 2143-51.

8 Cited in Amena Mohsin, 'Religion, Politics and Security: The Case of Bangladesh' in Satu Limaye, Mohan Malik and Robert Wiersing (eds.), *Religious Radicalism and Security in South Asia* (Honolulu: Asia-Pacific Center for Security Studies, 2003), 469.

9 Mohsin 'Religion, Politics and Security', 470.

10 Mohsin 'Religion, Politics and Security', 480.

11 van Schendel in this volume.

12 Sankaran Krishna, 'Cartographic Anxiety: Mapping the Body Politic in India,' in Michael J. Shapiro and Hayward R. Alker (eds.), *Challenging Boundaries: Global Flows, Territorial Identities* (Minneapolis: University of Minnesota Press, 1996), 193-214. In contempary Bangladesh, territorial anxieties abound. A recent example comes from a comment reportedly made by the Industries Minister and Ameer of the Jamaat-i-Islami (JI), Matiur Rahman Nizami. He is said to have claimed that country wide bombings in August 2005 were engineered by the Indian intelligence agency Research Analysis Wing (RAW), as part of a conspiracy to reintegrate Bangladesh into greater India. Meanwhile the apparent intractability of boundary setting continues to haunt official dealings between India and Bangladesh. In response to recent criticism by the current government about India's non-ratification of the Indira-Mujib Accord of 1974, the Indian High Commission in Dhaka issued a press release stating, among other things that, 'legislative requirements in India necessitate that the process of boundary demarcation be completed before ratification by the Indian Parliament.' India's ratification of

the Accord has so far not taken place because the process of boundary demarcation remains incomplete due to 'non-agreement on 6.5 kms of boundary,' *The Independent*, Dhaka. 7 February 2006, 16.

13 For details, see Mumtaz Ahmed, 'Madrasa Education in Pakistan and Bangladesh' in Limaye, Malik and Wiersing (eds.), *Religious Radicalism and Security in South Asia*, 101-15.

14 Riaz, *God Willing*.

15 Ibid.

16 Septuagenarian leftist intellectual Badruddin Umar contends, 'The basis of communalism was eliminated, to some extent, in 1947, and uprooted in 1971. Social basis of communalism no longer exists in this country. *The only form in which it survives here* [Bangladesh] *is anti-Indianism*. The Jamaat-e-Islami is one organisation based on religious ideas. But it cannot be called a communal organisation. Most people think that when you talk of religion and political use of religion, it amounts to communalism. But that is not true . . . Communalism has its own target—the other community. It is a conflict between two definite communities. Fundamentalism is altogether a different proposition. Fundamentalists try to implement basic principles of their religion. In that sense there can be Hindu or Muslim or Christian fundamentalism. So, apparently the Jamaat-e-Islamic people stand for basic principles of Islam and they want to implement tenets of Islam. That way they are not directly opposed to Hindus or Christians or anybody. But sometimes they make marginal use of communalism whenever the opportunity arises.' 'Badruddin Omar: Champion of Free-thinking,' *The Daily Star*, 23 April 2004. Emphasis added.

17 See Dina M. Siddiqi, 'The Festival of Democracy: Media and the 1996 elections in Bangladesh', *Asian Journal of Communication*, Special Issue on Media and Elections, 6: 2 (December 1996).

18 Nilufar Matin, 'Women's Rights: Freedom of Participation and Freedom from Violence' in Hameeda Hossain (ed.), *Human Rights in Bangladesh 2001* (Dhaka: Ain o Salish Kendra, 2002), 231

19 Amena Mohsin, 'Rights of Minorities' in Hossain (ed.), *Human Rights in Bangladesh 2001*, 251

20 Ibid.

21 Terrorist in local usage refers to 'outlaws, goondas and gangsters' without connotations of state-targeted violence or a specific ideology. The problem here is how to disentangle the 'terrorist' from the communalist and the politician.

22 See Amena Mohsin in Hossain (ed.), *Human Rights in Bangladesh 2001*.

23 Meghna Guhathakurta, 'Assault on Minorities: An Analysis'. Unpublished manuscript, 2003.

24 Ibid.

25 Paul Brass quoted in Jonathan Spencer 'Collective Violence' in Veena Das (ed.), *The Oxford India Companion to Sociology and Social Anthropology* (Delhi: Oxford University Press, 2003), 1575.

26 Meghna Guhathakurta compares this practice to the absentee landlordism typical of East Bengal's past. Guhathakurta, 'Assault on Minorities: An Analysis', 5.

27 Ibid.

28 For details, see Nurul Kabir, 'Desecularising Bangladesh?' in Dina M. Siddiqi (ed.), *Human Rights in Bangladesh, 2003* (Dhaka: Ain o Salish Kendra, 2004).

29 Ibid., 64-65

30 As reported in Shahriar Kabir (ed.), *White Paper: 1500 Days of Minority Persecution in Bangladesh* (Dhaka: Committee for Resisting Killers and Collaborators of 1971, 2005), 12.

31 Ibid.

32 In the debates over violence facing Hindu women in Bangladesh, little attention has been paid to shifting constructions of Hindu women's sexuality in the majoritarian imagination. An imperceptible shift in generational attitudes to Hindu women can be discerned. In the years just before and after Liberation, Hindu women were associated with overt friendliness/sexual availability, dubious morality and looseness in all spheres including the domestic. The image of the free/hypersexual Hindu woman has been replaced in recent times by the stereotype of women 'victimized' by their own men/culture/religion. I speculate that it is no longer politically correct to openly classify Hindu women as sexually and morally dubious. Whereas the 'victim of their own cultural practices' allows one to be progressive (demanding a uniform civil code etc.). This is a sanitized form of Othering that keeps Hindus in their place and allows Muslims to feel better about how they treat 'their' women.

33 Spencer, 'Collective Violence', 1569

34 Perhaps the biggest fear is that Bangladeshis will be refused US visas or have their resident status rescinded.

35 Ayesha Jalal, 'Reclaiming Religion: The Profanity of Partition

Violence,' paper presented at the Violence and Democracy workshop in Amherst, MA, May 2004.

36 One generalized anxiety turns on the dangers of the Bangladeshi media being flooded with Indian cultural products. Typical of such anxiety is the recent debate over the desirability and implications of having Aishwarya Rai's face grace billboards in Dhaka. Carried out in the letters section of the Weekend magazine of Bangladesh's leading English language newspaper, *The Daily Star*, readers pondered the possible negative effects on 'our' culture of having a non-Bangladeshi (read Indian) model on display in the capital city, and the need to promote local actresses. See *The Daily Star Weekend Magazine*, 2 February 2006, 2.

CONTRIBUTORS

RAVINA AGGARWAL teaches anthropology at Smith College, Massachusetts. She is the author of *Beyond Lines of Control: Performance and Politics on the Disputed Borders of Ladakh, India* (Duke University Press, 2004). She has also edited *Into the High Ranges*, an anthology on contemporary writings on the mountains of India (Penguin India, 2002) and *Forsaking Paradise: Stories from Ladakh* (Katha, 2001).

AMRITA BASU is the Paino Professor of Political Science and Women's and Gender Studies at Amherst College. She is the author of *Two Faces of Protest: Contrasting Modes of Women's Activism in India* (University of California Press, 1992) and of several edited and co-edited books, including *Community Conflicts and the State in India* (Oxford University Press, 1998) and *Appropriating Gender: Women's Activism and Politicized Religion in South Asia* (Routledge, 1998).

PAULA CHAKRAVARTTY is Assistant Professor of Communication at the University of Massachusetts-Amherst. She is the co-author of *Glo balization, Communication and Media Policy: A Critical Perspective* (with Katharine Sarikakis, Edinburgh University Press and Columbia University Press, 2006) and co-editor of *Political Economy of Global Communication: Towards a Transcultural Perspective* (with Yuezhi Zhao, Rowan & Littlefield, forthcoming 2007).

J. DEVIKA teaches and researches at Centre for Development Studies, Thiruvananthapuram, Kerala, India. She has worked on the history of gender and individualization in early modern Kerala, and on gender and social development in post-independence Kerala. Her publications include *Her-Self: Early Writings on Gender by Malayalee Women* (Kolkata: Stree, 2005); and *En-Gendering Individuals: The Language of Reform in Early Modern Kerala* (Hyderabad: Orient Longman, forthcoming).

ZOYA HASAN is Professor of Political Science and is currently Director of the Programme for the Study of Discrimination and Exclusion at the Jawaharlal Nehru University, New Delhi. She is a scholar of Indian politics with a strong interest in the state, political parties, social movements and the politics of representation. She is the author and editor of eleven books including *Quest for Power: Oppositional Movements and Post-Congress Politics in Uttar Pradesh* (Delhi: Oxford University Press, 1998); *Unequal Citizens: A Study of Muslim Women in India* (co-authored with Ritu Menon) (Delhi: Oxford University Press, 2004), *Parties and Party Politics in India* (Delhi: Oxford University Press, 2004). She has also published several articles.

SRINIVAS LANKALA is a doctoral candidate in Communication at the University of Massachusetts-Amherst. His research interests are in the field of popular culture and nationalism, and in the discourses around labour in the information economy. He has an M.Phil degree from Jawaharlal Nehru University, Delhi and an MA in Communication from the University of Hyderabad.

MARTHA C. NUSSBAUM is Ernst Freund Professor of Law and Ethics at the University of Chicago. She is appointed in the Philosophy Department, Law School, and Divinity School, and is a Member of the Committee on Southern Asian Studies and a Board Member of the Human Rights Program. Her work on international development has led to the books *Women and Human Development: The Capabilities Approach* (Cambridge University Press, 2001) and *Frontiers of Justice* (Harvard University Press, 2006). Her *Democracy in the Balance: Violence, Hope, and India's Future* will be published in 2007 by Harvard University Press.

RAKA RAY is Associate Professor of Sociology and South and Southeast Asian Studies, and Sarah Kailath Chair of India Studies at the University of California, Berkeley. Her scholarship focuses on gender, social movements and inequality. Her publications include *Fields of Protest: Women's Movements in India* (University of Minnesota Press, 1999), and *Social Movements in India: Poverty, Power, and Politics* (edited with Mary Katzenstein) (Rowman and Littlefield, 2005) as well as several articles. She is completing a book, with Seemin Qayum, called *Cultures of Servitude: The Making of a Middle Class in Calcutta and New York*. She is at present the Chair of the Center for South Asia Studies at UC Berkeley

SRIRUPA ROY is Associate Professor of Political Science, University of Massachusetts-Amherst. She is the author of *Beyond Belief: India and the Politics of Postcolonial Nationalism* (Duke University Press, forthcoming 2007) and of articles that have been published in *Comparative Studies in Society and History*; *Journal of Asian Studies*; *Contributions to Indian Sociology*; *Interventions: the International Journal of Postcolonial Studies*; and *South Asia*.

WILLEM VAN SCHENDEL is Professor of Modern Asian History at the University of Amsterdam and heads the Asia Department of the International Institute of Social History. Recent books include *The Bengal Borderland: Beyond State and Nation in South Asia* (Anthem Press, 2005) and (edited with Itty Abraham) *Illicit Flows and Criminal Things: States, Borders and the Other Side of Globalization* (Indiana University Press, 2006).

DINA M. SIDDIQI received her Ph.D. in Anthropology from the University of Michigan, Ann Arbor in 1996. She is a South Asia specialist, with particular expertise on Muslim women in Bangladesh. Dr Siddiqi's research and publications are concerned with globalization and labour, Islamization, and violence against women. She divides her time between the US where she teaches, and Bangladesh where she works with gender and human rights organization. Dr Siddiqi has worked on gender related projects for UNDP, UNICEF and NORAD. She is Senior Associate at the Alice Paul Center for the Study of Women and Gender at the University of Pennsylvania.

USHA ZACHARIAS is Assistant Professor of Communication at Westfield State College, Massachusetts. She works on the biopolitics of media, gender, and citizenship based on fieldwork with displaced/marginal communities in India. She is co-editor of the Commentary and Criticism section of the journal, *Feminist Media Studies*. Her writings appear in *Critical Studies in Media Communication*, *Social Text*, and *Cultural Dynamics*.

INDEX